Managing Technology

Managing Technology

Social Science Perspectives

Liora Salter & David Wolfe eds.

Garamond Press · Toronto

The publisher gratefully acknowledges
the financial assistance of the Canada Council
and the Ontario Arts Council.

We gratefully acknowledge the financial assistance of the
Social Sciences and Humanities Research Council of Canada
to undertake the research on the Management of Technology
and contribute to the publication of this book.

Printed and bound in Canada.
Typeset at The Coach House Press, Toronto
Designed by Phoenix Productions Int'l.

A publication of Garamond Press

Garamond Press
67A Portland Street
Toronto, Ontario M5V 2M9

Canadian Cataloguing in Publication Data

Main entry under title:

Managing technology: social science perspectives

Includes bibliographical references.
ISBN 0-920059-89-9 (bound)   ISBN 0-920059-79-1 (pbk.)

1. Technological innovations – Canada – Management.
I. Salter, Liora.   II. Wolfe, David.

HD45.M35 1990   658.5'77   C90-094146-4

Contents

Contributors

Liora Salter is currently Vice-President Academic (Acting) and a professor in the Department of Communication at Simon Fraser University. Beginning in the fall of 1990, she will join the faculty at Osgoode Hall Law School with a cross-appointment into the Faculty of Environmental Studies at York University. Her books include *Public Inquiries — Canada* and *Mandated Sciences: Science and Scientists in the Making of Standards*, and her current research is in the fields of communication law, standards, regulatory issues and science policy.

David Wolfe teaches in the Department of Political Science at the University of Toronto. His recent research has focused on the implications of technological change for skills, occupational requirements, education and training. He has recently conducted research in these areas for the Labour Council of Metro Toronto, the Social Planning Council of Metro Toronto and the Council of Regents for the College of Applied Arts and Technology in Ontario. He is currently completing a book on political and social responses to technological change in four industrial countries.

Meric S. Gertler is currently associate professor of geography and planning at the University of Toronto, where he has taught since 1983. He obtained a bachelor's degree in geography at McMaster before pursuing graduate studies in city and regional planning at the University of California, Berkeley and Harvard University. He has worked in the Ontario ministries of Industry and Tourism, and Housing, as well as in DREE, Ottawa. His current research focuses on spatial industrial reorganization, technological change, labour, and regional economic development in North America and Western Europe.

Richard Hawkins recently completed graduate studies in the Department of Communciations at Simon Fraser University. Previous to this, he was involved for some 20 years in the international music industry. His area of academic interest is science and technology policy, particularly as applied to communications and information technologies. He has prepared and taught a course at S.F.U. focusing on the role of standards in public policy formulation, and is co-author (with Liora Salter) of a Communications Canada report on communications and information technology standards.

Uschi Koebberling obtained her Ph.D. from the Department of Communications at Simon Fraser University in 1981. Prior to emigrating to Canada, she worked as a radio journalist at the Sender Freier Berlin in West Germany. Academic research work has focused on the application of communication technologies in Canada's Inuit communities. Contract work included a report for the Inuvialuit Communications Society in Inuvik and various literature reviews and annotated bibliographies on research and development in Canada, social and cultural implications of communication technologies, and international experiences with legislative and regulatory compliance. In the fall of 1989, she joined Wescom Communications Research International as a senior consultant.

William Leiss is Professor of Communication and Director, Centre for Policy Research on Science and Technology, at Simon Fraser University. He is the author of *The Domination of Nature* (1972), *The Limits to Satisfaction* (1976), *Under Technology's Thumb* (1970), and other publications.

Camille Limoges was born in Montreal in 1942. Doctorate in the history of sciences, Université de Paris (1968). Assistant professor, Université de Montréal (1968-1971); associate professor, The Johns Hopkins University (1971-1973); back to Université de Montréal and founder of the Institut d'histoire et de sociopolitique des sciences (1973). Visiting professor at Harvard (1978) and at Johns Hopkins (1979). Went to Quebec Government as Assistant Secretary for Scientific Development (1961), Deputy Minister for Science and Technology (1983) and for Higher Education and Science (1985). Professor at the Centre de recherche en évaluation sociale des technologies, Université de Québec à Montréal since 1987. Has published widely in the history of biology, in science policy and in social assessment of technology.

Richard Smith is Research Director at the Centre for Policy Research on Science and Technology at Simon Fraser University. He is also a Ph.D. candidate in the Department of Communication at S.F.U. His research area is risk communication with a focus on agricultural chemicals, stakeholders, and the media. His most recent research, for the Science Council of B.C., is on the commercialization of research.

Preface

Caroline Andrew

It is a real pleasure to be writing a preface to this volume on the management of technology. This book is important in a number of ways—it outlines the shape of the field as currently constituted by researchers in Canada, it raises questions and stimulates debate about the strengths and weaknesses of the research being done on the management of technology in Canada, and it clearly lays out the importance of social science and social scientists to this research area.

It is an ambitious task to attempt to define the shape of such a rapidly changing and inclusive area of study as the management of technology. But, at the same time, it is vitally important to do this task, because it is in this way that we can increasingly recognize the contours of the field and, from this, the existence of a defined and therefore definable field of research. There will of course be questions about the drawing of boundaries—why were certain areas included and others left out? But the more important point is, I believe, to look at the broad range of research topics that are clearly part of the area of the management of technology.

This book is intended to encourage debate about the nature of the research enterprise in Canada, specifically as it relates to the management of technology. This state-of-the-art is clearly not intended to be a sort of neutral compendium of research. It is supposed to look critically at research being done, evaluate the questions being asked, and relate this to the information about the research process—who funds it, what support is given, how is this support structured—in order to better understand the relationship between the shape of the field and the nature of the support for research in this area.

Finally—and most centrally—this book is an argument for the importance of the study of the management of technology to the social science research community and, conversely, the importance of the social science research community to the management of technology. This is an area of great importance to the development of Canada; even the most extravagant cliches can sometimes understate the importance of our being able to increase our capacity to integrate and guide technological developments. The social sciences have the intellectual tools necessary for this task—we are able to look at issues from multifaceted points of view and to bring a variety of perspectives to bear on the issue. In addition, we are able to link theory and practice—to better understand the management of technology in order to better manage technology. The research enterprise is related in a fundamental way to being better able to choose our collective future.

As can be seen from this book, the social sciences are deeply involved in all aspects of the management of technology. Yet all too often the social sciences have been seen as pertinent only to questions about the social impact of technology. It is, of course, true that we have much to say about the social impact of technology and about how it can be examined, but we also have much to say about innovation within the firm, technology transfer, labour process, training policies, science policy, the impact of technological change upon gender relations, etc. Social scientists have a major role to play in the exploration of these issues; considerable research already exists or is underway, but at the same time, an expanded research effort is clearly needed.

This project was initiated by the Social Science Federation of Canada, in response to the creation, by the Social Sciences and Humanities Research Council of Canada, of a one-time experimental program to demonstrate the actual and potential contribution of research in the social sciences and humanities to the resolution of national policy issues. In submitting a proposal to examine the field of the management of technology, the Social Science Federation saw an opportunity to reinforce our argument as to the importance—both in terms of social pertinence and of intellectual rigour—of research in the social sciences for the overall development of Canadian society. We are delighted with the study and very grateful to the researchers who worked so hard, during the long hot summer of 1988, to map out the field—the research and the researchers. We are pleased that Garamond Press has agreed to publish the manuscript to make it available to as wide an audience as possible. We thank the Social Sciences and Humanities Research Council for their special grant to facilitate the communication of the research findings to the broader community. The management of technology concerns us all. As Past President of the Social Science Federation of Canada, as a social scientist, and as a citizen, I would like to thank the editors and contributors for this book and to recommend it for your reading.

Caroline Andrew

Chapter One

Introduction

The phrase "managing technology" is a recent addition to the literature of the social sciences. It has its roots in public discourse, and in the speeches of politicians. In this context, it reflects three contentions: that this is "the new information age," that the pace of change is accelerating, primarily because of technology, and that there is a need for a social and political response to the opportunities and problems that the new age creates. The phrase "managing technology" has also found its way into the technical literature of scientists and engineers, and into the curriculum of business schools. In this context, it has a slightly different meaning, referring to the technical capacity managers need, and the managerial abilities that engineers require, to handle technology transfer and innovation within the firm. Finally, the phrase has found its way into union research reports, and occasionally onto the factory floor, where it refers to job dislocation, to changing job skills, to training and retraining, and to problems in the work environment.

Among social scientists, however, the phrase "managing technology" has, as yet, little currency. This is unfortunate, because social scientists have a particularly important role to play, regardless of whether the phrase refers to the new information age, changes in management philosophies, or changes in the labour process. Social scientists have long contributed expertise about managing change within the work environment, about social and environmental dislocations and their remedies, and about trends and opportunities in the global economy. Moreover, there are public policy issues involved in the management of technology, questions pertaining to the regulation of risks, the import of research and development funding, the effect of the industrial strategies followed by different nations, and different provinces within Canada, and the assessment of policies for the conduct of science. These are matters of great concern to social science.

There are reasons why social scientists have been relatively silent in the current discussions about managing technology, in spite of their significant expertise in many aspects of the problem. In the past, their research on managing technology has not been funded at a level commensurate with the importance of their potential contribution. As well, their research has not been coordinated, and the researchers themselves are seldom in regular contact with each other. This situation is deplorable, and it has serious implications if, indeed, Canada is serious about its participation in the new era. It means that the conclusions of social science research will not be brought to bear on critical decisions that governments, workers, industries, and members of the public must make about the management of technology. It is this situation that gave rise to a study of the management of technology by the Social Science Federation of Canada in 1988.

The initial purpose of the study was to make recommendations to the Social Sciences and Humanities Research Council of Canada (SSHRCC), which had funded the research. For SSHRCC, the task was to identify researchers in the management of technology, and to facilitate the creation of a working network among them. It was also hoped that it would be possible to create a relationship between social scientists and participants from the public and private sectors, working together on the problems of technology development and diffusion.

In the spring of 1989, a decision was made to publish the completed study as a book. Although the original purpose was primarily to make recommendations to SSHRCC, the study accomplished a wider purpose. It commissioned eight state-of-the-art papers outlining the research being undertaken by social scientists in a variety of fields in the management of technology. Taken together, the papers indicate the scope of the field, and the areas of possible convergence within it. Furthermore, it provided a list of research questions that researchers and others found to be worth pursuing. If social scientists have been relatively quiet, and if their considerable efforts have not received recognition, a book such as this one can draw attention to the many important contributions that social science does make to the management of technology. The variety of work brought together in this volume, the multiplicity of studies reported here and the scope of research can, and should put to rest the misguided notion that social science has no role in the management of technology. It should demonstrate quite conclusively how social scientific research might be integrated into more general discussions of technological innovation and its social and economic consequences.

The original study was carried out over a six-month period. It included the identification of researchers in the management of technology through a review of the literature, a review of the SSHRCC strategic grants in the areas of the Human Context of Science, Technology, and Managing the Organization, and a review of general research grants to identify researchers working in the management of technology (or closely related studies). Personal contacts were made or letters sent to each of the individuals so identified. The technology-related granting programs of several government departments were identified. Interviews were then conducted with more than sixty individuals from Halifax to Vancouver. The researchers also participated in meetings, conferences, colloquia and conferences related to the management of technology—approximately twenty-five meetings in total. Because one purpose of the study was to explore opportunities for research funding, meetings were held with potential partners in the natural sciences and engineering, in government agencies, in private organizations (labour organizations for example), quasi-government agencies (International Development Research Commission [IDRC], Science Council), and industry in order to assess their willingness to join in management of technology research.

As noted, the study was conducted under the auspices of the Social Science Federation, and three representatives of the Federation were members of its steering committee. The steering committee members were Mark Abbott, Caroline Andrew, Brenda Beck (who wrote another volume in the report), Marshall Conley, William Leiss, Camille Limoges, Christian Pouyez, Liora Salter, and David Wolfe, to whom the authors of this report owe a considerable debt of gratitude. The Federation administered the project. The assessment and views expressed in this report are those of its authors, however. It could not be otherwise. The Federation, like SSHRCC, has a complex process of consultation and approval that must take place before it can adopt its official policies and recommendations. In the six month period when this study was conducted, it would have been impossible to subject the final recommendations of this report to the scrutiny of the Federation and its members, given the demands of the research itself.

The organization of the book is as follows. Chapter Two presents an overview of the management of technology, seen from the perspective of social science. The overview includes a discussion of the prevailing paradigms (or perspectives) on the management of technology, of the topics and issues in the field and their representation in research, and of the network of researchers and research centres. It also includes an assessment of the role of social science and scientists in the management of technology. Chapters Three through Ten are devoted to the state-of-the-art papers. A bibliography, organized by topic area, is included at the end of the book.

One final note in introduction: the new initiative taken by the Social Science Federation in conducting the study, and by SSHRCC in funding it, was equally a new initiative for its researchers. It is not uncommon to be asked to conduct a state-of-the-art assessment of one's own specialization. It is quite a different thing, however, to conduct a state-of-the-art assessment of a new field of endeavour, and in doing so, to attempt to give intellectual shape and coherence to a diverse body of material. The task was made more interesting, in the sense of the Chinese proverb, by the requirement to work between the two cultures of social and natural sciences, the two cultures of scholarly and pragmatic research, and the two cultures of the university and the private sector. We have included no extended discussion in this book about the importance of the management of technology. Our willingness to embark on a project of this magnitude in light of all the attendant pressures represents our statement about the significance of the field and its national and strategic importance.

Chapter Two

Overview of the Field and its Researchers

Liora Salter

Introduction

Although the theme of technology runs through all social and humanities disciplines, from philosophy to economics, there is little agreement about what should be included under the rubric of the management of technology. In some cases, humanists and social scientists treat technology as a metaphor for society in general, and in other instances, they focus on the detailed implementation of strategies to encourage technological innovation. There are several ways to illustrate the various conceptions of the management of technology. Three have been chosen to give an overview of the field—namely, the paradigms, the topics and issues, and the network of researchers.

The term paradigm requires some explanation. Paradigm in this context is used in its limited, sociological (or Mertonian) sense to mean simply the list of questions that orient a program of research. At one level, paradigms are heuristic devices, designed only to provide a glimpse of the range of work in the management of technology and a guide to some of the debates within the field. At the same time, the paradigms in the management of technology are not simply abstract constructions, but do seem to represent four networks of researchers in Canada conducting studies on the management of technology. Indeed, individuals working in the same topic area often have little knowledge of each other's work, a situation which can be attributed, at least in part, to the different paradigms.

In correspondence with David Wolfe and myself during the course of the study, Harvey Kolodny and Lorna Marsden both made the point that the paradigms used in this study are robust as heuristic devices, but seem to be less useful when applied specifically to categorize research topics or researchers. For this reason, a description of topics and issues in the management of technology is also necessary. This method of encapsulating the various strains within the field can also be criticized, however, because the boundaries between the management of technology and related disciplines is a "fuzzy" one. For example, the management of technology shades into organizational behaviour, the sociology of work, the economics of trade and international aid, the study of public policy and regulation, and so on. Individual researchers draw the boundary lines quite differently in terms of the topics and issues they consider to be indigenous to the field.

A third way to characterize the field is to focus directly upon the network of researchers within it. Again, even the most casual observer will see that each "network" has no fixed boundaries, and that different conceptions of its "core" produce different pictures of the field. With these limitations in mind, it is still useful to describe the field in terms of its paradigms, topics, and researchers.

The Paradigms

There are four quite different paradigms in the management of technology: the theoretical paradigm, the business paradigm, the labour process paradigm, and the social science paradigm.

The theoretical paradigm

The theoretical paradigm is perhaps the best developed of all the four paradigms, although it is virtually absent from the current discussions about the management of technology. Simply put, it is the study of the relationship of technology to society, and it claims adherents from every social science and humanities discipline, plus others who are interdisciplinary in their orientation. Books and articles about "the information society", "the conserver society", and the "technological society" fall roughly into this category, as do such Habermasian concepts as "technical rationality" and "instrumental reason". The Frankfurt School and critical theorists are its most well-known contributors, but there are others. George Grant, Arthur Kroker, Robert Paelke, in Canada, and Jacques

Ellul, Lewis Mumford and Daniel Bell are names that come to mind. Several emerging disciplines, such as communications, are also distinguished by their strong interest in the relationship between technology and society/culture.

The basic premise underlying the very diverse work within the theoretical paradigm is that fundamental social changes are wrought by changes in the technological organization of societies or their economies. As is evident, the focus of attention is upon society in the macrocosm. Technology refers to something roughly equivalent in scope to the Marxian concept of the mode of production, but is different in orientation. In this instance, the focus of attention is upon the way in which technology influences how work is organized and wealth is generated. The assumption is that technological change is a key variable in each case.

In the theoretical paradigm, the changes generated by the new technological order cannot be easily measured or quantified. They cannot be understood in terms of measures of productivity, for example. Instead, technological change is manifest in changing social norms and values, in different modes of thinking or discourse, and in different social relations within societies.

Even though there are sharp divergencies of opinion among those who work in the theoretical paradigm, it is appropriate to characterize their work as critical in orientation. Historically, these scholars have viewed themselves as social critics and philosophers, rather than as social scientists. Their work is distinguished because of its breadth, and because it focuses on social transformation. The attitude towards technological change within the theoretical paradigm is not necessarily a negative one, however, because the various critics working in the theoretical paradigm view the changes wrought by technology in different lights; some see change in a positive light while others are more negative in their assessment.

The business paradigm

A recent American publication defines the management of technology as a field that combines the insights of business and engineering. The focus of attention in the business paradigm is on the firm, and more specifically, on how innovation and the adoption of technology can be fostered within the firm.

The basic premise of the business paradigm is that there should be a cross-fertilization of ideas and experience from the two disciplines of business and engineering. On one hand, it is suggested that managers should become more technologically-literate and capable of assessing the capacity, potential and impact of new technology. And, on the other, it is suggested that engineers should become sensitized to the dictates and demands of management. Not surprisingly, a good deal of attention is paid to education in the management of technology and, in particular, to the training of product managers and their colleagues both through the business and engineering schools and on-site within the firm. Research is focused on strategies and organizational processes for the management of technology.

If the theoretical paradigm is critical and wide-ranging in its approach, the business paradigm is its opposite. Of interest are the pragmatic problems faced by companies and their managers, and by individuals being educated to take their place in the new technologically-intensive industries. Of secondary concern are issues related to changes in the workforce and employment patterns, technology and R&D policies, standards and regulation. Within the business paradigm, there is little scope for either theoretical questions about the transformation of society or for social questions about the impact of technological change on society. Nonetheless, the business paradigm rests upon the assumption that technological change is beneficial to society, and indeed, many would claim that it is a social and economic imperative.

The labour process paradigm

The labour process paradigm originated in the broader literature concerning the transformation of the labour process under the conditions of modern industrial production. Following the work of Harry Braverman, the paradigm raises questions about managerial control of the labour process, and about the implications of change in production technologies for the skill content and definition of work.

Recently, the focus of attention within the labour process paradigm has shifted to encompass several new questions concerning the impact of technologies on the labour process, and the nature of the labour process that the new technologies create. As well, this paradigm has been extended to include a number of social issues arising from the labour process but less directly connected to it, namely health and safety, the status of women, and the environment.

The basic premise of the labour process paradigm is that technology does not exist independently of the actual social relations in which it is embedded. For example, those working within the labour process paradigm reject any notion that the current social and economic changes are caused by technology per se, and they stress the role of those with political and economic power in shaping the type of technological development that does occur. They see technological change as an outcome, rather than a cause, of conflict between those who control the labour process, and workers and their organizations.

The new wave of technological change that is sweeping across industrialized countries is seen to be connected with a broader set of economic changes affecting the global economy—the increasing international competition, the rise of the newly industrializing countries, and the industrial restructuring of mature economies. From the labour process perspective, the introduction of new technologies is viewed as one tactic among many employed by firms to maintain their competitive position in the face of economic pressures that are largely international in origin and related to the state of the economy in general.

Within the labour process paradigm, a number of different perspectives have emerged. Braverman and those most closely associated with his approach have emphasized the use of new technologies to eliminate the traditional skills of workers, and the adoption of new techniques, such as scientific management, to increase managerial control over the labour process.

However, another strain of more recent work has tended to champion a more open-ended set of conclusions about the results of the new technologies. The focus in this instance is on skill levels, job descriptions and job content, managerial control and issues related to the workplace (women's issues, health and safety issues), and the environment. It is claimed that the actual results of introducing new technologies emerge from the interaction of management strategies, the organized response of labour, and significant cross-national variations in organizational cultures. The results of the new technologies cannot be predicted in advance, nor in isolation from these other factors.

The labour process paradigm, then, is wide-ranging with respect to the issues it considers to be of primary concern, but many of its researchers have a very pragmatic orientation, not unlike those of the business paradigm in this respect. Issues of public policy, although of secondary importance, are relevant within the paradigm, because public policy sets the limiting conditions for the application of new technologies and the means to control their more deleterious effects upon the workforce and the environment. The labour process paradigm also offers a social critique, and a critical perspective on new technology. In recent work, there has been an interest in developing methods of introducing new technology to minimize its negative consequences. There is also a recognition of the positive economic and social benefits that can flow from the introduction of new technologies.

The social science paradigm

There is a body of research and researchers who fall outside the paradigms described above. They conduct research on a number of related issues in the management of technology. They share a commitment to empirical social science research. Many of their studies are designed to produce policy recommendations, but their research also contains analytical material which is scholarly, not practical, in orientation. For the purposes of comparison, this body of research will be described as the social science paradigm.

This paradigm is the least well developed conceptually, and least adequately described as a paradigm. It has no easily identified basic premises, and individuals working in this paradigm often draw from the other paradigms described above. It does not offer, as the other paradigms do, a clear perspective on the field, and it has yet to delineate research questions which define the management of technology.

Of interest to researchers working within the social science paradigm are such matters as the social impacts and consequences of technology; communication and information technologies; public policies for stimulating innovation and the adoption of new technologies; regulatory issues raised by the new technologies and their sometimes deleterious consequences; employment patterns and training needs created by new technology; and issues of national and regional economic development, trade, industrial strategy and foreign aid as these are affected by new technology.

As is evident from this list of interests, to the extent that the social science paradigm is unified, it is so by virtue of the fact that it draws upon the expertise of social scientists, and that it examines social, economic, and political relations in their most concrete sense. Although some of the specific studies are evaluative in orientation, in general the researchers from this paradigm take no explicit value position on technological change or the new technologies. For them, technology is neither beneficial nor problematic in the first instance. Its value arises from the manner in which it is developed and employed.

Topics and Issues

It will be useful here to provide an outline of the field as a whole, even if, as is evident from the following chapters, the state of research is uneven on different topics and issues. Eight topics have been highlighted. These eight topics should be viewed as "snapshots." They do not comprise all of the management of technology, but taken together they do indicate the scope of the field and its development.

In the first state-of-the-art paper, Camille Limoges provides an overview of work in Quebec. He suggests that there are three foci of attention in Quebec, namely, science policy, management of innovation at the firm level, and the regulation of technological activity. Initially, he states, science policy was conceived of as policy "for" science, and it remained the domain of natural scientists and engineers. The next stage saw attention being given to technology and innovation, but more recently the emphasis has been on the processes of science policy making. Two issues commanded attention: the economics of technological innovation, and the institutional arrangements that would be relevant for innovation policies. Concerning the former issue, economists have examined the impact of foreign investments, the international and inter-industry technology transfers, the relative level of Canadian provincial R&D spending, and the relationship between R&D and export performance. In the latter instance, the lack of stability of government programs is noted, as well as the lack of evaluation research.

Limoges notes that, in Quebec, research focuses on two distinct sets of processes in dealing with the management of innovation at the level of the firm. The first is the management of technology as a central element of the strategy of the firm, and the second is the organization and management of work. Recent studies have abandoned the model of innovation as a sequential process, internal to the firm. Market opportunities and the global environment are seen as critical factors. The environment also includes government policies and regulation, the availability of financing, and competition. More important yet, perhaps, is the emergence and success of high-tech endeavours which are dependent upon regional assets, such as clusters of other high-tech firms, research centres, high-level training institutions, and a critical mass of expertise.

The quick pace of technological change has had inescapable effects upon the workforce, Limoges notes. Many of the studies of this situation bear the imprint of the tradition of "critical" analysis which has been, and remains, so central to the ethos of the social sciences. Many of the local case studies have been examined in terms of the social contradictions and conflicts that are the core of the dynamics at the macrosociological level. However, this aspect of the field is changing, and there are now a number of microsociological studies of work at the firm level. Some emphasis has been given to the introduction of information technologies in the manufacturing as well as the service sectors to the work of women, and to issues of manpower training.

In Quebec, as elsewhere in Canada, risk and technological assessment comprise an important component of the management of technology. Risk studies are still in an embryonic state, Limoges suggests, but research is being conducted on toxic chemicals, biotechnology, and on the role of the media in risk perception. There has been little spin-off in terms of research on technology assessment from the mega-projects such as James Bay, however, and evaluation studies are still lacking. The most active areas of research are concerned with developing a framework for technology assessment (the social assessment of technology), with the evaluation of the repercussions of the new information technologies from the viewpoint of the law, civil liberties, and the cultural effects of these technologies, and with ethical issues related to biotechnology.

The anglophone research is more diverse, but not notably more developed than is the francophone research from Quebec. In his state-of-the-art paper on managing innovation, Wolfe suggests that the focus of this research has been on the effectiveness with which firms develop the institutional skills required to generate, adopt, and apply new technologies to enhance their international competitiveness. Some research deals with the relative merit of different efforts to stimulate R&D. But despite the potential importance of in-firm R&D, the most common source of new technology is through technology transfer from foreign sources. Industry associations can play a critical role, Wolfe suggests, in facilitating the process for technology transfer, and he cites the four Canadian industry research associations and some European examples. Government financial support and encouragement were instrumental in setting up each of these industry research associations.

Researchers also now believe that what is needed is not just better technologies, but also better management of the entire product innovation process. A great deal of emphasis has been placed in recent research on the linkages between the marketing and innovation skills of Canadian firms, as well as their expertise in new product development. Both attitudes within the firm and the adoption of sound new product development processes are key, as is developing appropriate relationships with customers.

Canadian companies lag seriously behind in the adoption and diffusion of new technologies, and recent research has emphasized the desirability of employing impact-analysis techniques to maximize the benefits and minimize the risks of introducing new manufacturing technology. The benefits to be gained from the introduction of new microelectronic technologies, such as CAD/CAM and CIM, are stressed, but it is noted that many companies' experience falls far short of published expectations. Organizational variables tend to have a significant effect on the effectiveness of these new technologies, and thus attention has been paid to the questions of work organization. A great deal of research is related to the quality of working life programs, which view the technical and human elements of an organization in a more holistic or systemic manner. The research on quality of working life has also received a good deal of attention from the federal and Ontario governments.

In the next chapter, Wolfe also surveys the research on innovation and the labour process. Here the emphasis has been on the impact of new technology on employment and skill levels, the degree of consultation—or lack thereof—over the introduction of new technology, and its implications for job descriptions, job content, and managerial control. Wolfe notes that there is a strong differentiation between studies that focus on the impact of new technology on the manufacturing industries and those on office and clerical work. Within the latter group, a number of studies have been particularly concerned with the impact of technology on the job ghettos where women have traditionally been concentrated. As well, attention has been directed to the collective bargaining process, and to the training prerequisites for successful innovation in the firm.

Consultation appears to be the critical variable, most of the labour process studies have found, with respect to the introduction of new technologies. The "best practice" recognizes the contributions made from the shop floor, but this "best practice" is often not followed in the implementation of new technologies. Wolfe notes that in the field trials conducted by the Department of Communications, planning for technological innovation was found to be essential, and even then performance often fell short of expectations. The user-friendliness of most systems was overrated, and a lack of integration was encountered in the systems.

One of the major issues that has been debated is the effect of technology on employment, but it has been difficult to obtain accurate measurements because other factors intervene. The situation is no longer viewed in alarmist terms, but the phrase "jobless growth" seems to apply. Some researchers have argued that the primary effect to date on employment seems to have been the increasing polarization of jobs, but results from various studies have been mixed. The effects vary from organization to organization and are often a function of management choices. A key issue is that of organizational flexibility, but here again the results are dependent upon managerial response. Several researchers found significant management resistance to change, and in such cases, technological change is likely to lead to deskilling, closer monitoring of individual workers, persistent efforts to speed up production, and high levels of worker-management conflict. Emphasis is placed on the concept of "user-driven" design to ameliorate these problems.

In Chapter Six, Bill Leiss and Richard Smith survey research on science policy, dealing with both industrial and R&D policies. Industrial policy is defined as the selective measures adopted by the state to alter its industrial organization. Although many such measures—such as government enterprise, direct financial assistance, regulation of competition and foreign investments, government markets etc.—exist, tariffs remain the most important factor in terms of their impact upon the economy in Canada, as in the other OECD countries. This is true despite the general decline in the impact of tariffs over the last twenty years.

The second most important aspect of industrial policy is associated with regional development. Together with tariffs, regional assistance forms the main thrust of industrial policy. Most attention, however, has been directed to the new technologies, where the benefit is seen to be to society and not just the firm. There is some disagreement as to what constitutes the barriers to technological innovation, with the Science Council, for example, arguing that foreign ownership plays a key role, and the Economic Council suggesting that tariff barriers are to blame. Jurisdictional arrangements also create a special case for Canada, and some commentators suggest that lack of coordination between the two levels of government is responsible for less than optimal results.

The argument for government support of R&D, which emerged in the U.S. after World War II, links R&D to economic growth, and suggests that industry lacks sufficient incentive to do more than a small part of basic research. This argument was based on generalizations that were not testable and were related mainly to the "R" of R&D. Theoretically, as well, prodigious amounts of money could be involved. Nonetheless, R&D is still seen to be a "good social investment". R&D takes several forms: direct government procurement of R&D products, support of basic or generic research, broad support of applied R&D, and narrowly aimed commercial programs. To date, no adequate assessment exists of the relative merit of each approach, and indeed researchers have argued that such an assessment can only be conducted on a case-by-case basis. Moreover, there is a high degree of instability affecting most aspects of each program.

There appears to be a differential importance for productivity gains of the various components of R&D—namely, basic research, applied research, and development—although this is a matter for further investigation. As well, investigation is required of the definitions of industrial policy currently in use, and the impact of free trade, if, indeed, tariffs are the primary tool of industrial policy. Tools for evaluation need to be developed, and the effect of instability gauged.

These four chapters provide the overview of the main body of research in the management of technology, but they do not cover the ground completely. Within each discipline, as mentioned above, there is further research on the management of technology. Geography has been chosen to illustrate the point, and Meric Gertler provides an overview. Gertler suggests that the dominant focus of geographers' research in the management of technology has been the spatial restructuring of production which accommodates or accompanies organizational change, enabling the technological change to occur.

Recent work appears to place a great premium on geographical concentration and agglomeration in stimulating technological innovation. This is the result not only of more flexible machinery and labour, but also of the complex set of transactions among producers. The relationship between technological change and spatial organization is mediated, researchers find, by pre-existing organizational structures and corporate strategies.

Geographers have examined the relationship between science and social policies, finding the objectives of the two sometimes in conflict. They have also looked at the role of different social and political structures of communities in generating innovation, the conditions for the stimulation of local entrepreneurship, the role of local venture capitalists, and of community support. Local expertise in particular areas seems critical, such as expertise in R&D, product design and engineering, managing, marketing, and advertising. Close contact with federal agencies is also key to the development of technologically-intensive firms. The federal presence provides an important source of demand, as well as assistance for development.

Chapter Eight provides an overview of research on standards, and some background information about this little-understood component in the management of technology. In fact, there are a number of relationships in the management of technology worthy of examination, particularly those associated with the capacity to move products in export trade. Three deserve special mention: standards, copyrights, and patents. In the case of standards, the commercialization of innovation, and its exportability, depend upon the development of standards in Canada and the compatibility of Canadian standards with standards in other countries. Patents and copyright provide innovators with the assurance they need that they will benefit from the risks incurred in the development of new technologies. In a complete assessment of the management of technology, a discussion of intellectual property rights, copyright, and patents would be included along with the material on standards.

In all these specific areas, the current state of research is poor. Even the basic information required by industry and government has not been gathered, and there is little scholarly analysis available. Standards, patents, and copyright research has fallen "between the cracks" with respect to research funding. It is neither conventional political science (it requires technical, engineering or natural science research, as well as social science research), nor has it been included in any of the federal government research programs on technology. In this specific area of research, there is an urgent need, and much room, for partnerships among government, universities, and industry.

Many social scientists are primarily concerned with the implications or consequences of technological development. They consider the phrase "managing technology" to refer to "society's" management of the consequences of technological development and change. From their perspective, issues related to the environment, the safety of the workplace, and the quality of life (and cultural development) are relevant to the management of technology. This perception, while not identical with the prevailing view in the field, is nonetheless reflected in a widespread agreement that at least the regulatory aspects of the management of technology should be included in any definition of the field.

The regulatory aspects of the management of technology have been addressed in the last two chapters. Chapter Nine deals with technology assessment, which is emerging as an area of specialization among policy makers and within the universities. Technology assessment incorporates the evaluative component of the research discussed thus far, and the regulatory procedures by which new innovations and mega-projects are approved. It also incorporates both environmental assessment and social impact assessment, both, or either of which may be required before a project or innovation is permitted. Koebberling notes that technology assessment has been given a great deal of attention, but the research is as yet underdeveloped. She suggests, and others concur, that a major effort is needed to develop appropriate methodologies for technology assessment and evaluation.

The same observation is made by Bill Leiss and Richard Smith in their discussion of risk analysis. Risk analysis refers to the process by which complex decisions about technology are made when potentially dangerous products or activities are involved. Risk analysis, Leiss and Smith argue, has four components: risk perception, risk assessment, risk management, and risk communication. The first and last of these deal with how information about complex technologies (their effects and potential dangers) is understood by the public, and how this understanding, and the views of scientists, industry, and policymakers, are fashioned into decisions about managing the consequences of technology. Risk assessment and management refer to the processes of gauging the risks themselves, and of identifying the regulatory options with respect to them.

Risk analysis is a relatively recent field of study in Canada, but research is underway in an increasing number of locations. Natural scientists (e.g. kinesiologists) and engineers are engaged in risk assessment along with social scientists, and most researchers are currently focusing their attention on specific cases studies (usually contract research) or on methodological questions.

The Network of Researchers

After a period of initial pioneering in Quebec in the 1970s, there was an emergence and consolidation of teams of researchers and research centres in the 1980s. University research is generally characterized by institutional and disciplinary insularity, and the management of technology was no exception for some time, but there are now clear indications of networking. The change has been caused partly by the increasing importance of technological issues in the media and the workplace, by the discussions generated by government involvement—or lack of it, and by the needs of government departments and advisory councils for expertise. It has been actively promoted by strategic granting programs of the funding agencies at both levels of government, a situation that is uncommon outside of Ontario and Quebec. It has also been encouraged by colloquia and conferences, organized by government and para-governmental organizations.

Some of the research units developed in organizations that were not dedicated to the analysis of the management of technology, but to broader objectives. This is the case, for example, with the Centre de recherche en développement économique (CRDE) at the Université de Montréal, and of the teams of researchers at the Ecole des hautes études (CETAI), and the Centre d'innovation industrielle-Montreal (CIIM) of the Ecole Polytechnique, which are also involved with technological development.

In other instances, such as the administrative sciences at UQAM (Université de Québec à Montréal), more or less formally institutionalized research units were created for the specific purpose of the management of technology. Such is the case of the Groupe de recherche en économie et en gestion des petites et moyens entreprises (GREPME) at the Université de Québec à Trois-Rivières and of the Institut national de la recherche scientifique (INRS).

In the wake of the strategic grant program of the Ministere de l'enseignement superieur et de la science, the "actions structurantes" program, three new research programs emerged at UQAM with the explicit function of linking researchers from different institutions: the

Centre de recherche en développement industriel et technologique (CREDIT), including researchers from Concordia and the Université de Montréal, active in technology policy and in studies on the innovative process; the Groupe de recherche en informatique et droit (GRID), working in cooperation with the Centre de recherche en droit publique of the Université de Montréal on the interface between law and information technologies; and the Centre de recherche en evaluation sociale des technologies (CREST), bringing together researchers from UQAM and the Ecole Polytechnique and working on the implications of technology for work and its organization, and on the social assessment of technology and of risk.

These centres notwithstanding, a substantial amount of university research in Quebec in the management of technology is still conducted by individual researchers, eventually assisted by a more or less stable small team of students and professionals.

Aside from the universities in Quebec, but in cooperation with them, the Institut de recherche appliquée sur le travail (IRAT), funded by the labour unions and the Ministère de l'enseignement superieur et de la science, conducts studies on the impact of technological change on workers and the workplace, and the Centre canadien de recherche sur l'informatisation du travail (CCRIT) of Communications Canada in Ville de Laval and the Centre francophone en recherche en informatisation des organizations (CEFRIO) in Quebec City, funded under the Canada-Quebec agreement for the area of communications, both support studies on the conditions and the effects of the introduction of information technologies in public and private organizations.

In the area of environmental assessment, the Bureau d'audience publique sur l'environnement (BAPE), under the responsibility of the Minister of the Environment, has developed considerable expertise on the assessment of impacts, and on the management of public controversy on environmental issues, and has served as a centre for research and its support.

Outside of Quebec, it is more difficult to describe research in the management of technology. Relatively few centres have been funded, and much work occurs outside of them at specific universities. Yet, here too, the initial impetus for much of the early research came from government programs. The Technological Innovation Studies Program established by the Department of Industry, Trade and Commerce in 1971 is one example. Funded initially at a level of $350,000 per annum (and $235,000 after 1978), the program produced 107 studies before its termination in 1985. The program was designed to provide research grants and scholarships to encourage studies in the area of technological innovation and technical entrepreneurship in Canada. The primary recipients of the grants were academics from economics, science, and engineering faculties, although several grants were also awarded to non-academics. In addition to the reports published directly as a result of funding under the program, numerous articles were also published by the researchers and several books were written as a result of assistance provided by the program. The program also contributed substantially to student training in Canada, and some of the former graduate students funded by it number among the principal researchers in the field today. An important figure in the evolution of the program was Thomas Clarke, a former director, currently of Stargate Consultants.

Research on the management of technology and innovation has received support from a variety of government sources. Although not a primary source of funding, SSHRCC's strategic grant program, Managing the Organization in Canada, provided support to a number of researchers. The federal government's Department of Regional Industrial Expansion continues to play a critical role through its funding of two major academic centres, the Management of Technology Institute (MTI) at McMaster University and the National Centre for Management Research and Development (NCMRD) at the University of Western Ontario.

MTI was created to promote the management of technology in Canadian firms as a means of improving their competitiveness. With its funding from the federal government, MTI operates with a national mandate to improve the quality of technology management in Canadian firms through the development of educational programs and materials, enrichment of the resource core of trainers, and the establishment of a national and international network of educators. MTI is still in its development phase, and although a number of important activities have been carried out, it has yet to establish itself nationally in any significant manner. Among the key academics associated with the McMaster program are Professors Robert Cooper, Christopher Bart, Elko Kleinschmidt, and John Miltenberg.

NCMRD operates with a national mandate comparable to that of MTI, only with the emphasis on the generation of research. It is designed to act as a focal point and clearing house for management research in Canada. Among the major research programs supported by NCMRD, the one with most relevance for the current investigation is Generating Profit From New Technology. The primary objective of this program, under the leadership of Professor Roger More, is to help managers of Canadian companies become more profitable by improving their capacity to manage and transform new technologies into new customers, profits, and growth. The three priority areas of the program are: improving management of new technology development; improving management of new technology adoption; and improving management of developer/adopter relationships. The program supports a network of activities by researchers at a variety of other universities including Chris Bart at McMaster, Carol Beatty and John Gordon at Queen's, David Boag at Saskatchewan, Hugh Munro and Hamid Noori at Wilfrid Laurier, and Isaiah Litvak and Tim Warner at York.

In addition to the two major centres with national funding, there exist a number of other research centres at several Canadian universities, primarily in Ontario. Included among these has been the Research Centre for High Technology Management at Carleton, which developed a highly focused set of concerns based upon its close relationships with the segment of the advanced electronics industry located around Ottawa. Among the key researchers at Carleton are Professors Anthony Bailetti, George Haines, David Cray, and John Callahan.

Another important centre located in Ontario is the Research Centre for the Management of New Technology at Wilfrid Laurier. Several of the principal researchers at REMAT, including Hamid Noori and Hugh Munro, enjoy a close working relationship with NCMRD. The Centre for Organizational Effectiveness in the University of Toronto's Faculty of Management Studies, whose members, including Harvey Kolodny, Martin Evans, and Daniel Ondrack, have concentrated their research efforts on design and implementation issues of sociotechnical systems and the management of innovation, as well as the problems of small high-technology companies.

Some of its members have also had a close involvement with the government-sponsored Ontario Quality of Working Life Centre. This centre also enjoyed close working relationships with a number of academics across the country, including Richard Long at Saskatchewan, David Conrath at Waterloo, and Don Nightingale at Queen's. The newly formed Centre for Technology Management at Dalhousie University focuses its research activities on improving management of, and management education in, information and related technologies, as well as improving management of the acquisition, commercialization, and international marketing of products and services based on new technology. The chief researchers at Dalhousie include M.A.H. Dempster, Andrew Peacock, Philip Rosson, and Michael Martin.

There is a strong interest in science policy at Dalhousie, where the Dean of Business, James McNiven brings considerable expertise. This is matched by work at Simon Fraser on science policy, risk assessment, technology assessment (including natural resource management), and standards (Stanley Globerman, Bill Leiss, Liora Salter, Chad Day). The Simon Fraser group has established a Centre for Policy Studies on Science and Technology, and has a long-standing research group on risk analysis. In the case of the Centre, the Simon Fraser researchers are joined by Ilan Vertinsky, Bill Stanbury, and Peter Nemetz from UBC, and they maintain contact with Elia Zureik and his colleagues at Queen's. In the risk work, the Simon Fraser effort, which involves academics from mathematics, kinesiology, computing, engineering, business, and communication, follows upon the lead established at Waterloo with the Risk Institute (Nils Lind and John Shortreed, in particular), and draws support from both government departments and industry.

Science policy is, of course, also of interest to the Science Council, which has expressed formally its willingness to be a partner in any new research initiative on science policy. The same expression of interest has been made by the International Research and Development Centre, which has a long history of science policy analysis, and by the Telecommunications Policy Branch of the Department of Communications. Similar interest is evident from within Investment Canada and the Department of Industry, Science and Technology, and indeed, one of Investment Canada's officials, John de la Mothe, has taken leadership in organizing conferences on science policy, and in the newly established North American and Caribbean branch of the International Science Policy Foundation.

An informal network of researchers interested in various statistical aspects of the management of technology also exists within the federal government. The network includes representatives from Statistics Canada; Industry, Science and Technology, Communications; Employment and Immigration; Labour; the Economic Council; and the Labour Market and Productivity Centre, as well as informal representation from the Social Science Federation of Canada. The network includes a variety of researchers and policy analysts within federal departments concerned with the quality of statistical data concerning the extent of use of new technology in Canadian industry, issues related to the diffusion of technology, and various aspects related to labour force skills and training needs.

As was mentioned above, the concern among the management and engineering faculties has not just been with promoting research in this field, but also with more actively disseminating the insights of that research to their students, who will become future managers, as well as to those currently working in the field. A key figure in promoting these concerns has been Mark Abbott, until recently Alcan/NSERC Professor of Management and Technology at Queen's University (Abbott, 1987,

1988a, 1988b), and now head of the Ontario Science Centre. A central locus for these efforts has been the National Workshop on Management and Technology which has met twice with deans from Canada's engineering and management faculties, as well as a significant number of chief executive officers of Canadian corporations.

At the second of these workshops, held in January, 1988, the participants focused on the need for team problem-solving and no-text courses; research and teaching in the management of technology; greater integration of engineering and business degrees in this area; general resource sharing between industry and university; better quality work terms for co-op students; and multidisciplinary programs (Fedorowicz, 1988: 55). The teaching of management of technology has recently become a key concern of the Science Council of Canada as well. On the basis of a recently commissioned study (Clarke and Reavley, 1987), it advocated the need for closer linkages between the university and industry in this area (Science Council of Canada, 1988: 44-45).

The largest single cluster of geographers working within the theme of managing technologies meets regularly under the rubric of the Industrial Geography Study Group of the Canadian Association of Geographers. Regular participants have included: Trevor Barnes (UBC), John Bradbury (McGill), John Britton (Toronto), Meric Gertler (Toronto), John Holmes (Queen's), R. Geoffrey Ironside (Alberta), Suzanne Mackenzie (Carleton), Glen Norcliffe (York), Damaris Rose (INRS-Urbanisation), and Guy Steed (Science Council of Canada). Another smaller cluster includes those working for the Science Council of Canada (Guy Steed, James Gilmour), and those who have completed studies for the Council under contract (John Britton).

Individual industrial geographers who have fashioned links with public or quasi-public organizations concerned with the process of managing technology in the workplace include: John Holmes, who has spoken at or helped to organize symposia in concert with both the Canadian Auto Workers and Canadian locals of the United Steelworkers of America; and Meric Gertler, who advised the Social Planning Council of Metropolitan Toronto on its project on labour market adjustment policy.

Within the labour process approach, the overwhelming majority of the studies conducted in the last five years have been sponsored by the Technology Impact Research Fund (TIRF) and, subsequently, the Technology Impact Program (TIP) of Labour Canada. In this program, priority was given to labour organizations, women's groups, and other organizations wishing to investigate issues of relevance to the workplace. In September, 1986, when Labour Canada announced the further extension of the program under the name of the Technology Impact

Program, a second objective to support demonstration and pilot projects that illustrate effective methods of cooperative development and implementation of technological innovation was added.

The TIRF/TIP programs produced a significant, and largely unintended, cross-fertilization between the academic community and the labour organizations in this country. Academic researchers were excluded from receiving direct support under the terms of the program. However, in many cases the labour organizations interested in conducting the research lacked the staff with the necessary skills to undertake the research themselves. Further, after the initial rounds of adjudicating research proposals, it became clear that Labour Canada was applying fairly stringent criteria of academic rigour in awarding the grants. These conditions of the program led to two indirect results. In some instances, academic researchers interested in the program approached labour organizations in a proactive fashion with proposals for the organization to sponsor. In other cases, unions interested in conducting research sought out sympathetic academics to collaborate with them, or hired freelance researchers with strong academic credentials. In both cases, the outcome produced strong partnerships that drew upon the expertise of the university community, while focusing this expertise on issues of direct concern to the sponsoring organization. The partnerships that resulted may not have been an original intention of the program, but appear to have been highly productive and satisfactory to all concerned. It has resulted in the creation of a network of university and labour organization-based researchers who share a common set of research interests and a common research experience.

As a consequence there has come into existence a very loose network of researchers in the field, some of whom interact and some of whom have very little contact with each other. As is usually the case, the networks are highly regionalized, with groups in different parts of the country having relatively little contact or overlap with each other. The network of researchers cuts across a variety of academic disciplines, drawing in members whose backgrounds range across law, labour history, sociology, psychology, political science, computer science, women's studies, and administrative studies. One name that comes up repeatedly among people working in this field, and especially among those in the trade union movement, is D'Arcy Martin, National Representative (Education) for the Communications Workers of Canada. Long an advocate of the need for greater study of the impact of technological change on the union movement, Martin is credited by some at Labour Canada with the original idea for the TIRF program.

At the core of the network is Labour Canada's Labour Outreach program. The administrator of the program, Ellen Cornell, is responsible for monitoring the ongoing state of the research grants administered by the department, and maintains a regular contact with the researchers. The department has never fully decided what use to make of the body of studies that have been completed to date. It did bring together almost eighty of the researchers involved in the first rounds of TIRF studies at a conference in Montreal in September, 1986. The discussions produced a very positive reaction among the researchers, and the department was urged by many to facilitate this type of interaction on a more regular basis.

Among the labour researchers themselves, a number of attempts have been made to build upon the findings of the studies. A key individual in coordinating the activities of a number of individuals working on TIRF projects in the Toronto region was Pat McDermott of the Social Science Department at York University. Professor McDermott conducted her own study for the Ontario Public Service Employees Union, assisted several other unions and researchers in obtaining their grants, and brought together a group of TIRF researchers in the Toronto area for regular meetings during 1986-87.

Another key researcher in the Toronto area is David Robertson, whose work with Jeff Wareham for the Canadian Auto Workers is held in universally high regard. A private researcher and writer, Heather Menzies, who has previously conducted research on these issues for the Institute for Research on Public Policy, has made the most extensive use of the resource materials collected in the studies. She has systematically reviewed all of the reports on file at Labour Canada and has incorporated the findings into her new book on the impact on society of new information technologies (1989).

Within the British Columbia region, a key researcher has been Elaine Bernard, formerly of the Labour Studies program at Simon Fraser University and now at Harvard. Professor Bernard conducted two rounds of studies herself for the British Columbia Federation of Labour and served as a consultant and advisor on a variety of other studies. Once again, within the Vancouver region there occurred a variety of lively meetings and debates among the various researchers. These interactions involved not just a discussion of research findings, but active debates on the political implications of the research for trade unions and on the strategies that should be pursued in light of the findings.

Another centre of integration for some of the labour process studies has been the Studies in Communications and Information Technology (SCIT) program at Queen's University. Two of its principal members, Professors Elia Zureik and Vincent Mosco (now at Carleton), conducted their own research project for the Communications Workers of Canada.

In addition, the SCIT program has conducted a regular seminar series for a number of years as well as several conferences that have included the results of some of the labour process studies. However, the SCIT program focuses much more broadly on the social aspects of communications and information technology, and on science policy.

There has been a certain, if limited, amount of interaction between a number of publicly funded bodies and the labour process researchers. The Ontario Quality of Working Life Centre published summaries of the results of a number of these studies in one of its final issues, but its untimely disbandment precludes it from playing a future role in this field. In addition, the Labour Resource Branch of the Canadian Labour Market and Productivity Centre has also published summaries of a number of the TIRF studies in its publication, "Labour Research Exchange". The Labour Resource Branch includes researchers, such as Ken Waldie, who also conducted a TIRF study for the Canadian Paperworkers' Union.

Finally, there have been several research projects sponsored by the Department of Communications' Canadian Workplace Automation Research Centre (CWARC) in Laval, Quebec. CWARC has sponsored research by a number of academics, including Professors Susan Clark of Mount Saint Vincent University and Peta Tancred-Sheriff of McMaster University, that shares the same concerns and interests characteristic of the labour process studies. In June of 1988, CWARC co-sponsored a conference on the individual, organizational, and social impacts of information technologies with the newly created Centre for Administrative and Information Studies at the University of Western Ontario that brought together a number of researchers, primarily interested in the impacts of office automation on the labour process.

The most striking feature of the networks in this area is the lack of any institutional basis of support for their activities within the academic community. The broad range of disciplines covered by the researchers makes academic interaction highly problematic. The connections between academic researchers and government bodies are equally casual; although a number have occurred, they have largely been on a haphazard basis. A critical failing has also been the lack of greater interaction between researchers in English and French Canada.

Analysis—The State of the Research

If one were to draw up a list of topics and issues in the management of technology, without respect for their relative importance or the amount of research on each, the list would be more or less as follows:

- the stimulation of innovation and R&D within the firm
- the management of the innovation process
- technology transfer within Canadian industry or from parent or foreign firms
- technology transfer for export
- technology transfer and foreign aid/development
- organizational adoption of and adaptions to new technology
- job classifications and job skills (related to technological change)
- the impact of technology upon the workforce, in general and in specific industries
- training issues and policies
- science and technology education
- public education concerning science and technology
- labour-management relations and collective bargaining (as affected by technological change)
- science policy—government stimulation of R&D
- industrial strategy
- trade policies
- the effect of the bilateral agreement on technology transfer into and out from Canadian industry
- standards
- intellectual property—patents and copyright issues
- regulatory issues—technology assessment (including social and environmental assessment)
- regulatory issues—risk analysis (including potentially dangerous products, technologies or industrial processes)
- office automation studies
- women and technology
- social impact of technology
- spatial impact of technology—
- regional and community development
- decision theory and decision-support systems

This list of topics and issues relates to the management of technology in general, but it also is reflected in studies of particular industries or sectors of the economy. For example, the communications and information sector have come under particular scrutiny with respect to their adoption, their export potential, their social impact and their regulatory issues. Potentially, however, any industry or sector could be examined with respect to any or all of these topics or issues. This list of topics can also be distinguished by the disciplines of the researchers. Almost any item on the list can be, or has been, subject to scrutiny in economics, political science, sociology, business administration, information studies, women's studies, communications, and even philosophy.

As is evident from the list, in theory at least, the management of technology is a very broad field. In practice, however, a smaller number of topics are usually grouped together for the purposes of research. Moreover, the organization of research by clusters of topics is at least in part a result of the organization of research funding. As noted above, different topics have been funded under different programs, with the result that cross-fertilization and synthetic work is rare. As is evident from the discussion of networks, there are a number of different departments, agencies, and councils involved. It will be useful to identify them, before commenting on the significance of research funding for the management of technology.

Labour Canada, the Department of Communications, and the Department of Industry, Science and Technology (ISTC) are actively involved in funding research, as has been the Department of Industry, Trade and Commerce, the Department of Regional Economic Expansion, and the Ministry of State for Science and Technology. As well, many of the policy advisory councils, such as the Economic Council, have funded research on such related topics as science policy, regulatory issues and standards, and the Royal Society has commissioned conferences and studies on risk assessment. Several private organizations are involved, for example, labour councils.

The National Sciences and Engineering Research Council (NSERC) has debated whether the management of technology should fall within its ambit, given the extensive involvement of scientists and engineers in some aspects of the research. And, of course, SSHRCC has funded related research through its general granting program, and through three of its strategic granting initiatives: Managing the Organization in Canada, Women and Work, and the Human Context of Science and Technology (HCST). NSERC and SSHRCC are now cooperating in a program that sponsors both Chairs and Masters Fellowships in the area of science policy, and SSHRCC has revised its strategic program on the Human Context of Science and Technology—in part as a result of this study—to incorporate the themes identified within the field of managing technology.

Historically, however, research commissioned or funded by any one of these bodies has often not been referenced by people funded through another, because the topics and foci differ in each case. For example, Labour Canada's Technology Impact Program focuses on the workforce, while the Technological Innovation Studies Program funded research on innovation and on the adoption of new technologies. Not surprisingly, the Department of Communications pays most attention to the communication and information technologies. To the extent that SSHRCC has funded the management of technology under its Human Context of Science and Technology program in the past, it has usually been with respect to the social impact of technology and risk analysis. By contrast, in SSHRCC's Managing the Organization program, the focus is naturally upon the management of innovation and the adoption of technology. The new SSHRCC strategic granting program in Applied Ethics, and the new initiative in Science and Technology Policy, are likely to provide considerably more support for the management of technology in the future, including support for humanists as well as social scientists.

There is nothing intrinsically wrong with the existence of different funding programs for a large area of research such as the management of technology. There are, however, three particular drawbacks in this specific case. The first is simply that several important topics and issues from the list have historically not been not included in any funding program. Not surprisingly, research is seriously underdeveloped (almost non-existent) in these areas. It has already been noted that there has been, as yet, almost no research in Canada being conducted on standards, relatively little research on analytical methodologies needed for risk analysis, few databases to support research on innovation strategies, and little research on matters related to intellectual property.

The second drawback is that the management of technology requires a coordinated effort, involving the public and private sectors, a variety of organizations, and both industrial and public policy decisions. When research occurs—as it has been in this case—in different forums, the information is not brought together. No single source of the relevant data on innovation or technology adoption yet exists, a fact that impoverishes a wide variety of research on related topics. Moreover, in the new global economy, it is no longer appropriate to separate individual sectors for examination in isolation from each other. For example, technological innovation in the communication and information sector has a direct impact on the competitive position of all other industries. In the past, the lack of co-ordination among various funding agencies and among government departments with responsibility for specific economic sectors has undermined the ease of co-ordination of their quite useful work in the management of technology.

There has been a further problem, most directly applicable to social science. As noted above, most of the social science research on the management of technology is funded through SSHRCC, but some of the important topics from the list have historically been funded only through its general research grants program. The result has been that research on topics such as women and technology or job automation is perceived thus far as distinct from research on the management of technology, because each has been funded under a different program within SSHRCC. In other words, the lack of co-ordination which has seemed to exist among funding bodies and government departments has been matched in the past by a similar lack of co-ordination among the researchers funded by SSHRCC. In this instance, the result has been that it is difficult for social scientists to conceive of themselves as engaged in a single program of study.

It is important to stress again that there are many benefits to be derived from the existence of a multiplicity of funding sources and programs for research on the management of technology. Moreover, one could not conceive of a situation in which any granting agency, government department or policy advisory body would withdraw from a field of research directly related to its mandate. The point to be made is a simple one. The field of the management of technology is a new one, comprised of many interrelated topics. The lack of a coordinated effort, of adequate means for integrating research, or of proper databases, has been costly. It has meant that some important topics have been neglected; it has meant that researchers—even those funded by SSHRCC—are often working in isolation. It has meant that, in spite of the attention paid to the management of technology in the political realm, the area as a whole is as yet underdeveloped. It has undermined the kind of interdisciplinary work necessary when global economic change is involved.

There is no need to argue for the national or strategic importance of the management of technology, for this is widely accepted. Without a concerted, integrated effort, however, the national and strategic need will not be met. Critical topics of research in the management of technology will be neglected; important research will not be brought to bear upon the strategic issues involved; research will proceed in a piecemeal fashion and remain largely inaccessible to both academics and those who need it most in government and the private sector.

Analysis—The Role of Social Science

Although social scientists are represented in all of the paradigms, are involved in each topic area, and are fully integrated into the networks, the management of technology remains a difficult area for social science. As Kolodny noted in his correspondence:

The training of many researchers in this field is originally psychology or industrial psychology with some engineers and relatively few sociologists and no political scientists. The latter two categories are increasingly important to the field, but have not had much impact as yet. The perspective of [the discussion paper] is broadly informed by people whose background is similar to these latter two categories than to those who currently dominate the field as I know it. (personal correspondence)

Indeed, there are some who claim that the field properly concerns engineers and those in management science, and not social science.

This situation is troublesome. It is useful to describe it in sharp relief, so the point will be clear. First, in virtually every social science discipline (and some of the humanities), the theme of technological change is considered to be intrinsic to the discipline. Moreover, since the focus is social science, not engineering or natural science, the issues of concern to the disciplines are the impact and management of technological change. Second, there are social scientists represented in each of the paradigms and topic areas. Third, the prevailing conception of the field (which Kolodny describes accurately) is that social scientists have had no role or impact upon it. Some even claim that the role for social scientists is, and should be, minimized.

Finally, however much researchers in the management of technology wish it were otherwise, this topic has not yet commanded much attention from the social science disciplines, or in the universities. It is only represented by course offerings in a few locations, rarely in social science departments. A survey of recent programs and journals conducted for this study suggests that management of technology is unrepresented in the programs of the annual meetings of such disciplines as political science, economics, sociology, and history, and it is rarely the subject of articles in their recent disciplinary journals. Only in the relatively new, emerging disciplines such as communication, information science, and natural resource management, and in a few schools of business administration, is the management of technology addressed in any continuing fashion, and even in these disciplines serious attention to it is the exception rather than the rule.

This situation creates a special mandate for social scientists. In addition to the national and strategic need to support research in the management of technology (in which social science is essential), there is a job to be done within the social science community itself. Part of this job is simply to focus attention on the management of technology, so that the researchers who do not now conceive of their work in this fashion (but whose work is undoubtedly relevant) will do so.

The other part of the job is less easily accomplished. There are some intrinsic problems facing social scientists in the management of technology. First, management of technology research requires social scientists to work closely with the business schools, an association which has often been shunned by both in the past. Second, and perhaps more important, the management of technology requires social scientists to work closely with natural scientists and engineers. The long-standing biases, stereotypes, and misconceptions that exist among social, natural, and technical scientists must be overcome in this new working relationship. Moreover, the seemingly impermeable barrier that has existed in the past between the two funding agencies—SSHRCC and NSERC—cannot remain in existence if social and natural scientists are to collaborate. The current differences in their criteria for research applications and their adjudication, and the lack of appreciation for their different standards, are matters that must be addressed if the two cultures are to be bridged effectively by interdisciplinary research in the management of technology.

Finally, the management of technology is, almost by definition, pragmatic, policy-oriented, and often evaluative in orientation. Traditionally, the granting councils—SSHRCC in particular—have been reluctant to engage in active partnerships with industry, or in research that is designed to produce recommendations for government. This is true in spite of the existence of the matching grants program (matching research funds with support from industry). There are reasonable grounds for resistance by social scientists to a funding policy that is either industry-oriented, or designed to produce highly pragmatic research, at least in part because scholarly work in general has been underfunded for several years. That said, management of technology will never receive the support and participation it requires from social scientists until the matters of research funding in general, and the relationship between basic and strategic research in particular, have been addressed both within the granting councils and among social scientists.

Chapter Three

Etat des recherches en gestion de l'innovation technologique au Québec francophone

Camille Limoges, avec la collaboration de Denis Veilleux

Introduction:

Cette revue ne vise pas à l'exhaustivité dans la description. Elle se propose seulement de faire le point sur les tendances actuelles de la recherche en gestion de l'innovation technologique au Québec francophone, et d'en identifier les foyers principaux. En outre, parce que ce travail a été conçu pour alimenter la rédaction finale du rapport commun, il présume que la présentation des problématiques et de l'état de l'art sur chacune des composantes de la recherche en gestion de la technologie aura été déjà développée par les autres auteurs. On se contentera donc ici de quelques précisions concernant certaines spécificités des travaux québécois.

L'enquête a démontré une activité de recherche diversifiée et relativement intense. Comme c'est d'ailleurs généralement le cas en milieu universitaire où les segmentations disciplinaires et institutionnelles, aussi bien que les traditions de la recherche individuelle, induisent un morcellement des champs de recherche, le vaste domaine de la gestion des innovations technologiques demeure passablement fragmenté et présente peu de liaisons organiques entre chercheurs provenant d'horizons divers et travaillant selon des problématiques parfois divergentes. Toutefois, il existe aussi de nombreux regroupements plus ou moins formels de chercheurs, et la tenue de nombreux colloques et conférences depuis le tournant des années 1980 a favorisé des rapprochements et des échanges plus ou moins soutenus d'information.

Ce chapitre propose donc une revue des problématiques, des méthodes, et des activités de recherche en gestion de l'innovation technologique au Québec francophone; il s'organise selon les trois composantes retenues par l'équipe de recherche de la Fédération canadienne des sciences sociales (voir annexe 1 pour une représentation possible de cette tripartition):

1. La politique scientifique et technologique;
2. La gestion des innovations technologiques au niveau de la firme:
   —management de l'innovation,
   —ajustement travail/technologie;
3. La régulation de l'activité technologique:
   —régulation des risques,
   —évaluation sociale des technologies.

La politique scientifique et technologique

Au Canada comme ailleurs, pour reprendre une distinction fameuse, la politique scientifique est passée du stade d'une politique pour la science à celui d'une politique par la science. Plus même, depuis le tournant des années 1980, ces politiques se sont de plus en plus nettement définies comme politiques technologiques, et en fait comme politiques de soutien à l'innovation.

Ceci n'entraîne toutefois pas nécessairement une négligence du soutien à la recherche fondamentale. Mais il est clair que pour un pays qui produit environ 4 pourcent de la science mondiale, le développement industriel ne peut s'affirmer comme dépendant principalement de la recherche autochtone. Ce serait, en effet, courir à l'échec que de développer une stratégie axée principalement sur la thèse d'un processus séquentiel de l'activité de recherche fondamentale, principalement universitaire, jusqu'au développement de procédés et de produits nouveaux. Si au Canada comme ailleurs une politique de soutien à la recherche fondamentale s'impose c'est plutôt à deux autres titres. La mission centrale des universités du point de vue d'une politique de l'innovation est de former des scientifiques et des ingénieurs de haut niveau; un tel objectif exige d'abord un milieu de formation bien informé des derniers développements aux frontières de la recherche, en contact actif avec les principaux centres mondiaux. D'autre part, ce soutien à la recherche universitaire apparaît aussi en quelque sorte comme le prix à payer pour développer une capacité d'utilisation efficace des autres 96 pourcent de résultats de recherche générés à travers le monde chaque année. La mobilisation de cette capacité aux bénéfices du développement économique requiert cependant des communications efficaces entre les universités et les entreprises, d'où l'insistance marquée et les expérimentations multiples conduites ces dernières années pour intensifier cette nécessaire liaison.

En même temps commence à se faire jour, comme le manifeste la préoccupation de développer la recherche en gestion de l'innovation technologique, la conscience que les sciences sociales ont à apporter une contribution spécifique au succès des politiques de l'innovation. En effet, les sciences de la nature mises à contribution dans la genèse des innovations se caractérisent par l'universalité de validité de leurs résultats. Il n'existe pas une physique ou une chimie qui serait vraie au Japon ou en Allemagne mais inexacte au Canada. En sciences de la nature, les connaissances, où qu'elles soient développées, sont applicables partout. Cependant les processus de l'innovation et les stratégies des firmes doivent tenir compte de conditions et de contraintes nationales et locales. L'apport des sciences sociales pourrait à cet égard s'avérer décisif par ses contributions à une connaissance approfondie des spécificités de ces caractérisques nationales et locales.

Une étude récente de l'OCDE (Science and Technology Policy Outlook 1987) soulignait que, malgré les efforts substantiels consentis par les gouvernements et par les entreprises depuis le début des années 1980, une fraction seulement des bénéfices économiques potentiels des nouvelles technologies a été réalisé. Les attentes, en ce qui a trait à l'augmentation de la productivité et à la croissance, n'ont pas été satisfaites. La diffusion des innovations a été lente et éparse. "Un déplacement de l'effort gouvernemental vers la diffusion et l'adoption des technologies semble devoir apporter de bien plus grands bénéfices économiques." Or les sciences sociales ont un rôle de premier plan à jouer dans l'élaboration de politiques équilibrant mieux les efforts de développement et les efforts de diffusion des technologies. Les obstacles, les freinages, ou les indifférences qui affectent la diffusion des innovations ne sont pas de nature à être levés par le recours aux sciences de la nature; ils ne relèvent pas non plus principalement de problèmes d'ingénierie. Les facteurs en cause sont des facteurs humains, de nature économique, sociale, ou culturelle: cultures d'entreprises, design des organisations, appréhensions des marchés, habitudes de consommation, modèles de formation, transformation des modes de vie et des aspirations, relations de travail, organisation du travail, ajustement institutionnels, réglementations, etc.

Les inerties, les verrouillages, la fragmentation et le défaut de fluidité des milieux, les perceptions déficientes des besoins et des opportunités, qui interdisent ou retardent la diffusion des innovations, sont largement d'ordre économique, social, et organisationnel.

Enfin, l'internationalisation des marchés et l'intensification de la concurrence requièrent une meilleure connaissance de ces marchés largement déterminés par des caractéristiques nationales et locales, connaissance à la contribution de laquelle le rôle des sciences sociales deviendra décisif.

La nouvelle politique scientifique, comme politique de l'innovation, va donc bien au-delà de la seule mobilisation des capacités de recherche scientifique et de développement technologique. Le cas du Canada, comme économie ouverte et de petite taille, pose des problèmes particuliers (Dalpé, 1988) dont l'examen a été sérieusement engagé depuis environ deux décennies. Ces travaux peuvent être examinés sous deux chefs: l'analyse économique et l'analyse des dispositifs et des politiques.

L'analyse économique

Les contributions québécoises à l'analyse économique de l'innovation portent principalement sur trois ensembles de questions (Bonin et Lacroix, 1987): les innovations technologiques dans le contexte international, la diffusion des innovations et le progrès technique, et la liaison de l'effort de R-D avec l'innovation technologique.

La structure industrielle, de même que le caractère ouvert de notre économie, appelait l'examen des effets des investissements étrangers, l'examen des transferts internationaux de technologie, et l'étude des incidences de la R-D sur la structure des exportations.

Certains des travaux pionniers ont porté sur l'accès aux technologies étrangères au moyen d'accords de type contractuels, (licences de fabrication ou entreprises conjointes), ou d'investissements étrangers directs au Canada (Bonin, 1967), sur les modes de transmission internationale de la technologie, et notamment sur le rôle des firmes multinationales (Bonin, 1973, 1981; Bonin et Duranleau, 1988). D'autres études incitent à une révision d'un certain nombre d'idées reçues sur les lacunes attribuées au poids et à la signification d'ensemble pour l'innovation canadienne des entreprises à propriété étrangère (Boismenu et Ducatenzeiler, 1985). Le transfert de technologie ne doit pas être interprété nécessairement comme un indice de dépendance. Au contraire, c'est souvent un trait des firmes innovatrices qu'elles sont particulièrement actives eu égard à l'appropriation de technologies développées à l'étranger. Une autre étude d'importance fondamentale a été celle de Lacroix (1971) portant sur la mobilité procurée par l'avantage procuré par la R-D et l'innovation technologique à l'encontre des avantages découlant d'une dotation, non-transférable, en facteurs locaux spécifiques.

Des études sur la relation entre la R-D et la capacité à l'exportation ont par ailleurs montré que si l'effort de R-D en valeur absolue ne paraît pas toujours déterminant, en revanche l'effort relatif d'une industrie par rapport à celui des autres pays peut rendre compte de la position concurrentielle internationale de cette industrie (Lacroix et Scheuer, 1977; Séguin-Dulude, 1978). Dans une recherche d'ensemble sur la capacité innovatrice de l'industrie au Québec, DeBresson (1986) a montré que les innovations sont très inégalement distribuées selon les secteurs; ainsi le centre du système technologique québécois est-il constitué par la production et la distribution d'énergie. Le secteur de la machinerie manifeste une faiblesse évidente. L'étude confirme également que les petites entreprises, celles qui comptent moins de deux cents employés, fournissent une contribution en innovations plus grande que celle de leur contribution aux ventes ou à la valeur ajoutée. En revanche, alors que les petites entreprises rencontrent fréquemment de graves problèmes de croissance et de financement, ce sont les grandes entreprises qui sont les plus grandes utilisatrices d'innovations.

En matière de diffusion des innovations, Leblanc (1976, 1977, 1978) a développé un modèle prévisionnel de substitution technologique appliqué ensuite à diverses industries. Martin (1979, 1981) a examiné les modalités de l'inégale diffusion interrégionale des innovations au Canada et au Québec; plus récemment ses travaux ont mis en évidence la faible relation entre l'effort régional de R-D et l'innovation, observations qui s'appliquent évidemment aussi à l'échelle nationale (Martin, 1982). Par ailleurs, dans des études particulièrement originales, Séguin-Dulude (1982, Séguin-Dulude et al., 1984) a mis en évidence la forte interdépendance technologique interindustrielle: loin d'être autarciques eu égard à la technologie, certaines industries sont au contraire presque entièrement dépendantes des autres secteurs industriels pour leur approvisionnement technologique.

Par ailleurs, c'est un fait connu que l'effort de R-D du Canada le place dans les rangs inférieurs parmi les pays de l'OCDE. L'effort québécois, également mesuré par la proportion des dépenses de R-D sur le PIB, reste constamment inférieur à celui du Canada. Cette question a été de façon soutenue analysée et débattue au Québec. Lacroix et Séguin-Dulude (1983) ont conduit une étude poussée de ces disparités, et remis en question l'opinion selon laquelle l'effort canadien souffre d'un financement relatif public anormalement élevé; ils ont aussi questionné l'efficacité des subventions de soutien à la R-D et à l'innovation dans le secteur privé (aussi, Hanel, 1986). La tendance actuelle du gouvernement québécois à substituer les mesures fiscales aux aides directes est cependant loin de faire l'unanimité et a été récemment critiquée (Conseil de la Science et de la Technologie, 1988a). De tels travaux, d'ailleurs souvent générés par la demande des gouvernements ou en réactions aux orientations de ceux-ci, constituent les matériaux de base pour l'élaboration d'une politique de l'innovation adaptée aux conditions locales.

L'analyse des dispositifs et des politiques

Le développement récent de l'analyse sociopolitique de l'action gouvernementale en matière de science et de technologie s'explique bien évidemment par le caractère plus visible et plus intense de cette action depuis le milieu des années 1970. Ces préoccupations ont suscité un bon nombre de travaux de chercheurs, et ont donné lieu aussi à la mise en place d'organismes et de programmes qui ont eu un effet d'entraînement sur le développement des travaux de politique scientifique. Des universitaires ont fréquemment été sollicités pour participer à l'élaboration de documents gouvernementaux et pour assumer des contrats sur des questions à caractère prospectif ou évaluatif. Les énoncés de politique scientifique du gouvernement du Québec et les avis de ses conseils consultatifs, principalement le Conseil de la Science et de la Technologie et le Conseil des Universités, ont donné lieu à de nombreuses réunions publiques, colloques, et débats qui ont eu notamment pour conséquence de mettre en relations plus fréquentes les chercheurs actifs dans le domaine.

Les principaux moments de cette impulsion donnée à la politique scientifique ont été la publication du livre vert *Pour une politique de la recherche scientifique* (1979), qui a donné lieu à près d'un an de consultations et de tenue d'ateliers publics; l'énoncé de politique scientifique *Un projet collectif* (1980), qui en découle; et la publication de l'énoncé de politique économique *Le virage technologique* (1982). Plus récemment a été publié le document de consultation *La maîtrise de notre avenir technologique, un défi à relever. Plan d'action Québec 1988-1992* (1988), donnant lieu à un colloque sous la présidence du Premier ministre. Par ailleurs, le Conseil de la Science et de la Technologie, en plus de publier de nombreux avis préparés en association avec des chercheurs externes, rend publique périodiquement une analyse évaluative de la situation québécoise sous l'angle de la politique scientifique et technologique (Science et technologie. Conjoncture 1985, (1986c), Science et technologie. Conjoncture 1988 (1988c).

On peut distinguer, en ce qui a trait à la recherche, deux grands axes dans ce domaine: les recherches portant sur les dispositifs et les arrangements institutionnels, et celles portant sur les politiques et les actions gouvernementales.

Les dispositifs gouvernementaux de politique scientifique sont notoirement instables, soumis aux aléas de la formation des cabinets, et au déplacement des accentuations de politiques et des restructurations ministérielles, dans la plupart des pays et singulièrement au Canada et au Québec. Duchesne (1978) en a examiné pour le Québec la première phase de mise en place, et les étapes subséquentes d'évolution de ces dispositifs ont été l'objet d'une attention persistante et critique (Carter, 1983; Conseil de la Science et de la Technologie, 1986b, 1988c; Davis et Duchesne, 1986a, 1986b; Landry, 1987). L'examen du rôle des organismes consultatifs, la participation du public, le contrôle de l'action gouvernementale ont jusqu'ici peu retenu l'attention (Landry, 1980-1981).

Mais il faut noter qu'au Québec comme ailleurs, les études de politique scientifique continuent à restreindre leur champ à la détermination et à la priorisation d'objectifs, à l'allocation des ressources et, dans une mesure beaucoup moindre, à l'évaluation de la performance des programmes. L'activité proprement gouvernementale de construction des politiques en contexte bureaucratique continue à être traitée plus ou moins comme une "boîte-noire" comme si elle était non pertinente pour l'analyse. Des travaux récents montrent comment la mise à contribution des acquis de la sociologie des sciences permet de comprendre l'élaboration des politiques et programmes comme un processus complexe de constructions internes à l'organisation gouvernementale, garanties par l'enrôlement de porte-parole des groupes d'acteurs externes (Cambrosio, Limoges et Pronovost, sous presse; Limoges, Cambrosio et Pronovost, sous presse).

Nous avons évoqué déjà, à la section précédente, les préoccupations relatives au financement des activités de R-D, et notamment de la recherche universitaire. L'étude de Lacroix et Séguin-Dulude (1983) demeure à ce jour l'enquête la plus poussée sur cet objet, bien que le soutien à la recherche universitaire ait fait l'objet d'assez nombreux travaux (Landry, 1978, Leclerc, 1986, 1987; Conseil de la Science et de la Technologie, 1987). La collaboration université-industrie dans la perspective d'une facilitation du transfert de connaissances et d'une mise à contribution de l'expertise des laboratoires universitaires au Québec, comme ailleurs au Canada, a fait l'objet d'une attention soutenue (Blais, 1980; Conseil de la Science et de la Technologie, 1986a; Forum Entreprise-universités, 1984, 1985, 1987).

Certaines initiatives gouvernementales, comme la politique québécoise, dite du "Virage technologique" (Chaussé, 1983; Landry,

1985b; Pascot et Price, 1983; Langevin, 1983), le plan d'action pour le développement des biotechnologies (Cambrosio, Davis, Keating, 1985; Conseil de la Science et de la Technologie, 1985), l'offre de programmes gouvernementaux à la R-D industrielle (Landry, 1985a, 1986), la politique canadienne de l'énergie (Gingras et Rivard, 1988; Duquette, 1988), celle de l'aérospatiale (Dalpé, 1985), ont fait l'objet d'examens substantiels. Il en va de même de l'analyse de l'action du gouvernement fédéral au Québec et des interactions, comme des carences de complémentarité, des interventions des deux niveaux de gouvernement (Conseil de la Science et de la Technologie, 1984, 1987; Gingras et Dufour, 1988; Julien, 1978; Landry, 1986).

D'autres domaines demeurent encore relativement peu étudiés. Ainsi du recours à la politique d'achat gouvernementale (Dalpé 1987). L'évaluation des programmes n'a donné lieu qu'à peu de publications. On doit cependant noter à cet égard une intéressante étude de Faucher, Blais, et Young (1983) sur l'ensemble des aides directes aux entreprises au Québec et en Ontario qui montre comment malgré leur multiplication ces programmes innovent peu et comment leurs critériologies d'application évoluent de façon largement indépendante des effets officiellement recherchés. Quant aux mesures fiscales, malgré la faveur dont elles jouissent présentement, l'analyse de leurs effets montre le caractère assez incertain de leur efficacité (Conseil de la Science et de la Technologie, 1988a), comme l'ont indiqué du reste d'autres études américaines et canadiennes.

Comme il a été dit plus haut, l'ensemble de cette activité, de développement récent, s'explique pour une bonne part par l'implication plus vigoureuse des gouvernements depuis deux décennies. Dans ce contexte, certaines universités ont mis en place de nouveaux programmes de formation et donné naissance à des pôles de recherche. L'Université de Montréal a logé, de 1973 à 1986, un Institut d'histoire et de sociopolitique des sciences qui a produit une soixantaine de diplômés de maîtrise et de doctorat dont la moitié en politique scientifique, diplômés qui occupent maintenant des postes dans les fonctions publiques fédérale et provinciales ou dans d'autres universités. L'Université Concordia opère depuis le tournant des années 1970 un programme de Baccalauréat en "Science and Human Affairs" et l'Université du Québec à Montréal a ouvert en 1986 un autre programme de premier cycle en "Science, Technologie et Société"; ces deux programmes incluent une substantielle composante de politique scientifique et technologique. C'est dire qu'il existe au Québec des dispositifs de formation susceptibles d'alimenter le développement du potentiel de recherche en politique scientifique.

En outre, les programmes de subvention à caractère stratégique, qui permettent un financement important et plus soutenu, ceux du CRSH, et surtout le programme des "Actions structurantes" du Ministère de l'Enseignement supérieur et de la Science, ont contribué à l'émergence d'entités de recherche nouvelles dans les domaines à caractère scientifique et technique où les pouvoirs publics interviennent (CREDIT associant chercheurs de l'UQAM, des universités de Montréal et Concordia, [Centre de recherche en développement industriel et technologique], CREST associant des chercheurs de l'UQAM et de l'Ecole Polytechnique [Centre de recherche en évaluation sociale des technologies], GRID associant des chercheurs de l'UQAM et de l'Université de Montréal [Groupe de recherche en informatique et droit]). Dans d'autres unités qui n'ont pas spécifiquement pour objet la politique scientifique, des chercheurs ont parfois de façon assez continue conduit des travaux dans le domaine; ainsi le CRDE [Centre de recherche en développement économique] de l'Université de Montréal, le Centre d'études en administration internationale [CETAI] de l'Ecole des hautes études commerciales, et le Centre de développement technologique de l'Ecole polytechnique et l'équipe dirigée par Réjean Landry à l'Université Laval. A ces groupes s'ajoutent évidemment de nombreux chercheurs individuels ou membres d'équipes distribués dans les universités, les ministères, et divers organismes paragouvernementaux.

Enfin, depuis quelques années, certaines firmes de consultants, auxquels sont parfois associés des universitaires, ont exécuté, sous contrat, d'importantes recherches pour les deux paliers de gouvernement, notamment à l'occasion de la préparation de sommets de consultation (SECOR).

La gestion des innovations technologiques au niveau de la firme

L'entreprise constitue le foyer de toute politique de l'innovation. Elle est le lieu où se nouent deux séries de processus que nous examinerons successivement: le management de la technologie comme élément de la stratégie de la firme, et la gestion de l'organisation du travail et des incidences des nouvelles technologies.

Le management de la technologie

C'est un trait intéressant des travaux récents en management de l'innovation technologique qu'ils s'appuient sur des modèles du processus d'innovation qui récusent la conception linéaire qui a longtemps prévalu, qui supposait des relations séquentielles et transitives entre la recherche fondamentale, la recherche appliquée, et le développement technologique. C'est d'ailleurs sur la base de ce modèle ancien qu'avait pu s'imposer la controverse sur les mérites respectifs des stratégies "technology push" versus "market pull." L'innovation apparaît maintenant comme un processus plus complexe, où jouent de nombreuses rétroactions, dont les éléments agissent le plus souvent en simultanéité, et qui requiert qu'on développe la technologie, ou qu'on l'introduise le monitoring, en continu de l'ensemble de l'environnement de l'entreprise (Miller, 1983; Blais, 1985; Bonin et Lacroix, 1987, Limoges, 1989).

Les études de cas sur des innovations québécoises restent peu nombreuses (Cambrosio, Mackenzie, Keating, 1988; Dalpé, 1984). Toutefois la grande enquête conduite par l'équipe de chercheurs coordonnée par Pierre-André Julien et Jean-Claude Thibodeau, sur l'"Impact des nouvelles technologies sur la structure économique du Québec," financée par le Bureau de la statistique du Québec et trois ministères, et portant sur cinquante-quatre secteurs et neuf professions a déjà livré de substantiels résultats. Bien qu'elle vise tout particulièrement à évaluer les impacts de l'introduction de nouvelles technologies sur l'emploi, ses résultats déjà connus s'avèrent riches en information sur les pratiques d'introduction de ces technologies.

La question du rythme de pénétration des nouvelles technologies dans les entreprises reste évidemment une question d'intérêt permanent (DeBresson, 1981; Julien et Hébert, 1986). Une analyse récente des facteurs qui favorisent cette pénétration, issue du programme de recherche de Julien et Thibodeau, adoptant une approche multi-critères utilisant des facteurs micro- et macro-économiques, conduit à identifier comme facteur-clé l'entrepreneurship, la volonté d'innover, manifestés par des directions déjà expérimentées, bien éduquées et informées, mais assez jeunes pour ne pas privilégier de façon réflexe d'anciennes attitudes et méthodes.

Le rôle-clé des nouvelles technologies informatiques de gestion, de conception et de fabrication, a suscité de nombreux travaux sur leur introduction et sur les conditions de réussite de celle-ci (Conférence sur l'électronique et l'informatique, 1985; Julien, 1985; Lefebvre et al., 1985a, 1985b, 1986a, 1986b, 1986c, 1986d, 1987a, 1987b; Fortin, 1982; Gasse, 1983; Raymond et Magnenat-Thalmann, 1981; Proulx, 1984; Groleau, 1986; Hurtubise et Pastinelli, 1987).

Mais il est clair que les succès à cet égard ne relèvent pas exclusivement du dynamisme et de la compétence des entrepreneurs; ils tiennent aussi à l'environnement de l'entreprise, et notamment à l'insertion de celles-ci dans des constellations régionales regroupant d'autres entreprises à caractère technologique, des concentrations d'expertises (laboratoires), et l'existence d'un bassin de personnel hautement qualifié (universités). Les analystes de l'incubation et du développement soutenu de telles constellations technologiques insistent sur la nécessité de fonder les stratégies, notamment sur les ressources et les capacités régionales, sur les entreprises d'origine locale, sur l'engagement à long terme des leaders des secteurs privé et public, sur le désenclavement des universités et l'enrichissement des liaisons universités-entreprises, et sur l'allocation par les entreprises de contrats aux autres entreprises de la région (Miller et Côté, 1985; Miller, 1983; Miller, 1985). A cet égard, les travaux sur la localisation des entreprises et sur les incidences des politiques de régionalisation, évoquées à la section précédente, prennent une importance et un relief particuliers (Martin, 1979, 1982, 1985; Lacroix et Martin, 1987).

Si à certains auteurs (Miller, 1988) il est apparu qu'au sein de l'entreprise, la gestion stratégique et celle même du processus d'innovation s'avèrent plus décisives que les attributs organisationnels de la firme sur lesquels les sociologues ont tendance à insister, en revanche quand il s'agit de comprendre les conditions de bonne gestion et de maîtrise des incidences des technologies introduites sur le travail, la vie organisationnelle de l'entreprise devient une préoccupation centrale.

La gestion de l'organisation du travail et des incidences des nouvelles technologies

Parce que ces questions sont au coeur des rapports de forces et des négociations au sein des entreprises, il n'est pas étonnant qu'elles soient le lieu de traditions socialement plus critiques que ce n'est le cas pour les préoccupations précédemment analysées. En fait, il n'est sans doute pas exagéré d'avancer qu'au cours d'une première phase, chez les sociologues principalement, et dans le sillage des travaux de Braverman ou plus largement d'une sociologie du travail d'inspiration marxiste, bon nombre des études, même de situations locales, se structuraient par le recours à une analyse en termes de rapports sociaux faisant en quelque sorte du niveau micro l'illustration des contradictions et des conflits macro-sociaux.

Bien sûr sans que ces analyses aient perdu toute actualité, on doit noter que non seulement la thèse de Braverman est maintenant ébranlée, notamment au coeur même de sa conceptualisation de la déqualification (Doray, 1987), mais que l'apport de la nouvelle sociologie de l'activité technoscientifique dont le recours s'est en quelque sorte naturalisé du fait du centrement sur les effets des technologies dans l'entreprise est en train de donner lieu à une nouvelle génération d'études microsociologiques, qui ne sont pourtant pas étrangères à la thématisation des rapports sociaux (Saint-Pierre, 1984a, 1987; Alsène, 1988; Denis et Alsène, 1988).

En somme, le champ des études sur les incidences de l'introduction des nouvelles technologies en entreprises apparaît notablement plus diversifié que ce n'était le cas il y a peu. A côté de vastes études horizontales, à caractère empirique, inspirées par les techniques de l'analyse économique et des sciences de l'administration, faisant appel aux techniques du questionnaire et de l'entrevue (Julien et Thibodeau, Lefebvre et al.), se poursuivent des travaux plus typiques d'une sociologie critique du travail et émergent des analyses portant sur les incidences de l'usage de technologies dans l'entreprise, considérée comme organisation technosociale.

Bien que ce domaine de recherche ait connu une impulsion nouvelle du fait de la priorité que lui ont reconnue les deux niveaux de gouvernement (programme des "Actions structurantes" du ministère de l'Enseignement supérieur et de la Science à l'origine de la création du GRID, du CREDIT, et du CREST mentionnés précédemment]; création du Centre francophone de recherche en informatisation des organisations [CEFRIO]; nouvel organisme financé par les deux niveaux de gouvernement dans le cadre de l'Entente Canada-Québec en Communications; Programme de Travail Canada, mise en place du Centre canadien de recherche sur l'informatisation du travail, à Ville de Laval), la recherche dans ce domaine est active depuis plusieurs années, du fait notamment du développement de la sociologie du travail en milieu universitaire, et de l'activité des syndicats eux-mêmes qui ont mis sur pied l'Institut de recherche appliquée sur le travail (IRAT) (financé conjointement par les syndicats et le ministère de l'Enseignement supérieur et de la Science). En outre, les transformations rapides des conditions de travail, notamment par l'implantation des systèmes informatisés, ont évidemment aussi contribué à donner un regain de vigueur à ces études (Frappier-DesRochers, 1986). Ainsi, une étude récente (Desjardins, 1985) révèle que plus de la moitié des conventions collectives examinées comportent des clauses plus ou moins élaborées relatives au changement technologique.

La soixantaine d'études sectorielles ou professionnelles déjà mentionnées, issues du programme de recherche coordonné par Julien et Thibodeau, ne porte directement, eu égard aux incidences des nouvelles technologies, que sur l'emploi, mais ces études fourniront de substantiels matériaux de base pour la compréhension de la diversité des effets, selon les industries et selon les technologies adoptées, sur l'organisation du travail.

Les nombreux travaux de l'équipe de recherche dirigée par Lefebvre (Lefebvre, Lefebvre, Ducharme, et Colin, 1986), en plus de fournir des données sur le rythme de pénétration des technologies informatiques, permettent également de tirer des conclusions sur les effets sur l'organisation, sur la productivité, sur l'emploi, de même que sur les perceptions et les comportements des directions d'entreprises.

Pour le secteur tertiaire surtout, il faut mentionner le programme de recherche sous la direction de Saint-Pierre, qui engage notamment une réflexion théorique et méthodologique d'ensemble sur les incidences des nouvelles technologies informatiques sur le travail et la gestion de son organisation (Saint-Pierre, 1984a, 1984b, 1985a, 1985b, 1987; Pinard et Rousseau, 1985; Tremblay, 1987; De Sève, 1985).

Face aux incidences des technologies sur le travail, les emplois apparaissent inégalement vulnérables ou précaires, et cette situation différentielle appelait une attention particulière aux effets des changements technologiques sur le travail des femmes. Comme l'indique une recension récente effectuée pour le Conseil du Statut de la Femme (Bisson, 1986), cette question a fait et continue à faire l'objet de plusieurs recherches, notamment sur la qualité de vie au travail et sur les conditions propres à l'assurer (Roy, 1983; Billette et Piché, 1985; Jacob et Lorrain, 1985; McNeil, 1982, 1985; Dumas, 1985); ces recherches sont souvent centrées sur une technologie particulière, comme celle du traitement de texte (Benoît, 1985; Benoît et al., 1984). Ici encore, certaines des données recueillies et analysées dans le cadre des travaux du GREPME, comme celui sur les transformation du métier de sténo-dactylo (Hébert et Lorrain, 1987), fournissent un éclairage horizontal, c'est-à-dire intersectoriel.

L'ubiquité des nouvelles technologies de l'information engendre d'ailleurs aussi des transformations dans l'univers des professionnels. L'Office des Professions du Québec en a fait réaliser un examen d'ensemble (Office des professions, 1986), alors que le GREPME a traité la question en ce qui a trait aux ingénieurs (Julien et Hébert, 1987).

Dans ce contexte de redéfinition du travail et de ses qualifications, les questions relatives à la formation et au recyclage prennent évidemment une acuité renouvelée. Le Conseil supérieur de l'Education (1987) a publié une étude d'ensemble sur le perfectionnement de la main d'oeuvre au Québec. Mais ces questions avaient déjà, évidemment depuis longtemps, préoccupé les syndicats et l'Institut de recherche appliquée sur le travail (IRAT) (Bernier et al., 1983; Centrale de l'enseignement du Québec, 1985; Bernier et Cailloux-Teiger, 1988). Les processus de redéfinition et de négociation des décisions concernant les programmes de formation technique sont l'objet d'un programme de recherche dirigé au CREST par Doray (Doray et Cambrosio, 1989; Doray et Dubar, 1988; Doray et Lapointe, 1988).

La régulation de l'activité technologique

La responsabilité des pouvoirs publics en matière de régulation des activités technologiques vise la protection de la santé publique et de l'environnement (évaluation et gestion des risques), de même que l'évaluation sociale des technologies ("technology assessment").

La recherche sur l'évaluation et sur la gestion des risques reste encore peu développée au Québec. Elle émerge en ce qui a trait à l'évaluation de la gestion de crises relatives à des accidents causés par des produits toxiques (Denis, 1989), et à l'évaluation et à la gestion des risques associés aux biotechnologies (Limoges et al., 1989a, 1989b). L'évaluation des technologies ("technology assessment") n'est pas non plus encore un domaine très développé, mais la recherche y est plus vigoureuse et davantage institutionnalisée.

Des expériences importantes d'évaluation des technologies et de leurs impacts appréhendés, comme celles liées au développement de grands projets, tels l'exploitation hydroélectrique de la Baie James ou la construction de l'aéroport international de Mirabel, n'ont pas eu d'effet d'entraînement durable sur la recherche au Québec, ni n'ont fait encore l'objet d'aucune analyse évaluative. Cependant avec la création du Bureau des audiences publiques sur l'environnement (BAPE) en application de la Loi sur la qualité de l'Environnement, des critères et des procédures ont été mis en oeuvre en ce qui a trait à la réalisation d'évaluations environnementales et à la gestion des controverses publiques qu'elles suscitent. Ces activités ont suscité de nombreuses études méthodologiques et de contenu, et permis la consolidation d'un nouveau domaine de recherche.

Par ailleurs, la politique québécoise dite du "Virage technologique" s'est accompagnée de la promotion, et de l'identification comme priorité, de la recherche sur la "maîtrise sociale des nouvelles technologies." C'est à ce titre que le programme de subventions stratégiques "d'Actions structurantes" du ministère de l'Enseignement supérieur et de la Science a permis l'émergence de deux nouveaux centres de recherche, le "Groupe de recherche en informatique et droit" (GRID) et le "Centre de recherche en évaluation sociale des technologies" (CREST).

De fait, surtout depuis les cinq dernières années, les travaux sur l'évaluation et la gestion des incidences sociales des nouvelles technologies se sont multipliés. Ces travaux portent sur cinq domaines principaux:

(a) la révision du cadre théorique et méthodologique du "technology assessment" au profit du développement du programme d'une évaluation sociale des technologies (Kaufman, 1988; Limoges, 1987, 1988a, 1988b; Cambrosio et Limoges sous presse);

(b) la gestion et la régulation des impacts sur l'environnement (Marceau recherche en cours, Université Laval; Grandbois, 1986; Denis, 1989);

(c) les incidences de l'informatique sur les libertés civiles et leur régulation juridique, au GRID, en collaboration avec le CRDP, (GRID, 1986; Péladeau, 1989);

(d) l'appropriation culturelle et sociale des nouvelles technologies (Proulx, 1988; Proulx et Tahon, 1986, 1989; Proulx, Levesque, Sanderson et Tahon, 1989; Veillette recherche en cours, Université Laval; Tremblay, 1983, Tremblay et Sénécal, 1987; Dagenais recherche en cours, Université Laval; Blais, 1983; Lalonde et Parent, 1984);

(e) les nouvelles technologies de la reproduction (Vandelac, 1986, 1987; Volant, recherche en cours, UQAM; Roy à l'Institut de recherche clinique de Montréal; Deleury, recherche en cours, Université Laval).

Conclusion

La gestion de l'innovation technologique constitue un domaine complexe et polymorphe. Notre revue des activités a mis en évidence pour le Québec francophone une substantielle quantité de travaux de recherche. Ce sera sans doute pour les années à venir une tâche majeure que de promouvoir, de faciliter et d'intensifier les échanges entre les chercheurs, et entre ceux-ci et les utilisateurs potentiels de leurs résultats. Malgré sa relative fragmentation, le domaine apparaît déjà doté cependant d'un bon nombre de foyers institutionnalisés, parfois déjà en contact plus ou moins organiques les uns avec les autres, qui pourraient servir de point d'appui pour la constitution et la consolidation d'un véritable réseau. Un tel réseau, à l'échelle du Canada, devrait être encouragé par la mise à disposition de ressources pour des programmes conjoints de recherche, pour des visites et des échanges de personnes, des colloques ou séminaires, et peut-être aussi un bulletin de liaison.

Dans le domaine de la politique scientifique, plusieurs questions appellent un traitement de façon urgente. Les dépenses publiques en soutien à la R-D demeurent difficiles à corréler avec le lancement d'innovations commerciales réussies. Le développement de la recherche évaluative, des analyses en profondeur de l'efficacité et des incidences des diverses modalités des programmes gouvernementaux (subventions, dispositions fiscales, recherche gouvernementale, etc.) devraient contribuer à clarifier ces questions. D'autres interventions gouvernementales comme le tamisage, le contrôle ou la facilitation de l'acquisition de technologies étrangères, la coordination des actions des secteurs public et privé, la coordination des actions des différents niveaux de gouvernement, le degré d'extension et de compréhension souhaitable des politiques publiques, le degré d'ajustement aux besoins des entreprises innovatrices méritent aussi examen. Finalement, au-delà des questions traditionnelles sur les objectifs, la priorisation, et l'allocation des ressources en politique scientifique, des études devraient être encouragées sur les processus même de définition et de mise en oeuvre, en contexte bureaucratique, des politiques scientifiques.

Dans le domaine de la gestion des technologies au niveau de la firme, les spécificités de l'environnement canadien par rapport auxquelles s'élaborent les stratégies d'entreprises devraient faire l'objet d'enquêtes systématiques. En particulier, de nombreuses nouvelles études devraient être conduites sur les avantages et les contraintes selon les régions, sur les constellations de firmes et d'institutions incubatrices, et sur des cas d'innovations ayant abouti à des échecs ou des succès commerciaux. L'étude comparative des systèmes industriels, du comportement des entrepreneurs et des cadres, des structures organisationnelles, des enquêtes aussi bien horizontales que longitudinales paraissent aussi s'imposer à ce stade de développement du champ.

Quant à l'analyse des incidences de l'introduction de nouvelles technologies en milieu de travail et sur les conditions de travail, les études microsociologiques au niveau de la firme ou de l'organisation pourraient bien être la meilleure voie pour poursuivre le renouvellement des problématiques. Une telle démarche n'exclut nullement des recherches horizontales ou longitudinales, lesquelles demeurent malheureusement, du fait de la pénurie de resssources, encore très exceptionnelles. Les travaux sur les négociations sociales auxquelles donne lieu la définition des contenus, et la mise en oeuvre des programmes de formation ou de recyclage de la main-d'oeuvre, prenant en compte leurs assises institutionnelles, devraient aussi constituer un domaine majeur de recherche.

Alors que beaucoup d'énergie a été depuis vingt ans consentie, surtout en Amérique du Nord, au développement de méthodologies rigoureuses pour l'évaluation des technologies aux fins de leur régulation publique, il demeure que ces travaux se fondent sur des bases théoriques encore incertaines ou fort discutables. Beaucoup d'efforts devraient maintenant être consacrés à la clarification des concepts fondamentaux, surtout en ce qui a trait aux incidences sociales et culturelles de ces nouvelles technologies. Les formes organisationnelles et les modalités des procédures aussi devraient faire l'objet d'une attention particulière, alors qu'il devient de plus en plus clair que l'évaluation sociale des technologies engage bien davantage que la seule application de méthodes analytiques. La dynamique et la gestion des controverses publiques et de leur clôture, au coeur des processus à travers lesquels se définissent les risques et s'effectue la négociation de leurs modes de régulation, apparaissent également comme méritant tout particulièrement l'attention des chercheurs. Finalement, l'imputabilité publique en ces matières affectant la santé publique et la protection de l'environnement émerge aussi comme une question-clé, indissociable des obligations d'une prise en charge démocratique des développements démocratiques.

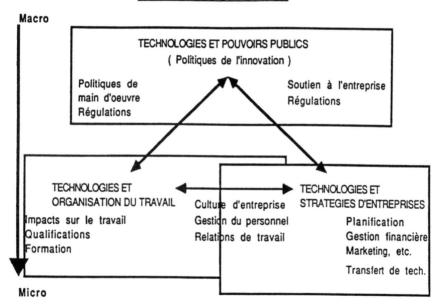

LA GESTION DE L'INNOVATION

Figure 1

Chapter Four

The Management of Innovation

David Wolfe

Introduction

At the core of studies of managing technology is the question of the relationship between organizational structures (organizational behaviour)
and technological innovation. The process of organizational adaptation
within the corporate and work environment, where innovation occurs
and is implemented, has a crucial bearing on the success of the outcome.
Increasingly, research from both a management and labour process perspective indicates the importance of distinguishing between the introduction of new hardware and the effective transformation of the organizational environment. Research indicates that firms that emphasize the
former at the expense of the latter fail to capture a significant portion of
the potential gains to be made from the process of innovation.

Organizational adaptation is crucial to the effectiveness of new technology. Such adaptation involves the entire range of activities that concern the firm, from managing the innovation process to job redesign and
job enhancement schemes. The increased significance of technological
change for the competitive success of firms, and its impacts on the workforce, has led to a recent increase in the volume of academic and applied
studies by social scientists in this area.

Since the early 1970s, the management of technological innovation has emerged as an area of study and concern within the faculties of engineering, management, and administrative studies at North American universities. However, the sense of urgency associated with the research and teaching of this subject has increased dramatically in the current decade as a result of the greater competitive pressures that have been felt in the economies of both Canada and the U.S. These pressures have led to an intensification of research efforts among academics and greater emphasis being placed on the teaching of the management of innovation among both business and engineering faculties. The discussion of the current state of the art of research in the management of innovation adopts the following definition:

> Management of Technology is a field that links engineering, science and management disciplines to plan, develop and implement technological capabilities to shape and accomplish the strategic and operational objectives of an organization. (Abbott, 1988b; cf. also the discussion in Roberts, 1988).

This working definition is extended by the following key elements of Management of Technology in industrial practice.

1. The identification and evaluation of technical options;
2. Management of research and development itself;
3. Integration of technology into the company's overall operations;
4. Implementation of technology in a product and/or process; and
5. Obsolescence and replacement of technology (Abbott, 1988b)

The concern with the management of innovation in Canada has focused as much on the need to improve the teaching of the subject in Canadian universities as it has on the purely research questions. While primary emphasis will be placed on the research that has been done to date, some consideration will be given to the teaching component in the discussion of the existing networks.

The Management of Innovation

The focus of research in the field of management of technology has centred on the effectiveness with which firms develop the institutional skills required to generate, adopt, and apply new technologies to enhance their international competitiveness. Canadian companies have had difficulty in translating the development and adoption of new technology into global competitiveness. This capacity is constrained to some extent by the predominance of foreign-based multinationals in the Canadian economy; the greatest potential for R&D jobs and innovation in Canada lies with indigenous, domestically controlled industries. However, management attitudes towards innovation also represent a serious constraint. The isolation of top management from conditions on the factory floor, as well as from customers who might influence their thinking about new technology, is an illustration of this problem. Canadian management has a great deal to learn from Japanese practice in this regard (Munro and Noori, 1987; cf. also Ontario Premier's Council, 1988, and Miller et al., 1988).

A background paper prepared for the National Conference on Technology and Innovation spelled out the requirements for Canadian firms to succeed. They must undertake aggressive programs to innovate, to adapt technology, and to integrate new skills into their business systems. Four broad imperatives were suggested as essential to building the institutional skills that corporations will need to meet the technological challenge: 1) attack, don't defend; 2) invest in knowledge and skills; 3) broaden horizons; and 4) instill a spirit of change.

The root cause of attitudes that inhibit dynamic innovation lies in the way that corporations organize themselves. They emphasize speedy results rather than the time and patience required to realize the fruits of technological innovation and adaptation. They foster organizational forms that reinforce individual fear of failure, rather than accept failure as part of the innovative process. And they create structures designed for order and predictability, rather than allowing room for innovation, which is necessarily more random, unpredictable, and chaotic (Schofield and Thomson, 1988).

R&D Activities

The conduct of in-firm R&D is one essential contributor to the innovative potential of Canadian firms. The role of foreign enterprise in the Canadian economy has long been a subject of interest, and its relevance for R&D activities is of particular importance. The ratio of R&D spending to gross domestic product in Canada is lower than in other industrial nations, including the U.S., Japan, Sweden, Belgium, and the Netherlands. Several authors have pointed out that the relatively low level of R&D spending in Canada may be the result of the structure of Canadian industry. Since close to half of manufacturing industry is foreign owned, Canada benefits from a large amount of R&D performed outside the country (Mansfield, 1985; cf. also Palda and Pazderka, 1982, and Rugman, 1983).

Several early studies of the industrial machinery sector found that industrial R&D activity was strongly correlated to firm size, not just foreign ownership. Larger firms tended to employ more R&D personnel. An important distinction was noted between the R&D behaviour of integrated companies versus holding companies, whether foreign-owned or Canadian. The former tended to allow little opportunity in the way of R&D activity, while the latter displayed the same degree of autonomy and research activities as did domestically owned firms. Changes in management strategy could exert a significant impact on the overall innovative strategies of the firms, although on balance, foreign-owned firms were not as sensitive to domestic market conditions as Canadian-owned ones (Ondrack, 1975, 1980).

The relationship between R&D and patenting activities has also been the subject of study. In the period between 1972 and 1982, Canada's share of patents granted relative to six other leading industrial nations remained relatively stable, while those of several European nations fell and Japan's rose. At the same time, Canada was responsible for only a very small proportion of the world's inventions. Canada's propensity to patent and to exploit its own technology abroad remains poor compared to most of the other leading industrial nations.

Using this evidence, a study prepared for the Macdonald Royal Commission maintained that current market mechanisms for responding to changes in active and stagnant technologies appeared to be working well for all nations, including Canada, and warned against the feasibility of governments trying to pick "winners" and "losers" in new technologies. However, it did note the desirability of developing policies and programs to take advantage of the growth of alternative sources of technology by providing Canadian purchasers with information to facilitate the identification of competing suppliers and technological options (Ellis and Waite, 1985).

Using information extracted from Canadian patent data, another study investigated the relationship between foreign ownership and patenting activity. It examined over a six-year period the activities of the twenty-five largest multinational enterprises that are Canadian patent holders. The companies studied gave evidence of highly centralized R&D structures in their home countries, with American multinational enterprises showing the greatest degree of R&D centralization. In general, the relationship between patenting and R&D activity is a very strong one, but patenting is much more centralized than R&D. Further centralization is achieved through the tendency to pool patents from the subsidiaries in home countries. Patenting appears to be a mechanism by which multinational enterprises control access to R&D and technology generating activities (Etemad and Seguin Dulude, 1984).

These results are best understood in the context of a later, more comparative study by the same authors. Comparing the patenting activities of subsidiaries in a wider range of multinational enterprises, they noted that the multinational enterprises' regions of origin account for significant differences in the patterns of decentralization of their patenting activities. The European multinational enterprises show the greatest tendency to decentralize, followed by the North American ones, with the Japanese multinational enterprises exhibiting the lowest tendency to decentralize. Furthermore, the overall intensity of inventive activity contributes to the degree of decentralization. Finally, the authors note that inventive activity remains singularly less decentralized than other aspects of the firms' activities, such as production and employment (Etemad and Seguin Dulude, 1987: 101-19).

Conversely, a subject of concern in the literature has been the relationship between market pull and the location of R&D activities of small and medium-sized Canadian enterprises. A study done for the TISP examined the tendency of these firms to locate their R&D activities at home or abroad. There is a strong tendency to maintain control over these activities close to the domestic base of the firm, especially before the firm reaches a level of $25 million in sales. After that point, the firm may consider locating some of its activities abroad as part of a broader strategy of growth. While exports may be used initially to service the U.S. market, the pull to assemble or manufacture in the U.S. becomes stronger.

At this stage, the performance of some R&D in the U.S. may be suitable to adapt the product to American markets, but concern about centralization tends to keep this to a minimum. However, once sales reach the next critical threshold of $100 million, the pull of the market may become much more irresistible and part of the corporate infrastructure, including R&D, may be moved out of Canada. While no firm conclusions are reached on this prospect, the authors argue it is worth examining the experience of large Canadian multinational enterprises, such as Nortel or Alcan, more closely in this regard (Litvak and Maule, 1984).

An important issue for small and medium-sized domestic firms is the source of financing for their R&D activities. Research indicates that small firms performing R&D do relatively little debt financing and obtain a high proportion of their financial needs in non-bank forms, while medium-sized firms employ an average amount of debt, usually supplied by the banks. There do, however, appear to be significant gaps in the availability of financing due to the high cost of funds or the existence of lags in meeting new needs, sometimes due to government regulations. One way to overcome this would be to expand the role of non-bank financial institutions to increase the potential source of funds for small high-technology businesses (Poapst, 1986).

Although R&D activities by firms located in Canada represent an important source of innovative activity, they are not the only or necessary source for it. As the pace of technological innovation accelerates, and as the Japanese experience confirms that innovation need not be directly tied to R&D, the study of the process of technology transfer has become more important. Recent research has suggested that the equation of technological intensity with the level of R&D activities may be seriously flawed. Rather, an industry's technology base includes its own-performed or direct R&D, free access to research of foreign affiliates, intramural research by government which is assignable to industry, and equally assignable university research. Empirical studies indicate that this broader definition of technological intensity provides a more appropriate measure (Palda, 1985). It has increasingly come to be recognized that the mechanisms for transferring the results of that activity into commercializable prospects by Canadian firms is every bit as important as the conduct of in-firm R&D.

An important potential source of commercializable R&D is the research conducted in federal laboratories. Federal-sponsored research has recently been subject to criticism from a variety of sources, including the Ontario Premier's Council Report (1988) and the NABST (National Advisory Board on Science and Technology) Industry Committee report (1988). However, it has also been suggested that the problem of managing R&D activities in government labs stems from underfunding, bureaucratic management that doesn't allow for the special needs of R&D activities, hiring freezes and staff reductions, and a poorly designed reward system. The study found that although increased emphasis has been placed on technology transfer from government labs to industry, inadequate resources hamper the labs' ability to carry out this role. The solution to these problems requires that the designers of government policy in this area be more knowledgeable about what constitutes a creative and productive environment for high quality R&D (Clarke and Reavley, 1988; for a recent survey of the broader literature on this issue, cf. Badaway, 1988).

Another potential source of commercializable R&D is university-based research, but recent examinations of the potential of this source indicate that there are a number of obstacles that must be overcome. Typically, the transfer of R&D from lab to product development requires a product champion, but, with a few notable exceptions, there is no one to play this role in a university setting. There are a number of reasons for this failing, namely that academics are generally unwilling to devote the time required for this process, that they are reluctant to work with the business partners necessary to commercialize the research, that they are not primarily motivated by the drive for profits, and finally that they are not usually willing to leave the university setting to pursue a profitable venture.

Overcoming these barriers may require a major commitment on the part of universities to allocating resources to prototype development, market research, and industrial design. However, study of the existing university innovation centres in both the U.S. and Canada suggests that this process is fraught with problems and an adequate model has not yet been developed (McMullen and Melnyk, 1988).

Technology Transfer

Despite the potential importance of in-firm R&D, government research labs, and university-based R&D, the most common source of new technology is through technology transfer from foreign sources. A major study of 283 of the most profitable products and manufacturing processes introduced between 1960 and 1980 found that 87 percent of expenditures on manufacturing processes and 75 percent of expenditures on products were accounted for by subsidiaries of foreign firms. When this was broken down, subsidiaries were responsible for 75 percent of expenditures on products based on in-house R&D and 84 percent of processes based on in-house R&D. Similarly they accounted for 97 percent of expenditures on products and 93 percent of processes based on external technology.

The main source of technology for these profitable innovations in the period of study was foreign multinationals, both as R&D performers and as importers of technology. Most transfers of external technology were effected in the form of blueprints, designs, software tapes and specifications, plus direct contacts, rather than in the form of transfer of equipment. Joint ventures were found to be relatively rare as a mechanism used for technology transfer and licensing of technology occurred in only 10 percent of the 283 cases studied (Wills, 1982).

A recent conference on this subject generated a number of articles that provide additional insights into the question. A contribution by Mac-Charles argues that lower levels of R&D activities by Canadian subsidiaries are not necessarily a negative indicator. Concentrating basic R&D in the parent may represent a desirable form of specialization for the multinational enterprise. The results of the centralized R&D are freely available to the subsidiary since it is profitable for the multinational enterprise to fully utilize intra-firm knowledge and thereby maximize its rents. Theory and evidence both suggest that Canadian subsidiaries do have access to the results of R&D produced by their parents, and that it is both high in quality and available at minimum cost.

To the extent to which there is a problem of poor international transmission of technology and knowledge in Canada, it originates with management attitudes. There is a general lack of knowledge on the part of managers about how significantly the environment around them has changed and how best they can adapt to it. The need for increased specialization, exporting, and use of foreign suppliers requires a redirection of corporate philosophy. Managers in subsidiaries have been slower to adapt to these changes than managers in Canadian-controlled firms. This is clearly the area in which rapid changes are most urgently needed (MacCharles, 1987: 53-69)

Two methods that can be used to facilitate the transfer of technology between firms are licensing and joint ventures. The conditions under which licensing can prove a viable strategy for Canadian firms have been analysed, and conclusions have been reached about the extent to which a weak domestic R&D effort can be compensated for by the acquisition of licences. Buyers of technology do not face great constraints in the acquisition of licences, nor, however, do they learn a great deal from their licences or get access to growth areas. In addition, such agreements often include restrictive clauses. On balance, it is unlikely that licensing arrangements will improve the situation faced by the host country with respect to subsidiaries, in terms of access to technology (Killing, 1980).

Joint ventures can represent a potentially useful mechanism for technology transfer, and as access to the latest innovations becomes more critical, they are receiving greater attention. Both in their own right, and as a mechanism for technology transfer, joint ventures are fraught with difficulties, and great care needs to be taken to ensure that they are managed effectively. Joint ventures as well as helping to facilitate technology transfer allow companies to develop new markets, gain access to raw materials, share the skills and finances needed, and achieve economies of scale.

Studies of successful joint ventures indicate that a strong degree of managerial autonomy for the venture is a key ingredient. For joint ventures to succeed as a mechanism of technology transfer, the firm involved must first know what it needs, have some minimum level of technological competence, and be skilled in joint management ventures. Joint ventures should not be used to solve temporary management problems, such as lack of familiarity with the target market (Killing, 1983).

Recent research has also called attention to the potentially critical role that industry associations can play in facilitating the process of technology transfer. A precedent for this type of activity, and for government support, is to be found in a number of European countries, such as France. While the model has not become predominant in Canada, there are a number of important exceptions. A study of four industry research associations, in plastics, steel, gas, and pulp and paper found that their range of responsibilities includes product testing, maintaining links with government laboratories and universities, sponsoring and conducting scientific and technical symposia, and helping to sub-contract research projects on behalf of industry members. In effect, they performed a technology gatekeeper and brokerage role for the members of their associations.

Significantly, government financial support and encouragement was instrumental in setting up each of the industry research associations, and government officials were involved in some working capacity in all four. All of the industry research associations maintain close working relations with federal government departments and laboratories, with universities, and with some provincial research organizations (Litvak, 1985).

The Innovation Process

The major problem faced in many technology-based companies is the successful development of new technologies, their translation into competitive new products and services, and the generation of profit from the adoption of these products by customers. This subject area has become one of intense study among Canadian researchers in recent years, and evidence indicates that what is required is not just better new technologies, but better management of the entire product innovation process. A great deal of emphasis in recent research has been placed not only on expertise in new product development in Canadian firms, but also on the linkages between marketing and innovation skills.

The case studies that have been conducted on successful entrepreneurship and innovation emphasize the importance of strategic market planning and of concentrating efforts on products in which a technical edge can be maintained. A number of common features have been identified in successful firms. Their product technologies at the time of start-up were at a fairly high level of development. Avoiding direct competition with larger companies and concentrating efforts in areas where they enjoyed a comparative advantage was critical. Successful firms tended to concentrate on specialized, rather than mass markets catering largely to industrial users in newly developing industries. Successful diversification out of the small Canadian market was often the route followed to sustain growth (Litvak and Maule, 1980, 1982; Rosson and Martin, 1985; Martin and Rosson, 1986).

A critical factor that has been found to contribute to the success of innovative firms in high-technology industries is the role of government procurement. A recent study of the factors contributing to the success of entrepreneurial high-tech firms examined the experience of a sample of start-up firms in the Canadian microelectronics and communications industry between 1965 and 1980. It surveyed the effects of a variety of factors, including tax incentives, grants and subsidies, government research and licensing, and training programs, but found that the winning of government procurement contracts was the most important determinant of success. Firms supported in this way tended to become larger on average than those who were not public sector suppliers; they were found to be more export-oriented, slightly better organized, and to operate in markets similar to those of their founder's previous employer (Doutriaux, 1988a, 1988b).

A central focus in the study of the innovation process has been the integration of R&D activities within the overall structure of the firm. Successful innovation must overcome a series of managerial, institutional, and scientific roadblocks. These include a poor understanding of the needs and strategies of the business, absence of a sponsor in the business system, failure to respond to the time frame demanded by the business, absence of good project discipline, and an overloading of key technical personnel. In order to succeed, R&D activities must be integrated effectively into the strategic management of the firm.

One means to accomplish this is by using the concept of a corporate technical strategy, which is defined as a strategy that integrates the total technical resources of the business into a coherent, directed force to commercialize a continuing flow of technology in order to remain competitive. The implementation of an effective technology strategy involves several related measures: (1) redefining R&D roles within the corporate technical organization; (2) taking a total-system view of technology; (3) establishing discipline and methodologies for joint activities between R&D and the rest of the firm; (4) frequent and effective project reviews and technical follow-up; and (5) creating a climate for outstanding work (Richardson, 1985, 1986).

The problems have been found to be even more acute for mature industries than for emerging firms with a concentration on technologically-intensive products. Some mature companies have recognized that their inability to innovate stems from a managerial failure to see the R&D results through the necessary subsequent steps of design and piloting that lead to commercialization. There are a growing number of instances in which mature companies have set up temporary design and demonstration organizations to determine the viability of new technologies.

One Canadian company, Alcan, has taken the design and documentation function one step further by creating a permanent design and demonstration organization to pilot the more risky aspects of new manufacturing processes and materials. Since its inception, it has made a notable contribution to the commercialization of new technologies within the company. Successful implementation of the design and demonstration organization requires that the corporation recognize the complexity of commercializing innovations. To succeed, the firm must have a high tolerance for a variety of management styles (Frontini and Richardson, 1984; for a broader statement of Alcan's commitment to the role of innovation, cf. Culver, 1988).

Studies of the determinants of successful corporate innovation found that entrepreneurship can be successfully fostered by the attitude projected throughout the firm. Failure needs to be not only tolerated, but expected, and procedures established to instruct personnel on how to proceed with their ideas. In general, corporate entrepreneurs tend to be as well trained technically as their counterparts in private firms, but they spend a lot of their time and energy defending their ideas within the corporation. A corporate sponsor is often useful to assist them in this process (Knight, 1985, 1988).

One organizational device that has been suggested to help firms deal with the problem of innovation is the new venture unit, a separate division of the firm created specifically to house new product or new business ideas and initiatives. A recent investigation into the effectiveness of these units suggests some measures to help ensure that they are used to best advantage. They should be used to produce and market unrelated new product types; great care must be taken to establish a corporate reward system that recognizes success without stifling risk-taking; the move into a new venture unit must be carefully thought out and planned for well in advance; once established, the units should be allowed to operate with a relatively high degree of autonomy (Bart, 1987).

Marketing Issues

A recurring concern in a variety of studies is the link between the innovation process and the marketing activities of the firm. The greatest constraint on Canadian threshold firms, those with sales under the $25-million mark, is not the lack of R&D support from the government, but a lack of entrepreneurial talent and marketing skills on the part of the firm's managers (Dermer, 1984; cf. also Dermer, 1986). Empirical research on this question has produced somewhat mixed results.

The creation of a distinct product advantage in international markets is a multidimensional process that can be controlled and managed. An empirical study of the determinants of product advantage dimensions in the Canadian electronics industry concluded that a functional technical advantage is an important, but not dominant factor. More important are the considerations that the product meet customer needs and incorporate a superior industrial design. Although R&D efforts were strongly correlated with measures of export performance, this does not necessarily hold true for all areas of R&D activity. Patents, for example, are held in low regard in the electronics industry because innovation is too fast moving.

Another study also found that strong marketing expertise in the founding teams of young high-tech firms helps achieve good results at start-up and facilitates entry of the firm into foreign export markets. However, after the initial comparative advantage fades, firms face an ongoing dilemma of balancing technological priorities and marketing (Kleinschmidt and Banting, 1984; Doutriaux and Simyar, 1988).

Other studies indicate that Canadian high-tech companies frequently have difficulty assessing their market or getting skilled marketing managers. These managers find it difficult to identify the market and to perform the appropriate research, promotions, and distribution. The marketing mix is considered less important than other activities, and there are marketing gaps and lags, especially with respect to forecasting markets and analysing competitors' strategies. There is a definite need to upgrade the skills of Canadian managers in this area (Knight, 1986; Boag and Munro, 1986). One study, however, asserts that contemporary marketing concepts such as target marketing and market positioning are being effectively utilized by the management of advanced technology companies in Canada (Barnhill et al., 1986).

Comparisons of the strategies that can be used effectively to market high-tech products with those used to market more conventional products suggest that many of the basic approaches are transferable (Fauman and Weiss, 1986). Where more effective marketing control systems were used by high-tech companies, they have been found to correlate highly with stronger market performance as measured by absolute sales, sales growth, cash flow, and profitability (Boag, 1987).

Financial Management

Financial management represents a serious problem for companies in developing new technologies. Given the long development periods and the uncertainty associated with this process, the decision to commit major resources to developing or adopting a particular technology is problematic. Managers need to find appropriate budgeting guidelines to facilitate the adoption of new technology in light of the internal opposition they may face from engineers or accountants.

One method is an "option" approach to capital budgeting that favours risky, long-range investment. In addition, managers can adopt their budgeting guidelines to permit recognition of the value associated with future investment options and can encourage the downward adjustment of the hurdle rate (net present value). The adoption of accounting devices such as these can help move the firm into a position that is both technologically aggressive and financially responsible (Hill and Dimnik, 1985; cf. also Bart, 1987).

Technology Development

A standard approach to understanding the evolution of existing products and the emergence of new ones has been the technology life cycle model, originally developed by Utterback and Abernathy with reference to the automotive industry (1975). Recent examination of this model by Canadian and British researchers has suggested a number of significant modifications. Radical changes in technological and economic conditions require that managers should not necessarily regard the common practice of the past as the most appropriate practice for the future. Discontinuities in production and technology occur more frequently than is portrayed in the original model.

Exclusive concentration on the technology life cycle model may distract the attention of the firm's managers away from the strategic implications of technological innovation. To take account of these potential discontinuities, firms are advised to follow a mixed or combined mode strategy: upgrading existing operations in stable production mode while seeking profitable new market niches. This requires that product managers simultaneously pursue defensive strategies for evolving existing products, while keeping an eye on possibilities for initiating projects that will exploit new opportunities (DeBresson and Lampel, 1985a, 1985b; cf. also Clark and DeBresson, 1987, and Bennett and Cooper, 1984).

A critical issue for the management of technology within firms is the new product development process. Increasingly, management studies are coming to indicate that intensive R&D alone is not necessarily a guarantee of success in this area. Robert Cooper's research on the new product development strategies of firms indicates that there are a variety of different ones that have been pursued. The results achieved by firms in the development of new products are closely linked to the strategies they pursue.

A number of dimensions underlie an innovation strategy: (1) the orientation of the firm's new product program; (2) the types of new products the firm seeks; (3) the types of markets the firm seeks with its new products; and (4) the commitment to the program. Analysis of the strategies actually pursued by firms reveals a number of different approaches: a technologically driven strategy; a balanced strategy; a technologically deficient strategy; a low budget, conservative strategy; and a high budget, diverse strategy. The best new product performance is based upon a strategy that links technological intensity with a strong market orientation.

There are a number of important conclusions derived from this research. Overall, the balanced new product strategy that yielded the highest results included a unique program orientation, selected certain types of markets exclusively (non-competitive, high potential, high growth), and developed very specific types of products (premium priced, with a close fit into current product lines). Adopting some, but not all, of the elements of a winning strategy is not adequate. A technologically driven strategy by itself is as weak as a conservative and cautious approach. An overall balanced approach produces the best results (Cooper, 1984a, 1984b, 1985a, 1985c, 1985d).

The research on the new product development process emphasizes the importance of strategic corporate planning and management of every stage of the process. Product superiority is a critical determinant of success, and a strong project definition at a very early stage of development, especially the predevelopment stages, helps ensure this outcome. Increased synergy between the technical and marketing functions of the firm is necessary at every step of the way. Certain key activities at these early stages help guide the project in the right direction. These include market studies, initial screening activities, and preliminary market assessment (Cooper and Kleinschmidt, 1986, 1987).

Investigation into the timing of market research in new product development shows that most companies expended their resources relatively early in the development process. They did earlier research in situations involving less situational similarity of the marketing tasks and decisions, in situations where they perceived they had less competitive advantage, and in situations involving higher risk to the adopting organization (More, 1984a).

Recent work in this area has attempted to synthesize this development process into a systematic series of stages that can be adopted and pursued in any innovative situation. In some Canadian companies, most notably Bell Northern Research, this innovative strategy has come to be referred to as the gating process. The key to new product success involves taking the product through a series of developmental stages, each of which involves a gate (a set of measures, criteria) that must be successfully cleared before the product can proceed to the next stage of development.

The questions and hurdles that must be cleared deal with various facets of the project, including: does the project continue to make economic and business sense? have the essential steps required to pass the gate been cleared? is the project on time and on budget? what steps or tasks need to be undertaken in the next phase or stage of the project? The answers to these questions at each gate can produce one of three outcomes: kill, go, or hold. The compression of product life cycles and the greater time pressures that are exerted on the innovation process have resulted in the adoption of parallel processing techniques for new product development. Various divisions of the firm-business management, R&D, manufacturing, sales and marketing must work in tandem through the gating process.

One model of this process specifies six specific gates that must be cleared for the successful development of new products: (1) the initial screening phase that commits resources to a project; (2) the preliminary assessment that brings in better market and technical information; (3) the pre-development business analysis that reaches agreement on things like the target market, the product concept, the positioning strategy, the product features, and even its specifications; (4) the pre-test review that follows development of the product and poses the question of whether it is still a sound business proposition; (5) the pre-trial review that reviews the results of lab and user tests; and finally, (6) the pre-commercialization business analysis that precedes moving the product into full production (Cooper, 1985b, 1986, 1988).

Customer Relations

A key problem experienced by firms in the development of new technology is the creation of appropriate relationships with their customers. The nature of these relationships and their impact on this process has also been the subject of recent study. Forecasting adoption rates for new products and technology has been a difficult problem for many managers, in part due to a failure to understand the customer's organizational buying process. Firms may fail to adequately specify the competitive advantage of a new product to the key buyer in the customer firm, or they may fail to appreciate the influence of an unidentified member of the buying team.

In order to improve adoption rate forecasts, managers must develop more sophisticated models to analyse customer reactions and their influence on adoption rates. By so doing they will be better able to focus their strategic resources on customer types that are likely to be faster adopters of the new products and technologies (More, 1984b, 1986b).

This concern with developing appropriate relationships with customers has been generalized into a broader set of research concerns focusing on the developer/adopter relationship with respect to new technology more generally. Roger More has employed a conceptual framework to identify, map, and manage different patterns of these developer/adopter relationships, and has successfully applied this model to several different new technologies, such as hardware/software systems, CAL systems, and CAD/CAM systems.

The model specifies three fundamental processes that must be recognized in dealing with these relationships: (1) the development sub-process, (2) the adoption sub-process, and (3) the interface sub-process. By identifying similar generic processes that must occur in both organizations, it becomes possible to specify the decision interdependency between them. In applying this framework to the analysis of new technology situations, some very different types of relationships are identified, namely, supplier-driven processes, user-driven processes, and co-development processes. Managers require better ways to plan for the kinds of relationships they must have with other organizations concerning the development and adoption of new technology (More, 1986a, 1986c, 1986d).

Technology Adoption

A critical area of research has focused on managing the implementation and adoption of new technology by Canadian firms. The evidence that exists indicates that Canadian companies lag seriously behind in the rate of adoption and diffusion of new technologies. This lag is correlated with the relatively poor level of performance of R&D in Canadian industry and the overall negative trade balance achieved in manufactured goods, especially high-technology products (Economic Council of Canada, 1987; Conklin and St. Hilaire, 1988: ch. 2, 3; cf. also Globerman, 1981). Some of the more recent evidence, however, suggests that the time lag in technology transfer has shortened in recent years and that it is now no greater than the average lag for Western European countries (McFetridge and Corvari, 1985; McFetridge, 1987).

The difficulties experienced in the adoption of new technologies by Canadian firms result from obstacles that are many and varied, including management attitudes, manpower deficiencies, financial constraints, the regulatory environment, and the investment climate. As was noted above, the preoccupation of senior managers with existing operations and short-term problems can constitute a significant barrier to innovation (Litvak and Warner, 1986, 1987).

Recent research on the adoption and implementation of new technology has emphasized the desirability of employing an impact analysis technique to maximize the benefits and minimize the risk of introducing new manufacturing technology. The acquisition of such systems cannot be based solely on economic benefits, but requires a more comprehensive framework. Several variables are critical to the success of this undertaking: the fit between organization and environment in new technology; production technology and organizational design choices must interact; new technology must be part of a predetermined organizational and production policy (Noori, 1986a; Noori and Munro, 1985).

Decisions of managers to purchase and implement new technological systems can result from several factors. Traditional analysis has tended to differentiate between technology push and market pull explanations. However, recent data suggest that managers surveyed employed an integrative perspective in considering whether to adopt these technologies. The attitude of senior management in particular is a principal force in committing the organization to the adoption of these technologies (Munro and Noori, 1986).

The introduction of new microelectronic technologies, such as CAD/CAM and CIM, are having far-ranging impacts on North American industries. The significance of these technologies derives from the relative importance of economies of scale versus economies of scope; one based on volume and the other on variety. Recent investigation highlights the benefits to be gained from the economies of integration which realize both. This would result from maximizing the gains made possible by technologies that have substantially reduced the inflexibility of dedicated production processes, and allowed the complexities inherent in a large multi-product operation to be handled more efficiently (Noori, 1986a).

One point upon which the research conducted by those operating within a management perspective and that conducted by those operating from the labour process perspective begins to converge is in the area of the organizational adoption of new technologies. Extensive research with respect to the implementation of CAD (conducted by Carol Beatty, both alone and in conjunction with Peter Gordon of Queen's) confirms its significance. The experience of many companies has fallen far short of published expectations.

Based on Beatty's survey evidence and that collected by the Ontario CAD/CAM Centre, it is apparent that at least 50 percent of the problems experienced in the implementation of CAD/CAM systems were human and organizational, rather than technological in origin. The successful implementation of these systems requires that careful attention must be given within the organization to the support for the system, planning for CAD training, organization of the tasks within the system and the technology of the system itself. It is the attention to these details that is often lacking.

One problem that is frequently cited by managers who were interviewed is the integration of the CAD system with the rest of the design operation. Testing various hypotheses to account for relative success rates, Beatty found that operator performance on CAD systems was strongly influenced by motivation and skill levels, with role clarity contributing to a lesser degree. One factor that has contributed effectively to the successful implementation of these systems is the presence of a "high priest" of the technology, comparable to the role played by a product champion within the firm. These managers possess a combination of passion, persistence, technical and project management skills, as well as a strong degree of influence within the organization. They are generally effective in winning converts to the new technology (Beatty, 1986, 1987; Beatty and Gordon, 1987a, 1987b).

The results of Beatty and Gordon's research conforms closely to the results of a variety of other studies that have indicated that organizational variables tend to have a far greater impact on the effectiveness with which new technology both in the office and in the plant is employed by firms. An examination of the relationship between robotics technology and work design indicates the range of possibilities that are available.

Work can be designed from a holistic perspective to include programming and maintenance tasks along with the more basic monitoring tasks. Implementing this direction in job design will tend to make operators' jobs more meaningful and challenging. Further, the adoption of sociotechnical systems of work organization in conjunction with the use of robotics can help reduce the adverse effects on the working conditions of operators (Saleh and Pal, 1985).

The implementation of more comprehensive computer-aided manufacturing systems is also amenable to different forms of work organization and control mechanisms, depending on whether they replace human labour or dedicated machines, and on the patterns of coping mechanisms in place before the CAM was installed (Pal and Saleh, 1987; for a broader discussion of the implications of different forms of work organization on the use of microelectronic technology, cf. Senker, 1986).

An even stronger statement of the relationship between organizational enhancements and microelectronic technology is found in Tim Warner's work. Warner maintains that information technologies should be adopted only after conventional improvements and system reorganizations have been implemented. The need for information processing can be reduced in firms by increasing the degree of lateral coordination. It is often more effective to reduce the need for information processing by removing the condition that caused it in the first place than by throwing a computer at it.

The twin strategies of product design and production system design around conventional technologies can achieve the lion's share of the benefits associated with moving from a poorly organized production system to a world class facility. Firms should forego information-technology-based approaches to solving production problems until they have exhausted conventional approaches, and then move forward to flexible automation (Warner 1987).

Organizational Questions

Students of organizational behaviour have long maintained that technological innovation independent of the organizational context in which it occurs is likely to produce less than optimal results, as some of the studies cited above seem to confirm. Researchers in this field argue that design considerations are something more than just an add-on to technical concerns; rather, the sociotechnical perspective to which they subscribe holds out the joint optimization of both the social and technical subsystems of an organization as one of its basic principles.

Although organizational design has long occupied a central role in management studies, the significance of new, experimental forms of organizational design has been highlighted by the challenge of implementing technological change. A great deal of the research and field work that has been carried out in this area in Canada is related to quality of working life programs. Quality of working life programs evolved out of a series of developments in organizational theory during the 1970s. The concern with individual job satisfaction derived from the human relations approach was expanded to a more holistic focus that took account of the effect of managerial values and peer groups on individuals at work.

Quality of working life was further aided by the elaboration of "sociotechnical systems theory" in the U.K. Sociotechnical systems theory maintains that both the technical and human elements of an organization must be recognized as interdependent parts of the whole, which itself must be seen in relation to its external environment. For an organization to be optimally effective, the technical and social subsystems must be co-designed to fit together in such a way as to accommodate and support each other.

The fundamental need of technical systems is to control variances as quickly and as near to their point of origin as possible. People in an organization need autonomy and discretion, as well as opportunities for ongoing learning, social support, recognition, and the opportunity to make a meaningful contribution. In order to satisfy all of the above needs effectively, a high degree of self-regulation and participation must be built into the day-to-day operation of the organization.

The basic building block of the sociotechnical systems theory approach is the semi-autonomous work group, based on the concepts of group responsibility and self-regulation. Sociotechnical systems theory places great emphasis on the creation of structures and processes for ongoing organizational, group, and individual learning (Kolodny, 1987; Mansell, 1987). Examinations of the theoretical and organizational basis for workplace democracy also argue that self-directing work groups are one of the most promising forms of workplace democracy as management's rights are not directly threatened and work is the most salient aspect of work life for most employees (Nightingale, 1982).

Interest in the development of quality of working life schemes received strong support from both the federal government (through Labour Canada and the Treasury Board) and the Ontario government (through its Quality of Working Life Centre) in the late 1970s. Similarly, employers began to evince more interest in the approach as competitive pressures and technological change placed a greater premium on organizational effectiveness. The sociotechnical systems theory approach has been applied most extensively in capital-intensive, highly integrated continuous process operations. Since variances move very quickly through these operations and take on many different forms, response flexibility and speed are highly desirable. Quick, high quality decision making and execution can save a firm a lot of money (Mansell, 1987).

Among the best known and most studied quality of working life programs in Canada are those in the petrochemical industry. The academic studies that have been conducted of actual quality of working life programs note that they have frequently met with mixed results and need ongoing renewal efforts to sustain them. Among the results noted are that the introduction of quality of working life programs tends to meet with greater success in greenfield sites than in existing plants, although they must be preceded by careful planning and development of the management philosophy and accompanied by effective training.

In one case study (which did not involve a greenfield site), the researchers found that the application of the sociotechnical systems theory approach was limited by the resistance of some supervisors to change (Evans and Ondrack, 1983; Tucker and Taylor, 1984). In the design of the system for a new plant, management decided upon an organic form of organization, a climate of mutual trust, a commitment from top management, and a team system approach at all levels of the plant. Due to the careful planning that went into the implementation of this scheme, it proved highly successful in its initial operation, although it was subsequently thrown off balance by political and economic developments within the industry (Ondrack and Evans, 1984).

A systematic comparison of worker attitudes and perceptions was undertaken in five petrochemical plants with quality of working life programs, others in the industry without quality of working life programs, and some non-petrochemical plants. The study found few differences between the petrochemical plants, with or without programs, but some differences between the petrochemical and non-petrochemical plants. The authors conclude that the programs may not have been implemented properly, or that the employees have become habituated to the effects of the program and they now seem routine (Ondrack and Evans, 1986).

Another study noted that difficulties are encountered in sustaining quality of working life initiatives because they are often introduced and just left to run. A prerequisite for success is continuous renewal in the form of a commitment to review and appraise quality of working life programs to ensure that they respond to changing needs and employee expectations (Nightingale, 1984; cf. also Long, 1984a).

The importance of interrelating technological and organizational innovation has been highlighted in the recent report of the Economic Council of Canada:

> ... successful adoption of those technologies, with their attendant requirements for a flexible, versatile and committed work force, depends upon more participative organizational designs that realize the potential, and reflect the needs, of all stakeholders. [ECC, 1987: 90]

In a paper that lays out some of the assumptions that underlie the Economic Council's position, Keith Newton draws on sociotechnical systems theory to argue that new microelectronic technology is less deterministic than other technologies that have affected work and workers. It is important to investigate the way in which the introduction of new technology is accompanied by organizational innovation that maximizes the benefits to be had (1984).

A review of several case studies where programs to enhance

employee participation were introduced in conjunction with the techno-logical changes found that the programs changed how employees approached their work. Employees identified and solved problems in their work areas and required less supervision and assistance from staff groups. The authors conclude that these programs can contribute signif-icantly to successful technological innovation (Portis et al., 1988).

Some interesting and stimulating research has been done drawing comparisons between changes in work organization in Sweden and North America. In the 1970s, the Swedes were leaders in pioneering sig-nificant changes in several areas of work organization. In more recent years, Swedish companies have engineered a revolution in the technol-ogy of small-batch production, based on both technological and organi-zational innovations. The primary objective is to achieve the kind of increased flexibility made possible by microelectronics.

A number of different organizational changes have been used to accomplish this, including the use of partly unmanned manufacturing, decreased product throughput times, and reorganized materials hand-ling. The use of these new production techniques parallels changes in organization that increase the emphasis on manufacturing cells, or group technology and on product shops, or small units organized around the product. The focus is on holistic organizational units dedi-cated to particular products (Kolodny, 1984, 1985, 1986).

Theorists in the U.S., Sweden, and Canada suggest that experiments in new forms of work organization are laying the basis for the emergence of a new model, based upon the principle of high commitment by the workforce (cf. Walton, 1983). One attempt to synthesize this research describes a model that builds on three key subsystems.

A legitimization subsystem involves that part of the change process in which key decision makers establish new work philosophies by actively examining their own and society's stable and changing values about work. Within the framework of the design subsystem, design teams are established, tasks and problems identified and solutions pro-posed; strong statements of principle are developed with as much employee participation as possible. The details of the design are devel-oped as consistently as possible with these principles.

The work subsystem completes the change process, producing goods or delivering services in ways that build and sustain the commitment of all involved. The model presumes that work systems designed in this fashion are never complete and that mechanisms for learning from expe-rience and feeding back that learning to a continuous design process are essential (Kolodny and Stjernberg, 1986).

Variations on the sociotechnical systems model have also been devel-oped to facilitate the introduction of new technology into the office. A recent summary of some of the main insights derived from these models emphasized the need to include the following four steps: (1) the formation of a strategic information policy group within the firm to establish the strategic, technical, and human resource parameters for information technology, and to oversee the change process; (2) the establishment of a mechanism, such as a joint union-management technology committee, to engage the union in the process of change; (3) the creation of a general environment conducive to change; and (4) the formation of user design groups to assess the potential for application of information technology and make recommendations to the information policy group. The importance of the feedback loop was also emphasized in the form of continuous evaluations of, and modifications to, the system (Long, 1987: 251).

Directions for Future Research

There are a number of areas in the field of managing innovation that could be important targets for further research.

Quality of data

There is a pressing need to improve the quality of data, particularly concerning the current utilization and diffusion rates of new technology to help public policymakers frame more effective responses. This is an area of concern for those within relevant government departments, especially Statistics Canada; Industry, Science and Technology; Communications; and Employment and Immigration. An initiative from SSHRCC to collaborate with these departments in improving the quality of our technological database would probably be most welcome.

Relative benefits

Another area in need of further research involves the question of the relative benefits to be derived from the various sources of new commercializable technology, in-house R&D, research from government labs, university-based research, and technology transfer from other countries. While the traditional assumption in most public policy statements is that in-house R&D is the most effective, some academics in this field strongly believe that technology transfer from other countries provides an equally effective source.

Public policy

If the research were to confirm that benefits are greater from the latter, the question remains as to what public policy mechanisms should be employed to best facilitate the process. A related question concerns the relative roles played by indigenous and foreign-based firms in innovation. Public policy sources, such as the Ontario Premier's Council Report, strongly support the superior benefits to be derived from indigenous firms, but other research suggests that multinational enterprises have played a role in facilitating technology transfer in the past. Further research is needed on this question to provide a stronger direction for public policy.

The Bilateral Trade Agreement

One gaping area of concern is the effect that the Bilateral Trade Agreement with the U.S. will have on the process of technological innovation in Canada. The recent ratification of the agreement provides an opportunity for social scientists to monitor its effects on an ongoing basis. A strong, well-researched body of findings on its short- and medium-term effects could provide an important basis for a future assessment of its impacts and help formulate the appropriate public policy responses.

Entrepreneurial success

Some of the most effective research to date concerns the factors that contribute to relative entrepreneurial success within the firm. Critical among these has been the identification of the need to link strategic marketing concerns with the development of technology. Also identified as a critical factor of success has been the ability of indigenous firms to make the transition from competing in domestic markets to competing in global ones. The further reduction of trade barriers and the heightening of international competition will make this an even more important area for further study. It will undoubtedly be useful to focus research efforts on a comparison of the practice and experience of Canadian firms with those of firms in other nations, both within North America and beyond.

Public policy: enhancing skills

There has been a general reluctance on the part of most management theorists to link management practice with government policy. While there seems to be a strong consensus on the problem of overemphasizing R&D at the expense of a broader range of management skills, there is little consideration given as to how the public policy environment can be changed to help foster the desired set of skills within Canadian management.

Organizational change

Finally, a crucial area of concern is the need for more in-depth studies of the type of organizational changes that have proved most conducive to the adoption and implementation of new technology, both in manufacturing and in the office. Studies of the introduction of robotics, CAD/CAM, and other new technologies have identified the problems that result from a lack of attention to organizational criteria, while studies of organizational design have devoted more of their attention in the past to continuous process operations, such as the petrochemical industry, rather than to the introduction of microelectronic technology throughout industry.

In addition, there is a scarcity of case studies, and a need to investigate the link between financing and entrepreneurship, and the effect of government policies in this regard at the level of the firm. There is also a need to integrate the research within the field of managing innovation. Collaboration between some of the management theorists and those working within the labour process perspective might prove fruitful. Although their respective research is frequently divided by a number of important differences, greater cross-fertilization of approaches might prove stimulating for both.

Chapter Five

Innovation and the Labour Process

David Wolfe

Introduction

Within the general framework of the labour process approach, the recent spate of empirical work has tended to reach an open ended set of conclusions about the effects of the adoption and diffusion of new technologies. The focus in this growing body of research has been on the impact of new technology on employment and skill levels, the degree of consultation, or lack thereof, over the introduction of new technology, its implications for job descriptions and job content and questions of its implications for the exercise of managerial control over the workplace.

Within this broad approach, a number of different foci have emerged. There is a strong differentiation between studies that focus on the impact of new technologies on manufacturing industries and those that have focused upon its impact on the office and clerical work. Within this latter category, a number of studies have been particularly concerned with its impact on the job ghettos where women have traditionally been concentrated. Within the general framework of labour process studies, one specific area of concern has been the question of the relationship between technological change and the collective bargaining process. A final area of concern has been the training prerequisites for successful innovation in the firm. This has been a general theme that runs throughout many of the labour process studies, but there have also been a number of studies that have specifically focused on this question and these will be summarized separately.

The Impact of Technological Change

One of the most consistent themes that emerges repeatedly in the body of labour process studies is the fact that workers experience technological change as something that happens to them in the workplace, rather than as a process that they are integrally involved in directing and controlling. Contrary to popular expectations, the attitudes displayed by workers towards technological change in the majority of studies was quite positive (Peitchinis, 1983).

In 1986/87 the Labour Council of Metropolitan Toronto sponsored a study of the impact of technological change on secondary manufacturing industry in Metro Toronto. Workers interviewed in the study recognized that technological change tended to be a critical factor in the competitive success of their firms. Consequently, many of the workers interviewed expressed greater concern over a lack of investment in new technology in their plants, recognizing that this could mean that their jobs were potentially at risk (Meurer, et al., 1987). Workers at those plants that are innovating, and moving into new market niches, or expanding their market share, seem to have a much more sanguine view of the effects of the technology than do those at plants who have not enjoyed the same degree of economic success—even in instances where the other plants may have more beneficial terms written into their contracts, ie. permanent employment guarantees (Vancouver Typographical Union, 1987).

Similarly, some of the studies conducted in the service sector, or those that focused on office automation, concluded that workers tended to have a generally positive attitude towards the technology, but the results were not always unambiguous. The evaluations of the Department of Communication's field trials noted that employees generally found their systems superior to what they had before and were reluctant to return to the older equipment (Taylor, 1985).

In a study conducted for the Public Service Alliance of Canada, clerical workers reported that many of their tasks were easier and faster to accomplish and that computer technology allowed easier access to information, as well as access to a greater amount of information. However, for many of them as well, computerization had meant a greater standardization and fragmentation of their work (Swimmer et al., 1987). In the study conducted for the Nova Scotia Government Employees' Union, the respondents to a survey displayed generally positive attitudes towards new microtechnology in the workplace. A majority of the respondents considered that their jobs would be "more difficult" to perform without the equipment (Clark et al., 1986a).

Some important variations on this theme were also noted, however. In the study conducted for the Ontario Public Service Employees Union, responses varied considerably in relation to the type of work being done with the computer equipment. Workers in data entry and word processing jobs (categorized as "screen based" work) complained that their work was frequently more routine and stressful, whereas those with jobs in scientific and systems analysis, data-based or visual work (categorized as "screen assisted" work) found that computers had eliminated the more repetitive, routine parts of their work, enabling them to perform their jobs better than they ever had before (McDermott, 1987).

Another variation on this theme was noted in a longtitudinal study conducted of office workers in eight large organizations throughout the Metro Toronto area. The findings indicated that workers tended to start off with a generally positive attitude towards the new computer systems, but that these attitudes became more negative over time. Six months after the implementation of new computer systems, employees interest in their jobs began to decline, they considered the atmosphere in the office less pleasant and they thought that their relationship with their supervisors had deteriorated. These changes were of a moderate degree, however, and employees attitudes were still generally positive. A critical factor in shaping employee attitudes appears to have been the degree of choice workers felt they had in implementing and using the new equipment (Freedman and Park, 1986).

This last mentioned factor, consultation, was a critical variable that turned up repeatedly in the vast majority of the labour process studies. One of the most frequently repeated complaints on the part of workers with new technology, in both the manufacturing and service sectors, was the lack of consultation on the part of management regarding the implementation of the technology.

A basic tenet for most of the labour process researchers is that workers generate new skills and technical knowledge daily in the process of carrying out their jobs. This informal technology of working knowledge is a vital aspect of production in modern industry, but workers are continuously frustrated by management's inability to recognize and value the real worth of their tacit knowledge (DeBresson and Peterson, 1987: ch. 5). The Labour Council of Metropolitan Toronto study emphasized the negative effects that companies frequently suffered as a result of ignoring the valuable contributions that could be made by their own shop floor experts (Meurer et al., 1987).

A similar observation was made in the CAW study of Northern Telecom. The authors observed that there is a conception of "best practice" emerging in the literature on managing technological change. All too often this recognized "best practice" is not followed in the implementation of new technology with sub-optimal results, both for the companies involved and the workers affected by it (Robertson and Wareham, 1988).

The evaluations of the field trials conducted by the federal Department of Communications noted the critical importance of planning for technological innovation and the incredible gap between expectations and performance. Systems consistently failed to perform as well as had been advertised. The systems invariably took much longer to learn than anyone had foreseen. Everyone underbudgeted for training. The user friendliness of most systems turned out to have been seriously overrated. The worst problem of all was the lack of integration encountered in the systems. And ultimately, the expectations of the increase in productivity to be achieved through office automation were not realized (Taylor, 1985, 1986; cf. also Long, 1984c).

Many of these findings are illustrated in a case study conducted for the York University Staff Association of the effects of the introduction of new computer technology. The decision to automate the secretarial offices throughout several faculties of the university was made and carried out with little advance consultation with the workers affected. The staff were frequently overwhelmed by the demands of coping with the new technology and had difficulty finding sufficient time in the course of their normal working day to comprehend the essential aspects of computer technology, let alone the more detailed aspects of the applications software. The study concluded that effective implementation was impeded by the failure to consult with staff, the inadequate or inappropriate provision of training and the lack of time on the part of staff to learn how to use the microcomputers (Clement et al., 1987; cf. also Clement, 1988). Another study concurred, "Although end users have the most precise understanding of the specific requirements of their jobs, they seldom have any input into the decisions pertaining to the selection of the equipment they will be using" (Clark et al., 1988: 32).

Technological Change and Employment

One of the major issues that has been debated in the past decade in the labour process literature has concerned the impact of technology on employment. The early alarmist forecasts that gained wide credence in the late 1970s have given way to more sober and empirical surveys such as those conducted by the Organization for Economic Cooperation and Development, the International Labour Organization and the Economic Council of Canada (E.C.C., 1987: ch 2-4; cf. also Magun, 1986 and Peitchinis, 1984). Among the many conclusions emphasized in these studies is that it is often difficult to factor out the effects of technological change from the effects of other economic factors and that the employment impacts of the technology vary considerably with the type of technology concerned.

On the question of new technology and jobs, the majority of the labour process studies in Canada have tended to move beyond the alarmist view that characterized this perspective several years ago. There is a general recognition that the new technology tends to reduce the labour requirements for production—in other words, the technology tends to facilitate higher levels of output with the same number of, or slightly fewer, workers (Robertson and Wareham, 1987).

This point comes through even more strongly in the CAW's study of Northern Telecom. Although overall employment levels have increased in the past decade in line with the company's growth, productivity increases resulting from the automation of its manufacturing processes and the reduction in the number of parts in many of its products has dramatically reduced labour requirements in this area (Robertson and Wareham, 1988). The overall result of this phenomenon has come to be characterized as jobless growth.

There is a great deal of concern expressed in the studies about what the source of future employment growth will be, if it is unlikely to occur in traditional occupations, especially in manufacturing industry. A study conducted for the Manitoba Federation of Labour examined the employment effects of computerization in the grain industry at company head offices and grain elevators. The study noted that data processing staff at head offices has grown, while the need for manual processing of transactions has been reduced. In the elevators, computers allow consolidation of jobs through more efficient inventory control. Although employment levels had not been reduced, overall, there was a situation of jobless growth as grain companies were able to handle much larger quantities of grain while maintaining stable staffing levels (Novek and Russell, 1986; cf. also Menzies, 1981: ch. 7).

In the study of the telephone industry conducted for the Communications' Workers, the researchers found that although technological change had not reduced employment, the prospect for future employment growth was questionable and workers in certain occupational categories were quite pessimistic about their future job security (Mosco and Zureik, 1987). One area where there were some direct observations made of employment loss was in the study of the effect of microelectronic technology on women's employment opportunities by the Women's Skill Development Society of Vancouver. The study noted that the more pervasive use of this technology was associated with increasing cutbacks in women's employment opportunities and a growing tendency to shift from full-time to part-time work (Cohen and White, 1988a; for a broader discussion of the impact of technological change on women in the labour force, cf. Armstrong, 1984: ch. 7).

A recurring theme in the studies was the tendency for technological change to contribute to an increased polarization of jobs at opposite ends of the occupational scale. The study of women clerical workers observed three distinct trends: an integration of managerial/professional jobs with high level clerical positions; a reduction of the number of traditional middle-level functions; and the development of a pool of routinized clerical jobs, such as data entry. The result is a more polarized clerical workforce with jobs concentrated at opposite occupational poles and little opportunity for mobility between them (Cohen and White, 1988; Bird and Lee, 1987; Menzies, 1981).

The trend towards polarization of jobs was noted in a variety of different ways. Within the public sector, studies observed that technological change tended to eliminate the routine apsect of more highly skilled or scientific jobs, while at the same time it made data entry and wordprocessing jobs even more routinized (McDermott, 1987). In the electronics industry, the same polarization was noted: on the one hand, it has led to skilled and complex automation work in some occupations and on the other, it has led to unskilled, repetitive and fragmented work (Robertson and Wareham, 1988). The authors of these studies tend to concur that although working with new technology contains the potential to improve the quality of more highly skilled jobs, it also has the tendency to further denigrate the quality of less skilled ones.

More detailed studies of the impact of technological innovation on job structures and job classifications have concluded that the results are somewhat indeterminate. A study in the steel industry noted that job structures and classifications change in response to a variety of variables, including technological innovation. New technology may provide the opportunity to negotiate new job descriptions, but job structures are more profoundly influenced by the tenor of labour relations in the firm or industry.

Technological change may eliminate some old job categories and create new ones. It can convert previously unskilled jobs into more skilled ones and it may amalgamate what were once defined as individual jobs into one job. However, these job changes must be translated into new job classifications through the collective bargaining process. The study found that often the classification of new jobs was sharply out of line with the technical complexity and the levels of responsibility required by the work (Storey, 1987). Another study noted that management frequently tries to classify new technologically skilled jobs outside of the existing bargaining unit or else will find a pre-existing, but little used, job category within the unit to cover the new, more skilled and demanding jobs (Meurer et al., 1987).

Job Skills

Closely related to the question of the impact of technological change on employment levels and job structures is its implications for the skill levels of workers. This question lies at the heart of much of the research that has been conducted in the labour process perspective, particularly as it was influenced by the seminal thinking of Harry Braverman. Braverman argued that deskilling was inevitable under capitalism as managers strove to extend their control over the labour process. Technological innovation would contribute to this trend. A number of recent studies in the U.S., have tended to confirm Braverman's argument, although they don't insist that this trend is inevitable.

However, a different perspective among researchers in this field has also emerged. Larry Hirschhorn has argued that the demands of microelectronic technology will require that the worker as machine tender give way to the worker as problem solver,

> ... workers in cybernated systems cannot function as passive machine tenders, looking to instruction manuals for the appropriate response. This suggests an entirely new definition of work in a post-industrial setting. Skills can no longer be defined in terms of a particular set of actions, but as a general ability to understand how a system functions and to think flexibly in trying to solve problems (Hirschhorn, 1982: 45; cf. also Hirschhorn, 1984).

Many of the labour process studies conducted in Canada have been strongly influenced by the thinking of researchers such as Hirschhorn, either directly or indirectly. The impact of technological change on skill levels has been investigated in many of their studies and the findings are somewhat mixed. Some of the studies have noted the increasing polarization of the occupational structure of the workforce. The implication of these findings is that although there is some increase in skill levels occurring, there has also been deskilling.

However, the concept of skill is at best difficult to define and frequently questions of skill effects are intertwined with questions of changes in managerial control. One study suggests the adoption of a threefold categorization, linking changes in skill levels to changes in managerial control of the work process: upskilling occurs where both workers' autonomy and skill levels increase; deskilling where there is a loss of control over the work process and a loss of technical skill; and reskilling occurs in jobs which maintain or increase the technical skill content while control over the work process has been decreased (Cohen and White, 1988b).

The empirical evidence on the impact of technological change on skill levels across the spectrum of office jobs is somewhat mixed. The insistence on distinguishing between the skill and the control effects of technology reinforces the point that the technology itself is not determinant of these effects. The effects vary from organization to organization and are often a function of management choices.

Studies of the effect of automation on word processing note that the original tendency to concentrate the technology in secretarial pools along Tayloristic lines has often been superceded by the recognition that more productive results are realized by dispersing the technology throughout the organization with job and skill enhancing consequences. In the long run, the most routinized clerical jobs that might tend to be deskilled, such as data inputting, recording and retrieval, are the ones most likely to be eliminated by computerization. The residual jobs, even those where workers' autonomy is reduced, will likely demand higher educational levels and more analytical skills. The expansion of these higher skilled jobs will also be aided by the increased demand for information, especially that provided by organizations making the most effective use of new information technology (Long, 1987: ch. 6).

Similar effects were observed for the manufacturing sector, in studies of the auto industry, the pulp and paper industry and manufacturing in Metro Toronto. The impact of new technology on skills is ambiguous; it is often less determinant of skill than other factors, including the way work is organized and the way jobs are designed. While there is a general trend toward an upward shift in skill requirements, there are specific situations where work has been deskilled. Manual jobs are the most easily automated and their elimination results in an increase in general skill levels. In addition, computerization increases the skill requirements of many individual jobs although some traditional 'craft' skills are vulnerable to being made redundant (Robertson and Wareham, 1987; Taylor et al., 1987; Meurer et al., 1987).

One of the most intriguing observations about the impact of technological change on skill levels is found in the series of nine case studies of information and materials processing industries conducted for the B.C. Federation of Labour. Pursuing a line of argument similar to Hirschhorn, and clearly influenced by the thinking of socio-technical systems theorists, the researchers hypothesized that there was a general model, involving both technical and social elements, that applied to contemporary forms of automation in both types of industries.

The most significant transition occuring in these industries centres around the shift from an earlier stage of batch entry computerization to the current online stage of source entry. The key aspect of source data entry involves the automatic or near automatic capture at the point the data is created, virtually eliminating the role of the worker as an interface between the external world and the information system. This transition, and in particular, the progressive removal of workers from direct involvement in the production and handling of data has generated a variety of new skills, including the following: 1) watching for exceptional events and handling unexpected contingencies to achieve system goals (monitering); 2) judgement and analytical skills; 3) skills that relate to the system as a whole; and 4) abstract skills that involve dealing with informational representations of reality. The changes in skill requirements in the industries studied create the potential for workers to play a qualitatively different role in the work process. The extent to which that potential has been realized has depended to a great extent on the manner in which management has responded to the changes (Hansen and Bernard, 1986b).

In some of the case studies analysed, the results conformed very closely to Hirschhorn's cybernetic model, in which workers do not control routine decisions—which are fully automated—rather they 'control the controls', deal with exceptional circumstances, and anticipate problems or weaknesses before they enter the system. Another trend identified follows closely the pattern observed in the studies of women's clerical work. More routine, predictable tasks are absorbed by the computer, leaving the discretionary, monitoring work to be performed by workers, albeit in a highly centralized fashion.

Workers who operate systems demanding a high level of operator intervention can best serve the system when they are allowed to apply problem-solving methods to a wide range of events, to flexibly maintain the achievement of overall system goals. While responsibility for the main policy decisions is highly centralized, problem solving within these policies is highly decentralized. Control of the workers no longer occurs primarily through the external application of rules, but much more by the internal adoption of the requisite attitudes (Hansen, 1987b).

Organizational Flexibility

One of the central questions concerning technological innovation involves its effects on organizational flexibility. Frequently, the same technology can be adopted and implemented in ways that are more centralized or decentralized, especially in industries that involve the processing of large volumes of information, such as the insurance industry. Two different case studies reveal the range of potential organizational effects that follow from this aspect of flexibility. One study examined the introduction of a new on-line data processing system in a large insurance company in Toronto. The new system reversed the historical trend towards the fragmentation of tasks and the increase in the number of processing steps. This resulted in the progressive collapse of the processing chain, also allowing faster, more accurate response to customer requests. This change is also based on the trend towards capturing data at source (Clement and Gotlieb, 1987).

These developments were associated with a tendency by management to intensify their control over the work process. Managers oversaw every stage of the implementation of the new system and used it to obtain more detailed performance measures of their employees and regulate employees' access to information. Managerial control concerns were also a factor in the way tasks were integrated and the organization was decentralized along territorial lines (Clement and Gotlieb, 1987).

In contrast, a study of the process of change in the general insurance industry in the Quebec metropolitan region emphasized the interactive nature of the work that was allowed through the introduction of teleprocessing. The study argued that traditional forms of bureaucracy tended to decrease because of the flexibility of interactive teleprocessing. These changes resulted in both a greater degree of autonomous control exercised by employees after they gained access to interactive teleprocessing, while at the same time the centralized storage of all computer transactions facilitated a greater degree of control and supervision on the part of head managers (Billette et al., 1986).

While the Laval study concurred in the finding that computerization simultaneously allowed more flexibility in response to the market and more effective centralized control over the organization, it also maintained that this was compatible with greater degrees of employee autonomy. The results of these studies are indicative of the range of organizational changes that are compatible with the introduction of microelectronic technology. A general finding of many of the studies has been that the organizational consequences of technological change are highly dependent on the range of managerial responses (Robertson and Wareham, 1987).

The technology can be effectively accomodated within a range of different organizational structures and frequently, it is management's perspective that determines which of these structures will be adopted. In a study of computerization in small offices in Southern Ontario, the author concluded that the technology contains the potential for a much greater degree of control than is usually realized. The reason for this is the alternative range of social values and cultural systems that determine the structure of relationships within the office, often based on the engineering or professional authority of the owner of the firm (Marsden, 1987).

Other research that has recently been conducted on office workers' reactions to new technology also suggests that management choices can profoundly alter the way in which the technology improves office work. Data comparing the work effects of new technology in Canada and the U.S. indicates that intracultural differences do exist according to type of equipment used, gender and the heirarchical level of the office workers (Gattiker and Nelligan, 1988). Organizations should recognize the technology's effect on individual perceptions of career success.

The data suggest that individual's reactions to intelligent work stations are far more positive than they are for main frame terminals. Increased acceptance and effective use of computers may be greatly facilitated by installing intelligent workstations. It is suggested that managers should take note of the fact that productivity increases via computerization might best be achieved by providing employees with intelligent workstations that possess main-frame communications capabilities (Gattiker, 1988; Gattiker, Gutek and Berger, forthcoming).

The process of technological change has been accompanied by a great deal of organizational innovation in the workplace. In many instances, the organizational changes have been as signficant if not more significant than the technical ones. Included among these are a variety of systems associated with the current buzzwords of technological change—Just-in-Time, Quality Circles and a host of others. It is on this issue, however, that the labour process studies adopt the most skeptical attitude towards managements' intentions with respect to the introduction of new technology. There is little evidence in these studies that management has heeded the admonition of the Economic Council of Canada concerning the need to adopt more flexible forms of work organization to accomodate the increased potential of the new technology (E.C.C., 1987: 90).

Among the most critical of the studies have been those conducted for the B.C. Federation of Labour which observe a significant gap between the potential for a more flexible, participatory form of work organization based on the new technologies and the form that currently prevails. Their case studies overwhelmingly indicated, to one degree or another, a failure on the part of management to accept the social consequences which seem to flow from the introduction of the new technology—a process they characterize as 'management resistance to change'.

As was observed in the insurance industry cases discussed above, the ability of computers to generate increased volumes of information through data capture at source are used to maintain traditional forms of centralized control and supervisory systems, rather than to devolve the information analyzing and interpreting tools into the hands of the workers. "While the real potential of the new information technology is in the re-integration of work and expanded flexibility in operations and information use, in practice many workplaces are attempting to restrict flexibility and integration and are organizing the labour process in a neo-Taylorist fashion" (Hansen and Bernard, 1986b).

In a study of the Newfoundland deep sea fishing industry, the researchers found that, because of the continued dominance of Taylorist assumptions on the part of management, technological change is likely to lead to deskilling, closer monitoring of individual workers, persistent efforts to speedup production and continued high levels of worker-management conflict (Neis et al., 1987).

The more progressive and dynamic firms increasingly are coming to understand that organizational changes are as important as purely technological ones, yet there is considerable evidence that even some of the largest and most dynamic of companies, such as GM or Nortel, remain more committed to the form of organization innovation than to its actual substance. In other words, these employers are often quick to pick up on the buzzwords and the techniques of organizational change, yet tend to implement them in ways that maintain or reinforce the existing authority pattern and command heirarchy in the firm.

Quality of Working Life and Management Control

The labour process researchers tend to be highly suspicious of the effects of many of the organizational innovations discussed above by the management theorists, such as Quality of Working Life programs. A major study of QWL from this perspective argues that it is the opposite of what it says it is; QWL is designed to achieve greater power for management: over workers, the way they work and the product of their labour. QWL as implemented in the cases studied by Wells was not intended to increase workers' participation in the management of their plants through their unions. It was a managerial control strategy that involved four key elements: 1) the controlled delegation of authority to selected workers; 2) improved access to worker's skills and knowledge about their jobs; 3) the promotion of work group identity; and 4) the forging of a stronger identification between the workers and the product they produced. Although QWL programs are presented to workers and unions as "win-win" situations, in reality, they are subordinated to the overriding goal of increasing profitability. The most insidious effect of QWL is that in the long run, it attempts to transform the definition of workers' collective interests into individual ones. One of the most effective ways unions can respond to this challenge is by incorporating the promises of QWL programs into the collective bargaining process and involving membership more directly in determining the negotiating objectives (Wells, 1986; 1987).

Organizational changes featuring QWL programs have not been the only ones. They have been accompanied by the adoption of new management systems and techniques designed to increase productivity and use new technology more effectively. Most often modelled after the Japanese or—in cases such as the Nummi plant in California—implemented directly by Japanese management, techniques, such as the Just-in-Time system or the team concept, emphasize the gains to be made from increased flexibility. However, flexibility as defined in this approach often takes on radically different meanings than intended by workers or unions who argue for its benefits.

These concepts, termed "management by stress" by American researchers Mike Parker and Jane Slaughter, are based on the principle of methodically locating and removing protections against breakdowns and glitches. "To identify both weak and strong points, the system, including its human elements, operates in a state of permanent stress. The weak points break down, indicating where additional resources are needed.... points that never break down are assumed to waste resources" (Parker and Slaughter, 1988: 39).

Despite the fact that these organizational innovations are credited with realizing significant productivity gains, they deviate significantly from the goals and principles of socio-technical systems advocated by some management theorists. Consequently, they do little to enhance employees' sense of security in the light of ongoing technological change; in fact, the result is exactly the opposite. The combination of technological and organizational changes introduced with little or no direct employee input is experienced as highly stressful and generates increased insecurity. The results of research conducted by the labour process theorists suggest a substantial gap between the cybernetic model and the practice of many North American firms. They perceive the need for a fundamental choice to be made,

> ... in a computerized workplace characterized by a Just in Time production philosophy and an ongoing commitment to product and process improvements, production requires the timely and appropriate interventions of workers. Production requires fewer workers but it requires more from them. The question for management is whether the trust, security and confidence of workers is a precondition for the changes in the workplace and if so, whether flexibility will be a negotiated process or a resort to managerial prerogative (Robertson and Wareham, 1988: 237).

An area of growing concern for students of the labour process is the potential of computer performance monitoring and control systems (CPMCS) to measure and motivate employee performance in order to enhance overall productivity. These systems operate in a real-time mode, collecting data on things such as number of transactions processed, number of errors committed, transaction processing time, and operator connect time. At the simplest level, the system feeds performance data back to the employee to facilitate self-control. At the other extreme, they replace more conventional means of performance appraisal with seemingly objective measures to determine pay and promotions. However, in addition to simply monitoring employee performance, CPMCS interacts substantively with the organizational environment to alter the characteristics that affect motivation and performance (Grant, 1986).

Research on this issue was conducted in several TIRF studies. One study focused on the impact of CPMCS as perceived by individual service sector workers at three group claims department sites of a major insurance company. The results of the study indicate that with CPMCS measures, workers expect performance measures to be complete, accurate and appropriate. If they don't perceive these criteria to be met, there is greater dissatisfaction with the supervisory and appraisal process. When CPMCS cannot accurately measure an important aspect of performance, it tends to promote bureaucratic behaviour to conform to the system's standards. Employees tend to disregard dimensions of their performance that cannot be measured by the systems. Workers who internalize the standards may function more comfortably in the monitored environment than those who do not. Finally, CPMCS does not reduce the need for human supervision to improve the quality of working life and the overall level of satisfaction with control systems (Higgins et al., 1987).

In the study of workers in the telephone industry of four provinces, workers in every category, including repair and maintenance, operators, supervisory and directory assistance, as well as clerical, indicated that they believed technological change was associated with the increased monitoring of their jobs. One of the strongest findings of the study was the perceived relationship by workers between monitoring and increased stress on the job (Mosco and Zureik, 1987). In interviews conducted for this survey with some researchers active in the field, the issue of computerized monitoring was identified as one that was likely to grow in significance and as a source of controversy.

User Driven Technology

As a result of the findings of many of the labour process studies, a number of researchers have begun to advocate the need for greater emphasis to be placed on user-driven design to improve both the quality of working life for those affected by technological change, as well as the productivity of the firms involved. Labour researchers advocate that equipment must be designed not just in conjuction with the purchaser, but also with the users. Only the users can fully appreciate the skills and intricacies associated with their jobs. The numerous problems experienced with microelectronic technology that stem from flawed designs, not to mention the adverse effects on workers, can only be rectified if users are allowed to play a more direct role in design themselves (Bernard, 1983).

A number of the labour process studies actually undertook demonstration projects to design new technology from a user's point of view, or to help workers become acquainted more effectively with the technology they were expected to use. A demonstration project conducted by the United Food and Commercial Workers Union in B.C. created and installed a model checkout station for use in retail food stores based on occupational health data and on internationally developed ergonomic principles concerning repetitive motion tasks performed at checkout stations. The study compared the effects of the conventional checkout stand with the modified prototype.

The research indicated that the new design displayed significant improvements with respect to physical stress and allowed cashiers to spend 56% more time in their work cycle in an upright position. Ratings by cashiers also showed greater satisfaction with the new workstation (Stoffman et al., 1986; for a discussion of another demonstration project in an office setting, cf. Clement et al., 1987).

Innovation and Industrial Relations

An issue of great potential significance for the management of technology is the question of how the industrial relations system in Canada has adopted to the process of innovation. The question is of particular significance for union members and has been highlighted to some extent by the labour process and other researchers. However, the way in which the collective bargaining system deals with the issue of technological change has implications that go far beyond these narrow interests. As the Economic Council of Canada indicated in its recent report, the collective bargaining system can potentially play a major role in facilitating the process of adjustment to change within Canadian industry. The Council argued that participation by all stakeholders is a necessary ingredient for effective technological and organizational innovation. Genuine and constructive collective bargaining over the implementation of new technology is an important policy objective and there is a need to find better ways of achieving it (E.C.C., 1987: 109).

Research on the subject to date has indicated that both the legislative and contractual provisions for technological change in Canada are relatively limited. There are four jurisdictions in Canada with technological change provisions in their legislation—the federal government and three provinces. There have been relatively few cases decided under these provisions and in those that have, a number of problems with the provisions have loomed large. The first problem encountered by unions is defining a certain workplace practice to fall with the provisions of the respective labour code. This has proved difficult as the provisions are defined fairly narrowly. In addition, several of the codes have clauses that allow unions and management to opt-out of coverage and this weakens the effectiveness of the provisions. A third problem involves the requirement that technological change must affect a signficant number of employees to fall under the coverage of the code. A final problem is that the length of time companies are required to give for notice is not sufficient to enable unions to have a meaningful input into the changes (McDermott, 1987; cf. also Jain, 1983).

With respect to collective agreements, there are four main areas that have been included: the requirement for advance notice of technological change, provisions for the retraining of workers affected by technological change, the establishment of labour and management committees to deal with the consequences of technological change, and finally, the provision for wage and employment guarantees for workers adversely affected by technological change. The evidence presented in a major survey conducted for the Economic Council suggests that negotiated technological change clauses are relatively infrequent even in agreements covering large numbers of workers and that they have not become notably more frequent since 1972, when technological change legislation was first put into effect.

The failure of unions to bring these issues to the bargaining table and management resistance to worker involvement in the implementation of new technology helps explain the relative infrequency of these provisions (Pierce 1987). Even when unions have written tech change clauses into collective agreements, labour boards and arbitrators have generally, except to a limited extent in B.C., not enforced either the existing provisions in the labour codes or in the agreements (Knight and McPhillips, 1986; Gunderson and Meltz, 1987; Craig, 1988).

One current project underway attempts to link the process of technological change to broader transformations in the political economy of the country and to spell out its implications for the industrial relations system and the role of unions. This analysis views the process of technological change as part of a broader transformation associated with the decline of "Fordism"—the institutional set of arrangements that linked standardized mass production to a series of social and political institutions, including collective bargaining arrangements, in the postwar period.

The emergence of a new Fordism is linked to a general rationalization of production—the shedding of surplus labour, the introduction of new management techniques, such as quality circles, greater use of two-tier bargaining and contracting out, and the adoption of more flexible work processes. The threat posed by these changes for unions is that they will eventually weaken the unions' collective strength because they will lessen the apparent need for unions in the eyes of their members. These dilemmas are compounded by the shift of employment growth from the manufacturing to the service sector where unions have encountered greater difficulty in organizing. All of these changes constitute a grave challenge for Canadian unions and the form of collective bargaining system that has prevailed for the past 45 years. Unions must devise new ways of organizing and mobilizing their members if they are not to be left in a seriously weakened position (Drache and Glasbeek, 1989; cf. also Drache and Glasbeek, 1988).

Evidence gleaned from a review of the international literature also suggests a number of points worthy of note for both unions and Canadian public and private sector managers: workers tend to be more willing to cooperate in workplace change processes when they feel they have both a reasonable degree of job security and a genuine say in how such change is implemented; a greater degree of worker cooperation helps promote more complete and more effective diffusion of new technology; in those countries that have been most successful in adapting to new technology, specific national adjustment mechanisms for dealing with technological change have often gone hand in hand with active labour market and full employment policies. However, those countries tend to be the ones where unions have been strongest in the first place (Mahon, 1987).

Innovation, Training and Skill Development

An issue that is attracting increased attention from both a policy- and research-oriented perspective is the link between innovation, training and skill development. As detailed studies of the effects of technological change on employment have eased the worst fears of a decade ago, the recognition has also spread that the minimum consequence of widespread innovation will be substantial labour dislocation. This change is likely to place an increased strain on the existing resources that can provide for labour force adjustment—training and skill development programs. Within the social sciences, attention has been directed at these questions from two distinct disciplinary perspectives—economics and education—with predictably different results.

Economists generally recognize that technological innovation will have a significant impact upon the skills required by current and future labour force participants. However, they tend to adopt a relatively sanguine view about the prospects for existing institutional and market mechanisms to adopt to the demands for labour market adjustment that will be placed upon them. One analysis by a leading labour market economist argues that what are required are better information systems to monitor skill shortages and emerging requirements; modification of training facilities and programs to meet emerging needs; promotion of geographic and occupational mobility through provision of travel grants and portable wage subsidies; and income maintenance through unemployment insurance and enhanced early retirement pension provisions (Dodge, 1984).

Several background papers prepared for the Macdonald Royal Commission were even less concerned about the need for enhanced policy initiatives to respond to the challenge that innovation will create for labour market adjustment. One study concluded on the basis of its review of the literature on the skill effects of technological change that both the evidence available concerning retrospective and prospective changes did not make it appear that the case for massive retraining needs was compelling. Workers learn the vast majority of the skills they need on the job, rather than through any formal educational programs, obviating the need for massive retraining efforts (Globerman, 1986).

Another paper reviewed summarized the recommendations of recent government policy reviews and concluded that the evidence in support of a substantial need for increased retraining efforts appeared weak. A greater reliance on market mechanisms would lead to a situation where resources would be reallocated as required by changing patterns of demand. It did support the diversion of some federal funds from postsecondary education into support for vocational and on-the-job training, as well into educational tax credits for post-secondary students. It rejected the adoption of a levy grant system or system of paid educational leave in favour of a registered educational leave savings plan (Davis, 1986).

The view on these questions adopted by social scientists primarily concerned with adult education differs quite dramatically from those cited above. A discussion paper prepared by the Canadian Association for Adult Education for a roundtable sponsored by the Canadian Advanced Technology Association pointed out that the prospective decline in new labour force entrants over the next decade will mean that future labour market demands for skilled labour will be met by a greater emphasis on the recurrent education of the adult labour force. It summarized data from a recent Statistics Canada survey on the incidence of adult education in Canada and concluded that in comparison to some European countries, we lag behind (Morrison and Rubenson, 1987).

Adult educators who have reviewed the capacity of the Canadian educational system to cope with the demands that will be placed upon it by the competitive pressures of the current technological revolution are pessimistic in their prognosis. The lack of a comprehensive education strategy, the failure to appreciate the diversity of demands placed upon the educational system by current labour market developments and the hegemony of classical economic theory on policy development all contribute to a failure to take seriously the concept of recurrent education, as advocated by the OECD (Rubenson, 1987).

A number of the background papers prepared for CEIC's Skill Development Leave Task Force in 1983 examined some of the issues related to these problems in greater detail. Among the issues dealt with were the following: the barriers to participation in adult education programs (Rubenson, 1987) and the limitations of employer sponsored training programs in terms of access and duration (Paquet, 1983). Other background papers explored a wide range of policy options to deal with an anticipated range of adult training problems, including acquiring occupational skills, skills maintenance, transition into management, functional illiteracy and trade union training (Adams, 1983; Thomas, 1983).

The issues raised in a policy context with respect to training have more immediate significance for many of the workers directly affected by technological change. Workers in many industries in both the manufacturing and service sectors recognize that their future employment prospects are tied to their ability to gain the training they need to work with the new technology. Yet, they are increasingly frustrated by their inability to gain access to this training.

For its part, management in Canadian firms seems to display an overwhelming reluctance to invest in the training of its workforce. The recently completed study by the Economic Council of Canada concluded that there was little evidence of a major investment in skills development by Canadian industry in response to the wave of technological innovation that had already occurred (1987: 83). The attitude displayed by management suggests that it continues to see investment in training as a drain on current profitability rather than an investment in future growth and profits.

Several of the studies conducted for the TIRF program noted a variety of strategies that have been pursued by management in relation to the training question. One strategy favoured by management in many manufacturing sector firms favours hiring graduates directly out of community or technical colleges with some formal training in computerized equipment over the re-training of the current workforce. The advantages of this is that the new workers frequently have the computer and numerical skills needed and they can often be located outside the bargaining unit. The disadvantage, however, is that this practice overlooks the vast store of acquired or 'tacit' knowledge that is stored in its current skilled workforce. Often these tacit skills, which are highly valued in other countries, are lost to employers who adopt this strategy.

The right of access of workers to training for new technologically skilled jobs represents an important potential collective bargaining issue for the future. To date, outside of the larger industrial unions, appreciation of its significance has been growing slowly. At the same time, the practice creates a serious problem for public policy in that displaced older workers represent the component of the labour force most resistant to declining rates of unemployment and are likely to experience the most serious employment problems in the future (Meurer et al., 1987; Storey, 1987).

An area of pressing concern for some of the labour researchers has been the affect of technological change on older workers. Old workers are widely perceived to be one of the most disadvantaged groups in terms of the impact of new technology. They suffer from a widespread perception that they are slower to adapt, untrainable and less productive when compared to new entrants to the labour force. These biases pose particular problems for older workers in gaining access to the training required to facilitate their adjustment to new technology. In a TIP sponsored survey of affiliates of the Labour Council of Metro Toronto, the researchers found that 84% of the unions responding reported no training programs were available to their members. When asked how important their employers regarded the provision of training opportunities for their members over 45, they responded that it was not very high. Interestingly, these union leaders also perceived governments at all levels as not very responsive to the training needs of their members (Sobel and Meurer, 1988).

Several researchers have begun to examine the specific effects of industrial training techniques as they relates to technological change. The findings in this area have a crucial bearing on many of the issues discussed above, specifically with respect to questions of skill and the organization of the labour process. One study conducted on the development of training policies in and for the plastics industry has reached some conclusions that are highly troubling from a labour process perspective.

The research focuses on the implications of the shift of training activities from the locus of the colleges to private industry in Ontario and the role of the Skills Development Ministry in helping industry devise new training modules. In the new model for training that is being developed, there is an attempt to incorporate the nexus between training and the needs of industry into a comprehensive management structure. The organization of curriculum and training objectives around highly specific tasks and performance objectives makes it possible to train workers only for those tasks to be performed and in a relatively short period of time. Skills are thus tied tightly to the needs of the productive process and companies avoid having to pay for skills that are not required (Smith and Smith, 1988).

Other research that has been conducted in this area notes the dangers of this approach to training for clerical workers in general and women in particular. The conceptualization and organization of instruction along these lines leads potentially to an impoverishment of the substance of vocational knowledge itself and to the separation of skills from the power and status of workers. A competency based approach to skill training produces an organization of vocational training which fails to satisfy workers' needs and may in the long run serve to erode rather than enhance the stature of women's job skills in particular (Jackson, 1987; on the broader question of the relation between gender and skill as it bears on the training issue, cf. also Gaskell, 1987).

The implications of these findings lead in a direction that is quite different than the cybernatic model espoused by many labour process researchers and some management researchers. It raises questions about whether management is seriously committed to a model that might enhance workers skills and powers under new technology.

It also raises questions about which models of training, skill development and work organization will ultimately have the most positive implications for future increases in the productivity and competitiveness of Canadian industry. A recent survey of the comparative approaches to training in several industrial nations cautions against the pitfalls of adopting a narrow and restrictive approach to the concept of workers' skills with respect to the new technology (Muszynski and Wolfe, 1988). The entire area of training is one that is definitely in need of further research.

Directions for Future Research

The studies that have been conducted to date from a labour process perspective provide a wealth of data, mostly based on case studies, concerning the impact of technological change on workers and their working conditions. The information that has been collected has gone a long way towards resolving previous questions regarding the impact of technology on employment, skill levels, occupational structures, work organization and employee satisfaction. However, because so much of the data was gathered on a case study basis by specific unions, there is a pressing need to undertake further research that can aggregate findings across a wider range of sectors and industries in order to confirm or disprove the case study results.

A major obstacle to this development is the relative isolation from each other in which most of these researchers work. While the bulk of this research has been funded by Labour Canada, many of the people working in the field are social scientists. There is a pressing need for SSHRCC, ideally in conjunction with Labour Canada, to develop mechanisms that would allow a greater degree of interaction among researchers in this field and the establishment of a more tangible network of researchers that could operate at the aggregate level.

One of the most interesting outcomes of the labour process studies is the extent to which concerns have shifted away from an exclusive focus on the employment effects of technology and a preoccupation with the deskilling focus that predominated in the earlier literature. Most of these studies display a high degree of sensitivity to the relevance of the interaction between technological and organizational variables that is emphasized in the management literature.

As a consequence, however, many of the results tend to confirm the contingent nature of the relationship. What are required at this point are more detailed and specific studies of the impact of different forms of work organization on a range of variables: ease and effectiveness of the implementation of new technology; its impact on productivity and the competitive position of Canadian firms; the overall levels of employee satisfaction in working with new technology; the specific effect on workers' skill levels; and the general impact on the climate of industrial relations within Canadian industry.

One final point is worthy of attention. At several points in this review of the state of the art of current research, one is struck by the degree of convergence between the work of some management theorists and many of the labour process researchers. This convergence has been particularly stimulated by the growing influence of the socio-technical systems perspective, as mediated by writers such as Hirschhorn, on the work of the labour researchers. Despite this convergence, however, the work of the two groups remains segregated by a wide chasm based in large part on their professional affiliations, theoretical orientations and political commitments. Without either side abandonning their respective positions, the clear potential for a great deal of fruitful interaction exists. SSHRCC occupies a unique position that would allow it to promote future research projects with the potential to generate this interaction.

Chapter Six

Industrial Policy and Strategies for Research and Development

William Leiss, Richard Smith

Introduction

In this chapter, research and development (R&D) strategy is discussed in the context of overall industrial policy and is also dealt with at greater length in a separate section on R&D policy. The paper seeks to identify the relevant literature and the questions which need to be addressed in the field.

Industrial Policy *

Most of the relevant research on industrial policy has been conducted within the last thirteen years. In 1975 the Organization for Economic Cooperation and Development (OECD) published an influential paper comparing the instruments and objectives of "politiques industrielles." In that same year the Economic Council of Canada released a document which called for freer trade for Canada, and which included many of the elements of an "industrial policy" argument.

In the early 1980s, as an economic recession gripped the continent, North American interest in industrial policy grew rapidly. Commentators from both the American left and right proposed models for industrial policy (for example, Reich, 1982; Thurow, 1980). Early commentators

---

* We regret that we saw the new book by Atkinson and Coleman (1989) too late for inclusion in this review.

on the economics of industrial policy in Canada included William Watson (1983) and Richard Harris (Harris and Cox, 1984). The Canadian debate on industrial policy has been largely taken up with the differences between the perspectives of the Economic Council of Canada on the one hand, and the Science Council of Canada on the other.

It is important to distinguish between the debate on "industrial policy" and industrial policies themselves. While the former is a relatively recent occurrence, it is quite probable—given a generous definition of the term—that industrial policy has existed as long as governments have intervened in the economy. How, then, should industrial policy be defined? Adams and Klein (1983:3) work with a very broad definition:

> We intend to use the term industrial policy without preconceptions or biases. We are concerned with all measures that will improve on the economy's supply potential: anything that will improve growth: productivity and competitiveness.

This definition echoes that of the OECD: "Industrial policies are concerned with promoting growth and efficiency" (1975: 7). This definition may be too narrow because growth and efficiency are not the only objectives for industrial policy; social concerns (Hager, 1982) and political concerns (Zysman, 1983) also play a role. Blais (1986) suggests instead that the objective of industrial policy is to change the structure of industry. The state does this through the use of particular tools: "[Industrial Policy is] the selective measures adopted by the state to alter industrial organization" (Blais, 1986: 4).

The "selective measures" which make up the tools of industrial policy can take the form of government enterprise, direct financial assistance, tax allowances, tariff protection, regulation of competition and foreign investments, government markets, and special protection against imports. In Canada and the other OECD countries, tariffs remain the most important factor in terms of their impact on the economy. This is despite a general fall in the impact of tariffs over the past twenty years (perceptions of the "new protectionism" notwithstanding) and the relative rise in the importance of subsidies:

> The average tariff in advanced capitalist democracies will be around 4 percent in 1987, when the period of adjustment in the Tokyo Round of GATT agreements has come to an end. Direct financial assistance and tax allowances represent 3 and 1 to 2 percent respectively of the gross domestic product (GDP). Government markets, technical assistance and special protection (quotas in particular) have a fairly low overall impact. [Blais, 1986: 5-6]

In Canada, there are not only different tools of industrial policy but also different levels of government which can wield those tools. Although jurisdictional influences in the area of industrial policy are present in Canada, the role of the provinces remains smaller than that of the federal government, mainly because of the influence of the (largely federally controlled) tariff and tax systems. The apparent lack of coordination between the two spheres has led some commentators (Tupper, 1986, for example) to be concerned that this might preclude optimal results. This is an area where further research is required, however, as it is not known whether cooperation or competition is the better solution (Belanger, 1982).

If we look at industrial policy in terms of the targeted industries, it is apparent that agriculture and textiles get the most attention, chiefly in the form of quotas and tariffs. As a general rule, the industries that are affected most by the gradual lowering of tariff barriers are those with a large number of employees and who are facing stiff competition from abroad. From a more general perspective, it can be said that "industrial policy tends to support first declining industries and regions and then new technology" (Blais, 1986:12). Brenner and Courville (1986) stress the political necessity for aid to declining industries:

> There are risks, associated with domestic and international turmoil, that a government, by definition, is supposed to reduce. Industrial policies are one of the means by which such disturbances can be mitigated. In order to diminish these risks, people may be willing to pay, directly or indirectly, the cost of insurance by subsidizing some provinces, regions or industries [76].

Regional development, the second most important aspect of industrial policy, is strongly correlated with assistance to declining industries. If a declining industry is concentrated in one region it is more likely to receive assistance than an industry that is scattered all over the country. Without a doubt, regional development is a priority for governments and has experienced a reasonable success rate. According to the Economic Council of Canada, "The RDIA [Regional Development Incentives Act] part of DRIE expenditures does seem to work, in the sense that enough firms are encouraged to relocate by the grants to cause national output to be higher than otherwise, as a result of making use of labour that would otherwise be unemployed" (ECC, 1977: 172).

Managing the fall of declining industries and administering regional development may be the "meat and potatoes" of industrial policy, but the "cream" is promoting new technologies. This is what governments like to do and this is also, apparently, what the public likes to see governments doing: "Eighty percent of Canadians wish the federal government to invest large amounts of money in the development of new technology (Decima Quarterly Report, 1982-83, question 373)" (Blais, 1986: 33). According to an OECD report (1978), nearly all governments have set up incentives for industrial innovations. The two most common methods are preferential taxes accorded to R&D and government purchasing policies for high-technology goods and services.

In the context of an overall industrial policy, technology is targeted because it is felt to be one of the principal sources of economic growth. The creation and utilization of new technology, it is argued, benefits society to a much larger extent than it does the individual firm, so government involvement is justified (ECC, 1983: 40). The rationale for this is described by Leiss as follows:

> The main output of R&D activity is new information, and the total sum of benefits accruing to a society (indeed, potentially to all societies) from new information cannot, by its very nature, be restricted to the particular persons or firms—the domain of "private benefits"—once the information begins to be utilized. In other words, even with patent protection in place, all the gains from other innovative activities "spawned" by the new information, but not directly contemplated in a particular piece of research, cannot be captured by the original innovator. Thus social benefits are thought always to exceed private benefits, by a substantial margin." [Leiss, 1988, note 2]

For many commentators, Canada falls behind other industrial countries in the area of innovation (Science Council of Canada, 1979; Economic Council of Canada, 1975). Differing explanations or this phenomenon lead to different solutions. The Science Council identifies "truncation" as the main hindrance to innovation in this country. This theory attributes the lack of innovative verve to the extent of foreign ownership; foreign-owned firms do not participate to the full extent because their owners assign them tasks or markets and reserve non-innovative/innovative development for the home country. The alternative explanation, preferred by the Economic Council of Canada, is that tariff barriers make Canadian firms lazy by protecting them, and unable to compete in scale because of lack of access to markets.

These different explanations result in different R&D policy approaches: the Science Council advocates government backing for firms; the Economic Council feels competition and access to markets (free trade) is the answer. Both organizations, though they advocate different means, hope to improve the Canadian economy by making Canada more innovative and entrepreneurial.

The economic arguments about optimizing the collective rate of return on creating new technology versus utilizing existing technology (McFetridge and Warda, 1983) have not been decisively settled, but governments have moved ahead regardless, particularly since the 1960s. According to Norris and Vaizey (1973), much of the support for R&D is related to international competition, the desire to be seen as "modern" and "advanced," and to a widespread belief in Western societies that technology can solve problems (Treiman, 1977).

A growing percentage of government support for R&D is in the form of general tax incentives. Tax measures are costly but do achieve the goal of increasing R&D, according to McFetridge (1977). Tax measures have the added benefit of being general; high profile failures of specific industries or projects are very embarrassing for a government. Trebilcock (1986) states that general incentive measures represent the best economic policy toward industrial R&D that is attainable in our political system. Mansfield (1985) concurs, concluding:

> ... governments seem to be most successful in stimulating civilian technology when they emphasize relatively broad policies rather than attempting to make detailed decisions concerning which specific designs and types of commercial products should be developed and at what pace [98].

With the recent upturn in the Canadian and world economies, there are some who would argue that industrial policy will fade as a topic of interest. Brenner and Courville have pointed out that industrial strategies "all emerge and receive attention, in Canada as elsewhere, when economies suddenly perform less well than expected." (1985: 62-63). Even if economic pressures provoke governments into promoting entrepreneurship, it is quite possible that the pressures of a booming economy would see people advocating some dampening down of activity. This reveals one of the inherent problems with industrial strategy, namely,

> changing circumstances require changing goals. Promoting entrepreneurship may be perceived as appropriate at times, while promoting stability may be more suitable at other times. This leads to inconsistent strategies whose effects survive long after the circumstances which produce them have changed. [Brenner and Courville, 1985: 64]

Industrial policies change over time. The reason for that change appears to be linked to governments' twin desires for growth and stability—two objectives that are not always compatible. And while it is tempting to see industrial policy as the result of pressure group protectionism, the fact is that trade is generally more liberal now than in the past: "The strategy of governments seems then to have consisted in ensuring that the movement toward trade liberalization continued, while yielding to certain protectionist pressures in certain sectors and at times when the economic situation was particularly unfavourable" (Blais, 1986: 14).

R & D Policy **

The foundation for policies leading to sustained government support for research in science and technology emerged in the United States in the period following the Second World War. As described in detail by Harvey Averch (1985: 10-11), beginning in the late 1940s a series of influential advisors to government in the United States, such as Vannevar Bush, advanced the following propositions in a series of reports:

1. New knowledge is a necessary condition for economic growth;
2. New knowledge originates in basic research;
3. The supply of new knowledge is unlimited and is not subject to diminishing returns;
4. The government should support basic research directly due to its interests in national security, the condition of the economy, health, and so forth;
5. Industry lacks sufficient economic incentive to do more than a small part of the required basic research.

This argument attracted strong advocates over the years and led to commitments of significant resources from all national administrations. Once the argument was accepted, however, the great conundrum for policy makers was: How much support was enough? The scientific advisors who were pressing the case in Washington adopted the following credo: "A nation could never have too large a base of scientific and technological information" (Averch, 1985: 15).

A corollary position was that everyone who had the talent and the desire to pursue a scientific or technical vocation should have the support necessary for adequate training, as well as suitable lifetime employment opportunities. Finally, the government had an obligation (according to this argument) to ensure that the citizenry as a whole had a high

** This section of the paper reproduces the major part of Leiss (1988)

level of scientific "literacy," so that it could understand, appreciate, and support modern society's commitment to scientific and technological progress. It will be immediately apparent that prodigious resources would be required for this enterprise, and these same advisors did not shrink from accepting this part of their argument. During the late 1960s, for example, the U.S. Office of Science and Technology took the position that an annual 15 percent increase for research support programs was a "conservative austere minimum."

Almost always, of course, the grand designs of the advisors were whittled down by other government officials. But in a very real sense, this is the origin of what may be called "policy anarchy" in the government sphere. The idea of the great importance of R&D in a modern economy took firm root and was widely propagated, but there never emerged a firm consensus on how much R&D was enough, nor, more seriously, on how to allocate "rationally" some fraction of what it might be desirable to spend in an ideal world. This latter shortcoming was a constant source of aggravation.

For the most part, as Averch shows so incisively, the argument in support of intervention was composed of airy and shifting generalizations, framed to suit the imperatives of the moment (such as the Sputnik "scare"). There is an easy passage thence to the later state of policy anarchy in Canada, with its host of competing programs in different agencies of the same government and its lack of any comprehensive evaluation of the resulting expenditures.

Averch's historical approach to the making of science and technology policy in the post-war period raises another issue of considerable importance for still-unsettled policy debates, including those occurring in Canada at the present time. He shows that the argument in support of intervention was made with respect to "basic" (scientific) research only, and did not include what is called the "innovation" process—that is, the "D" (development) in R&D. This was not an oversight, but rather an explicit part of the assumptions built into the argument, namely, that market failure operated with respect to basic research only. It was assumed that, given optimum levels of basic scientific research as assured by government intervention, industry would then make the appropriate business decisions on applying this research to technical innovation and product and process development.

As the argument for intervention evolved from the 1950s onwards, it was generally recognized that the key assumptions in the rationale (among those discussed above) were: first, maintenance of productivity gains in the economy is dependent on steady growth of scientific and technical knowledge; and second, there is serious "market failure" here, for private firms will not invest sufficiently in R&D to meet the identified social goals for adequate levels of research. These two points have been elaborated as a series of propositions, as follows:

1. Technical advance counts for a large fraction of productivity growth.
2. The private rate of return on R&D is high, but the social return is believed to be even higher.
3. The gap between social and private return is largely a function of limited appropriability of results, externalities, limited rights of exclusion.
4. Risk and uncertainty inherent in R&D inhibit firms' investments.
5. Economies of scale and the need for pooling risk discourage research in smaller firms; non-intervention may result in R&D monopolies for larger firms.
6. There are "grey areas" between public and private sectors that offer limited appeal to the profit motive (Bozeman and Link, 1983: 95).

Averch states the basic conclusion of many economists, a good indication of why governments in all industrial societies believe that they have a high stake in rates of R&D investment:

The very large contributions of R&D to macroeconomic growth and productivity and the exceedingly large differences between the social and private returns of past innovations suggest that R&D is a very good social investment, relative to other social investments. To show the reverse, errors in estimates and calculations would have to be so large as to be incredible. [Averch, 1985: 38]

An important issue that is usually not discussed with respect to the rates of return on R&D is the relation of those returns to the interaction between research and development activities. The issue is one of differentiating between the relative impact of research versus development; for example, the timing of the impact of subsequent productivity gains might be quite different. We shall return to this point at the end of the paper.

The key idea is that R&D is a very good social investment; in other words, a nation's investments in R&D will have a large long-term payback in terms of general economic prosperity. By the same token, firms making private decisions will tend to under-invest in R&D to a significant degree. That is to say, their separate funding decisions, considered as a whole, will fall far short of a predicted optimum level.

Expressed in different terms, the work of Edwin Mansfield and other economists "showed that R&D expenditures by firms usually resulted in social returns substantially in excess of the profitability to firms performing the R&D" (Piekarz, 1983: 211). This provides the primary rationale for government intervention in the area of science and technology policy. With respect to tax incentives, for example, this rationale proceeds along a chain of expectations, to wit, that preferential tax treatment of R&D expenditures will result in increased R&D activity, which in turn will occasion a greater number of successful technical innovations, thus more commercially successful products, finally resulting in a higher standard of living (Bozeman and Link, 1985: 337-338).

With this set of rationales in place, the United States government embarked on a number of different courses of interventions, four of which are discussed briefly below (Nelson, 1983: 504-512). In different mixes and at different levels of expenditure, the governments of most other Western industrial societies, including Canada, have experimented with R&D support in roughly similar fashion.

Direct procurer of R&D products

In the United States, in at least three important industries (aviation, computers, and semiconductors) the federal government guided industrial development to a significant extent through (largely military) procurement contracts. According to Ric Nelson, this has three results:

It has placed the government in a position to define technology targets according to its own criteria; it has given the government leverage in gaining the expertise of the producers concerning the technologies in question; and in the eyes of the public it has legitimated official attempts to stimulate and guide the evolution of the relevant technologies.

In each of these industries there were important spillover benefits (piggybacking) for civilian industries, especially in the crucial early years of what were to become significant technological innovations. But, according to Nelson, the strongest advantages were derived when those spillovers were the unplanned consequences of government programs that were undertaken with their own objectives uppermost in mind.

Support of basic and generic research

Basic research is what scientists and technicians choose to do according to the imperatives of professional success in their own fields. Generic research defines a fairly large realm of activity that falls somewhere between basic research and the type of applied research carried out by industrial firms; the best example is the type of research in the agricultural, health, and environmental protection fields, which has been carried out in some areas (at universities and government research stations) since the nineteenth century. It is noteworthy that government support for basic/generic research is being discussed increasingly with respect to some high-technology fields, such as semiconductors and biotechnology.

Broad support of applied R&D

In some cases, support has extended beyond generic research to more specific applications; here agriculture is the chief (and perhaps the only major) example in the United States. The reason lies in the nature of the agricultural industry, made up of numerous independent producers who have a significant political influence due to regional concentration. However Japan's MITI (Ministry of International Trade and Industry) seems to fit this pattern: "The most striking feature of MITI's R&D assistance and coordination in support of the Japanese electronics industry has been the formation of applied R&D consortia of Japanese firms to work together, with significant financial aid, on certain relatively well-defined areas" (Nelson: 510). The Microelectronics and Computer Technology Corporation, formed by a consortium of large U.S. high-technology firms with the tacit blessing of the Justice Department's Antitrust Division, appears to be a response to Japan's strategy.

Narrowly aimed commercial programs

There are some well-known examples of this strategy, especially in the aircraft industry: the Supersonic Transport (SST) project in the U.S. and the British-French Concorde project, which did not result in successful commercial products, and the more successful European Airbus project.

Nelson concludes that choosing among the various types of support (including no support) in a sensible way can be done only on a case-by-case basis, taking into account the nature of a particular industry or type of innovation and the specific government objectives at a particular time.

Development of R & D Policy in Canada

In a study published in 1983 (McFetridge & Warda), Canada's tax incentive programs for research and development were compared with those of nineteen other nations or jurisdictions. The major finding was that only Singapore's incentives were more generous than Canada's. However, the authors went on to argue that even the level of support in Canada could be considered to be too low, in terms of the widely accepted industrial policy rationale for subsidizing R&D—namely, that social benefits far exceed private benefits. On the other hand, OECD statistics regularly show Canada's relatively poor standing, among OECD economies, with respect to the most frequently cited indicator of R&D effort, namely total expenditure on R&D as a percentage of GNP. The disparity between these two aspects of the situation has fueled much controversy over R&D strategy in Canada for a long time.

There are two major forms of R&D subsidy: tax incentives and direct grants programs. Both have been characterized by constantly changing rules. In a thorough study entitled "Tax Incentives for Canadian Research," John A. Zinn (1987) commented: "It is unlikely that there is any area of Canadian federal income tax law which has been the subject of more frequent and significant change over the past twenty-five years than that involving research and development." This environment of changing tax rules and grants programs in Canada obviously is a rather unstable one. Some of the consequences of this instability are:

Inhibition of long-range R&D planning by firms

Zinn sees this as a major drawback resulting from frequent changes to tax legislation. This may not be a hindrance for the largest firms, with both their established product lines and their long record of new product and process innovation. These firms will also have in their corporate structures a high level of legal and accounting expertise to keep abreast of, and to take full advantage of, the kaleidoscopic array of tax incentive and grants programs for research and development. But smaller and medium-size firms often do not have these advantages.

Tax incentive changes

The frequent changes in tax incentives make the task of evaluation almost impossible to perform, since various provisions are not in place long enough for meaningful comparisons with R&D performance to occur, even supposing that adequate data is being collected and analyzed. For example, the Auditor General's report to the Parliament of Canada has referred to the absence of reliable reports on the magnitude of tax expenditures (estimated at $30 billion annually), and especially to the lack of evaluation criteria for judging their effectiveness. (Of course tax expenditures for R&D support are only a small fraction of this total sum.)

Grants changes

What applies to changing tax incentives applies here also; well-defined protocols for assessing programs in place simply do not get developed. Abraham Tarasofsky, who undertook detailed evaluations of four major programs, comments:

As for the retrospective evaluation of a program's overall impact, this, too, is manageable once the many questions that need to be answered are clearly formulated and systematically addressed. Turning to the four subsidy programs reviewed..., the first and most important thing to be said about them is that their collective story to date has been one of failure to ask—let alone answer—the right questions. [1984: 65]

Plethora of program managers

At the federal level, the Department of Finance writes tax legislation, and the Department of National Revenue administers it. Many R&D support programs have been run until recently by the Department of Regional Industrial Expansion (DRIE), formed by the amalgamation of two earlier departments; now DRIE's programs are supposed to be shuffled into the new Department of Industry, Science, and Technology (ISTC) and still also to be funnelled through regional granting agencies.

Major R&D grants programs are run by a variety of departments; the major ones are Agriculture, Communications, and Energy, Mines and Resources, but most departments have at least one. The National Research Council and the academic research granting councils have reported to a variety of ministers over the years and the Ministry of State for Science and Technology, which has been doing "strategic analysis" for R&D policy on its own, is now also to be part of the new ISTC. Finally, there is also a new national council on science and technology chaired by the Prime Minister, the National Advisory Board on Science and Technology."

Multiplicity of objectives

The stimulation of R&D expenditures is often mixed with a variety of other objectives, especially regional development, employment assistance, "high-profile" ventures (such as the recent funding reallocations for space research), and Canadian ownership. Among other things, this makes it difficult to know what evaluation criteria to apply to each particular program.

Research or development?

So far as tax expenditures are concerned, one of the most difficult problems has been to know where to draw the line of demarcation that will distinguish the "experimental development" activities those which are eligible for incentives payments under the Income Tax Act from all other types of ordinary expenditures made by a firm in changing and enhancing its products and processes. For example, industry association spokespersons regularly suggest that all product development—no matter how routine—should be eligible for the tax incentive. Such a broadening would automatically increase the tax expenditures for R&D, and thus also the federal budgetary deficit, by a significant amount.

Such long-standing disagreements about the meaning of the basic components of R&D activity as well as the habitual avoidance by many participants in the ongoing debate of any mention of evaluation criteria are in part the logical outcome of two decades of R&D policy anarchy. In the view of many observers, they also result from the fact that, until now, too little effort has been made to forge a consistent and comprehensive national strategy for R&D programs.

Issues for Debate

Harvey Averch, commenting on the basis of his years of experience as a federal science administrator in the United States, describes what he encountered in this role as follows:

> In contrast to the doing of science, the doing of science and technology policy was casual. There were no standards for debate or argument. The most bizarre kinds of reasoning and the weakest kinds of evidence were offered in support of action recommendations. Scientists, engineers, and university administrators offered views and assertions that could not pass the minimum standards of rigor, if one accepted the canons of policy analysis developed over the last 25 years. [1985: ix]

Against this background, it should be clear that we mean to cast no aspersions on the efforts of anyone who has been involved with the development of R&D policy. There is no reason to believe that officials in North America were alone in this regard; it is a fair surmise that the entire discussion of R&D policy during the post-war period in Western industrialized nations, both inside governments and elsewhere, has been bogged down in the same quagmire of ambiguous conceptions and nebulous objectives.

What else recommends itself, in such a situation, save a resolve to extricate ourselves from this predicament with dispatch? Nobody seems to doubt the value of investing in research and development in an industrial economy, ideally at a level where the social benefits derived therefrom are fully realized. On the other hand, there are considerable doubts everywhere about the adequacy of our current levels of national expenditure on R&D, and about their effectiveness. We must question whether the resources we do expend are being allocated effectively, and in a cost-efficient way, to the appropriate industrial sectors.

The simple answer seems to leap from the page: government support in the form of both grants and incentives must be increased, perhaps dramatically. Yet this solution ignores some equally elementary truths about our current situation. In the first place, given existing national budgetary constraints in most nations, no such proposal can be entertained with equanimity by either officials or elected representatives. Even more salient, however, is the absence of any comprehensive strategy or evaluation criteria through which to define appropriate levels of support. The usefulness of any major increase in public expenditures alone at this time remains problematic.

Thus it appears we must stick to the duller task of further examining the nature of these doubts and questions before proceeding to recommendations for ways of resolving them. A few proposals along these lines follow. One of the most promising suggestions comes from the 1983 study by Bozeman and Link, entitled *Investments in Technology*. They refer to the widely observed, long-term decline in rates of productivity growth in the United States economy, and go on to suggest an explanation for it:

> We conclude that the slowdown in productivity growth is related to not only the temporary slowdown in the rate of growth of industrial R&D spending, but also to the change in composition of R&D away from both basic and product-related R&D to more short-term and applied ends. [1983:128]

What is contemplated here is opening up the whole issue of the adequacy of using aggregate R&D expenditures as a performance indicator. Bozeman and Link advocate disaggregating R&D into its three components—basic research, applied research, and development (experimental development).

This suggestion is in fact based on a prior conclusion by Bozeman and Link about the differential importance for productivity gains of the various components in R&D, and a thorough examination of this issue would constitute a second point for analysis. The evidence they have sifted leads them to the conclusion that it is expenditures on basic research that are correlated most strongly with productivity gains:

> Our assumption ... is that the stimulation of basic research would generate more value for the US economy than the stimulation of

applied research. That assumption stems from the fact that much of what individual firms do under the heading of applied research and development consists of little more than differentiating their products from the products of competitors; wholly new products or improved processes usually arise out of research of a more basic character, which largely explains why trends in measured productivity growth are highly correlated with trends in basic research spending. [:375]

The results of any further testing of this assumption could have enormous consequences, not only in the obvious dimensions of allocating incentives and grants to activities in the three R&D component areas, but more importantly in the possible attainment of national objectives for R&D performance and productivity growth.

Questions for Further Research

There remain many critical questions for further research. Among them, several can be identified, as follows:

What definitions of industrial policy are currently in use?

Definitions are vital for public policy discussions. All parties must have a common language in order to resolve differences. Industrial policy has often been defined with a goal-oriented definition, e.g. it is to promote growth and competitiveness. Blais (1986) makes a persuasive case for a more descriptive definition which allows for an industrial policy which focuses on stability.

*If tariffs are the primary tool of industrial policy,
what will be the impact of free trade?*

Recent research indicates a rising reliance on subsidies and quotas as tools of managing international impact on domestic economies. Will the Canadian government be further pressured into these areas because of a lack of alternative tools?

*How are the programs which provide the incentive to R&D
to be evaluated?*

As has been observed, changing rules and managers make before-and-after comparisons difficult. What, if any, economic rationales can be provided in these circumstances? It has been suggested that there are difficulties in the traditional approach of simply gathering aggregate R&D

funding figures; some commentators suggest that only sector-by-sector international comparisons are useful. Although there are some American studies in this area, Canadian examples could be examined. What effect will the negotiation of a subsidies code, or the failure to establish one, have on this question?

How can greater stability be achieved for R&D incentive programs and for the firms doing research?

Both federal and provincial governments urgently need to be persuaded, perhaps by the results from well-designed studies, that, whatever the aggregate level of government support is to be, the vital consideration for promoting innovation is greater long-term program stability.

Chapter Seven

The Socio-Spatial Dimension in Innovation: Contributions from Geography

Meric Gertler

Introduction

Economic geographers have for some time been interested in the process by which new technologies come to be generated and adopted, and the impacts of that adoption on the localities in which they occur. This is especially true of Canadian geographers, most of whom share an ultimate interest in the geography of employment—that is, the spatial distribution of employment opportunities and the geographical variation in employment fortunes across the country.

Four themes dominate current research by Canadian economic geographers on the general subject of the management of technologies. First, geographers are concerned with industrial restructuring and technological change in communities and regions. Second, they examine innovations within the workplace and spatial/organizational change. Third, they focus on the role of the urban and regional milieu in stimulating innovative activity. And finally, geographers are concerned with the interactions between regional policy and science policy.

The first of these themes emphasizes the (largely negative) local impacts resulting from the shutdown of plants containing older, often obsolete technologies, while the last three themes focus more explicitly upon the generation and impacts of emerging technologies in particular communities and regions. Because of this book's emphasis on the process of technological renewal, this chapter will say little of the work which falls under this first theme. However, illustrative studies focusing on the economic and social impact of corporate restructuring and technological change upon individual Canadian communities include work by Bradbury (1984; 1985; 1988) (at McGill University) on resource industries in Quebec, Villeneuve and Rose (1986; Rose, Villeneuve, and Colgan, 1988) (Laval and INRS-Urbanisation Montreal) on the labour force implications of industrial restructuring in Quebec and Montreal, by Mackenzie (1988) (Carleton) and Barnes and Hayter (1988) (UBC and Simon Fraser) on resource industries in the B.C. interior, by Webber (1986) (at McMaster—now at Melbourne) on steel production in Hamilton, Ontario, and by Gertler (1985) (University of Toronto) and Norcliffe et al. (1986) (York) on deindustrialization in the Toronto region. A further objective of these studies has been to determine those economic, social, and political characteristics of communities that influence where plant shutdowns, "downsizing" of production operations, and labour-replacing new investment might occur (Gertler, 1987).

Innovation in the Workplace and Spatial/Organizational Change

Although it is commonplace to conceive of technological innovations as the output of research and development laboratories in private firms or the university sector, the bulk of technical changes (whether to products or processes) actually arise on the shop or office floor, as an important byproduct of the production process itself (Gertler, 1988b). Social scientists from different disciplines have chosen to study this process in a number of ways. At the most aggregate scale are studies which analyze the level of total R&D effort in the national economy and its relationship to government industrial policy and economic performance (Abonyi and Atkinson, 1983). At the opposite end of the spectrum are studies which examine the process of innovation and technology adoption and its impact within the individual firm (Meurer et al., 1987; Mansell, 1987; Economic Council of Canada, 1987).

In contrast to these two approaches, geographers have tended to consider these issues somewhere between the individual firm and the overall economy, at the scale of multiple production establishments, whether they be different establishments of multi-locational (including multinational) firms, or different firms in the same or related industries. A dominant focus evident in the work of Canadian industrial geographers is the spatial restructuring of production which accommodates or accompanies organizational change in order to enable technological change to occur. Some have chosen to take a sectoral focus, examining this process within the context of a particular industrial sector. Others have attempted to look across a variety of sectors in a more explicitly comparative mode. While the bulk of this work concentrates on technological change within manufacturing industries, more recent studies have begun to focus on changes underway in office-related service activities.

Perhaps the prime exemplar of the sectoral approach is Holmes' (Queen's University) project to analyze the changing geography of the North American automobile industry as it continues to undergo major waves of technological renewal (Holmes, 1983, 1986, 1987, 1988). Working within the regulation approach, Holmes' analysis springs from the premise that locational shifts in automotive production since 1955 have been driven by that industry's response to major accumulation crises. This is true of both the industry's adoption and rationalization of Fordist mass-production during the 1950s, 1960s, and 1970s, and its increasing use of more flexible, Post-Fordist methods in the 1980s.

Furthermore, Holmes' work demonstrates a principle of central importance which has become widely recognized within industrial geography—that multi-plant producers' choice of technique is made simultaneously with their choice of a location at which a particular element of production will occur, in accordance with the production conditions (wages, labour supply, labour quality, history of labour relations) that prevail at each location. Hence, in the spatial division of labour which developed in the North American car industry during the 1960s, Canadian auto plants performed labour-intensive assembly and subassembly and production of low-value parts with their generally cheaper and lower skilled labour. At the same time, American plants retained the highly skilled production of higher-value parts, plus research and development and major decision-making functions.

More recent work by Holmes (1986, 1988) has focused on newly emerging forms of production organization, within and outside the automotive sector, which appear to place a greater premium on geographical concentration and agglomeration than ever before. This Post-Fordist form of production is founded not only upon more flexible machinery and labour, capable of rapid redeployment to produce a variety of goods, but also on a much more complex set of transactions between producers. These new inter-firm relations utilize subcontracting, joint venturing and putting out to a much greater extent than before, and are capable of being flexibly constituted and reconstituted as new production needs arise. Because of these characteristics, there is alleged to be a much greater need for geographical agglomeration to accommodate the greater frequency of small-volume, qualitatively varying transactions between interlinked firms. This phenomenon is said to be epitomized by the clusters of assemblers and parts producers bound together by just-in-time production systems which are currently being created by

American car manufacturers on both sides of the border, in response to Japanese success with this approach.

In a related vein, Gertler (1988a) has conducted an inquiry to determine the extent to which the organizational trends described above have actually taken place in a variety of sectors. He has also been concerned with the degree to which the actual geographical expression of these recent phenomena correspond to the predictions of Holmes and others. Not surprisingly, he finds that adoption of flexible production methods has been rather uneven and fraught with difficulty for producers. Furthermore, it remains unclear whether firms must necessarily adopt a more clustered form of organization with their suppliers in order to implement such methods.

These findings are also consistent with the work of Hepworth (1986) (University of Toronto, now at Newcastle, England) who examined the adoption of information technology (computers and telecommunications) in a variety of Canadian-based multi-locational firms to examine their consequences for the geographical distribution of employment. Studying firms in computer production and research, food and beverages, agricultural implements, petrochemicals, retailing, banking, transportation, and computer services, Hepworth was particularly interested in the changing location of information and non-information workers, and the information and non-information capital also used in production.

A number of key findings emerge: most notable is that the same information technologies are being applied in a wide variety of ways, producing many different spatial patterns of employment change. The implementation of this technology is clearly mediated by pre-existing organizational structures and corporate strategies, so that while some firms have utilized information technologies to geographically disperse certain production elements or decision-making, others have used it to increase the centralization of their operations. Hepworth's framework for analysis has now been adopted by others working on the developmental implications of information technology adoption in regions such as the Maritime provinces (Lesser and Hall, 1987) (Dalhousie, Economics), and has even been applied to the analysis of Toronto's integration with world financial markets and its local consequences (Dobilas, 1988) (London School of Economics).

The Role of the Urban and Regional Milieu in Stimulating Innovative Activity

An equally important theme within geographical research is the determination of those attributes of places, as collections of individuals, businesses, institutions, and infrastructure, which make them more likely to produce technological innovations. Within this broad theme are a number of subthemes that have attracted the attention of Canadian geographers.

One area of research centres on the role of the social and political structure of communities in the generation of new, innovative local economic activities. This concern comes through strongly in the work of Coffey and Polese (1985) (INRS-Urbanisation, Montreal), who analyze the necessary and sufficient conditions for the stimulation of local entrepreneurship in regions which have historically relied upon external sources for the provision of local jobs. They highlight the need for better access to information and finance, as well as the crucial role to be played by local development organizations in "animating" the indigenous population to act in more entrepreneurial fashion.

This same theme is picked up by Miller and Cote (1985) (UQAM, Technology and Management) in their observations on "how to grow the next Silicon Valley." Based on their analysis of ten high-technology clusters in North America and Europe, Miller and Cote advocate support of indigenous entrepreneurs through directed procurement from established businesses and governments in the region, and linkages between businesses and universities or other laboratories doing first-class applied research. Equally important are the presence of local venture capitalists who are able to dispense business advice along with finance, and a strong base of community support for high technology (e.g., a cooperative local government willing to provide expenditures to support high technology; support for technical universities within the local business and banking community).

Steed's (Science Council of Canada, 1982) analysis of technologically dynamic small firms in three regional clusters (Southwestern Ontario, the Prairies, and the Ottawa Valley) highlights the importance of subcontracting relationships between these firms and larger businesses in the same region. He points out, in a manner which foreshadows the later contributions of Holmes (1986), that, since technologically sophisticated products must frequently be custom-produced in relatively small batches, there is a strong need for such firms to be physically close to their major purchasers so that design specifications and modifications can be readily transmitted and understood.

In a follow-up study of the Ottawa Valley complex (Steed and De Genova, 1983) Steed emphasizes the key role played by close contacts with federal agencies such as National Defence, Supply and Services, the National Research Council, Industry, Trade and Commerce, and Communications in stimulating the development of technology-oriented firms. The federal presence provides an important source of demand, as well as information, assistance, and grants to support product development. Indeed, many of the current high-technology firms in the region have themselves spun off from government research institutions.

While the above studies remain fairly general in their level of insight into the process of technological innovation and adoption, a more recent thrust within economic geography appears to be more directly promising. This thrust focuses on the quality of the local base of specialized services oriented to meeting the needs of technologically dynamic firms (Britton, 1985, 1988) (University of Toronto). Of particular significance are local firms providing expertise in scientific research and development, product testing, industrial design and engineering, computer database and software services. However, not to be overlooked are services in the areas of advertising, marketing, and general management consulting, which provide the managerial expertise so often lacking in the scientist/inventor who originally develops a new product. The existence of these service firms is especially crucial for small and medium-sized manufacturers who cannot afford to hire this kind of expertise on a permanent, full-time basis, and usually only require strategic access to these services on an occasional basis.

The importance of these so-called producer services has recently been substantiated in the work of MacPherson (1988) (University of Toronto, now at SUNY, Buffalo), who has shown that small firms in five different manufacturing sectors in Toronto demonstrated significantly superior innovation and export performance when they made greater use of such services. Furthermore, it was usually important that these kinds of services be available within close proximity to the producers themselves, in order to facilitate the frequent, unplanned, and complex interactions which were normally required.

The Interaction Between Science Policy and Other Federal Policies

The fact that different policy initiatives by the same government might be in conflict with one another seems to have fascinated social scientists with a policy-analytic bent for some time. Geographers have shared in this fascination, naturally dwelling upon those policy initiatives that possess strong spatial consequences. Of obvious relevance to the current project are two particular policy interactions: between science policy and regional development policy, and between science policy and foreign investment policy.

On the first of these two themes, Britton and Gertler (1986) have raised the likelihood of conflict between the objectives of federal science policy and the reality of regional policy as it is currently practised in Canada. They point to the dual mandate of the late federal Department of Regional Industrial Expansion (DRIE) which saw the bulk of its funds going to prop up old, mature, (often foreign-owned) industries while it was also supposed to be assisting homegrown, fledgling firms employing or developing new technologies.

Similarly, DRIE's responsibility to stimulate development in relatively peripheral parts of the country seemed to be somewhat at odds with strategies to promote technological development, since the latter might best take place in those large metropolitan regions with the advantages of high-quality infrastructure, well developed producer service base, deep and varied labour markets, and institutional supports already in place.

The second interaction, between science policy and foreign investment policy, has also been the subject of research by Canadian geographers. One thrust within this general theme has been to draw attention to the state of relative technological underdevelopment of manufacturing in Canada as a result of the predominance of foreign ownership within that sector (Britton and Gilmour, 1978). Britton and Gilmour contend that foreign-owned firms perform far less research and development activity in their Canadian operations than they would in their home country, concentrating instead on the production of standardized products utilizing mature technologies.

In more recent work, Britton (1985) has argued that foreign-owned manufacturers also have a tendency to make use of producer services imported from their home country (either from their own headquarters or from the service firm designated by their head office), rather than buying such services from local providers. As a result, the indigenous producer service base remains somewhat underdeveloped in the absence of stronger demand from the manufacturing sector. However, the most unfortunate consequence may well be felt by small, Canadian-owned manufacturers who now have access to a significantly smaller local producer service base than would otherwise be the case, and whose export and innovation performance might suffer accordingly.

Directions for Future Research

A number of subjects remain unresolved yet worthy of further attention:

Flexible technologies

First, it will be important and instructive to extend research into the geographical expression and consequences of flexible technologies.

Currently, most of the geographical research has focused on the auto sector, but the extent of similar developments in other sectors remains to be explored. In the auto industry, the technological changes driving the spatial restructuring of production have been imported by foreign firms. Must a similar process of technology transfer occur in other sectors?

Territorial production complexes

A related question revolves around the local conditions—economic, political, social, and historical—which are most likely to attract or generate in situ the sorts of territorial production complexes of flexibly interlinked producers that have been recognized in countries like Italy. In fact, given the importance ascribed to the local artisanal traditions of the Italian regions where such clusters have materialized, it might well be asked whether and under what conditions such complexes are likely to take shape in Canada.

The geography of economic activity

Finally, we still know comparatively little about the process by which information technologies are adopted by existing organizations, and the implications of this process for the geography of economic activity. To what extent, and under what conditions, might this strategy enhance the developmental potential of more peripheral regions within the Canadian economy? At the intra-urban level, will such technologies contribute to the further suburbanization of office and manufacturing activity? (For an earlier more general perspective on these developments, cf. Menzies, 1981: ch.7.)

Chapter Eight

Problem Areas in the Management of Technology I: Standards and Standards-Writing in Canada

Liora Salter, Richard Hawkins

Introduction

Standards are often key factors in the commercialization of innovation, and in the adoption of technology. Indeed, some products cannot be commercialized simply because standards have not been developed for them, or because such standards have been developed too slowly to allow them to be competitive, or because there has been strong resistance to the development of standards. Standards determine whether new technologies will be compatible with existing manufacturing systems or with other consumer products. The standards adopted and used within any one country determine which markets will be accessible to its products; indeed, standards are often considered to be non-tariff barriers to trade. Finally, standards often also influence costs of production significantly.

Standards permeate all aspects of industrial action. The metric system, for example, is a system of standards for measurement. Standards are also used extensively for such everyday matters as pricing for example, when chickens or apples are graded and priced accordingly. Standards are a normal part of consumer product development. Kettles, irons, television sets, house wiring are all governed by standards. Standards are used extensively in food production (standards for the proportion of peanuts in peanut butter), food labelling (beer versus "light" beer), farming (chemical composition in fertilizers; the amount of fertilizer or drugs that can be employed), and agriculture more generally (pesticide residues, food additives). Standards are used—or actively avoided—in the development of new technologies. Standards also govern manufacturing processes and engineering. Standards play an essential role in insurance, both in the determination of rates and areas of coverage, and in the payment of claims. They also play a similar role in civil and criminal litigation.

In some of these cases, the technical specification—the standard—governs an activity rather than a product. Standards are the basis for occupational health and safety and environmental measures. The Canadian Standards Association (CSA) recently created a standard for risk assessment. In these cases, standards refer to how decisions should be made, not simply the levels of pollution and risk that are judged to be acceptable. Used either as guidelines or as rules, such standards set limits for airborne contamination or pollution, or provide for measures that reduce the dangers or deleterious effects; they also provide a process for making decisions about risks and environmental pollutants.

There are standards for noise levels, for low-level radiation, for vibration (from equipment), and for emissions from video screens and from hydro wires. There are standards for library systems, experimentation on human subjects, the proportion of Canadian programming on Canadian television stations, the manner of handling controversial topics on the news, and the conduct of professionals. In other words, there are standards for virtually every form of industrial activity.

It should go without saying that not all of these standards are accepted, enforced, or used in every instance. The mere existence of a standard is no indication of the actual level of standardization throughout industry, or of the level of government regulation involved. Standards go by many names: standards, consensus standards, rules, regulations, guidelines, protocols, criteria, etc. Each names implies a different level of coercion. Thus, for example, a regulatory standard is considered to be more coercive than a guideline standard. The naming of the phenomenon is of little significance, however. For example, many regulations are treated as if they were simply guidelines. What is important is that standards—of whatever type—set points of reference for an industrial activity.

In the realm of development of technological innovation, standards—or their absence—are used extensively as market strategies for the introduction of new technologies, for the control of their export potential, and for control over competition. The management of technology, its adoption and innovation, all require that attention be paid to existing standards, and to the development of new standards that might affect the costs of production and the compatibility, marketability, and exportability of the products or systems in question.

Given the importance of standards, it is surprising to find so little literature on standards and their origins. What literature exists is focused mainly on regulatory issues, and standards are seen to be synonymous with regulation. This perception is inaccurate, because the vast majority of standards are originated by private organizations (in which government representatives often play a role), and because many standards are used only as voluntary guidelines. A more convincing, yet equally inappropriate view is to see voluntary or consensus standards as alternatives to government regulations. In this case, standards are part of a debate about government intervention in markets. Again, this view obscures the fact that some standards are adopted as regulations, and that government officials often play an important role in setting voluntary or consensus standards.

A more adequate understanding of standards views them as neither synonymous with regulations nor as an alternative to them. In such a view, standard setting is a separate sphere of activity, a sphere in which some aspects of innovation and technology transfer are managed. This sphere of activity takes place in a number of different trade, national and international organizations, most of which are devoted exclusively to the task. It involves government participants, but often takes place outside of government agencies or departments. It involves industry, but usually takes place outside the individual firm. As such, standards development is something other than science policy, and it is not included in discussions about the management of technology within the firm. Standards constitute an independent area of research in the management of technology.

Standards can be studied in the context of broad subject areas, such as economics, or in terms of "interest areas," such as telecommunications, computers, or the environment. In each instance, the study may be undertaken on a case-study or on a general basis. Moreover, the study can focus on the technical nature of standards, the standards-setting process, or a combination of these approaches. As a broad guide to determining research questions, one should be mindful of Verman's contention that the subject of "standards" impinges on so many areas of study as to be worthy of consideration as a discipline in its own right (Verman, 1973).

The Classification of Standards

As has been discussed, "standards" is an easily confused term. In the first place, it can be applied to virtually anything—from technical specifications to morality. The situation is further complicated by the fact that terminology is often introduced which may be related to standards, but which is not directly germane to the study of standards and standard setting as such (codes of behaviour, for example). A number of commentators have offered different classification systems as analytical tools for understanding standards and their role in the management of technology. As a guide to the issues involved in standards, it will be useful to review these classification systems. Each provides a different picture of the critical issues in standard setting.

One classification system for coming to terms with the myriad of activities and specifications involved with standards is offered by Cerni (1984: 9). She distinguishes standards by virtue of what they are intended to accomplish. Thus, her classification is as follows:

1. Object Standards—These are descriptive of a physical entity and are used as references for mass, length, and time.
2. Documentary Written Standards—These include "definitions, diagrams, classifications, recommended practices, specifications, test methods, codes, etc." In contrast to object standards, documentary standards are susceptible to frequent revision.
3. Conceptual Standards—These include customs and traditions which, even if written down or transformed over time, remain essentially at the conceptual level. Social and personal standards of behaviour are examples.

Clearly, if one relies upon this system, it is the second of these classifications, documentary written standards, which requires primary consideration in the study of managing technology. At the same time, however, the seemingly simple object standards are of interest as well, since even systems of measurement can be controversial, and can influence management decisions about new technologies.

Another method of classifying standards also focuses on the application of the standards. Legget (1970), for example, lists five types of standards applications.

1. Standards of terminology, to ensure that essential information about an item is communicated.
2. Standards of quality, to describe a set of minimal characteristics that a material or product must display.

3. Standards of size and dimension, to ensure a measure of compatibility and interchangeability in commonly used items.
4. Standards of safety, which set out procedures to "protect ... from recognized hazards that may accompany advances in technology."
5. Standards of measurement, to "insure the integrity of the measurements made in the ordinary procedures of commerce." (Legget, 1970: 27-30)

This classification method has the advantage of recognizing such aspects of standards as their connection with safety, but it is less useful in dealing with new technologies, for which the standards often refer to systems or manufacturing processes rather than products.

A third method of coming to terms with the complexity of standards relies mainly on the process by which standards are set, and on the authority given to the resulting standards. In this vein, Legget cites two definitions of standards which emanate from documents of the International Organization for Standardization [ISO]. The first suggests that "standardization is the process of formulating and applying rules for an orderly approach to scientific activity for the benefit and with the cooperation of all concerned, and in particular for the promotion of optimum overall economy taking due account of functional conditions and safety requirements. It determines not only the basis for present but also for future development, and it should keep pace with progress" (Legget, 1970:23).

The second definition indicates that "a standard is the result of a particular standardization effort, approved by a recognized authority" (Legget, 1970:24). The picture, however, is not quite complete. Consider a third definition, which incorporates a role for the public at large, and greatly expands the purposes of the standardization effort. "[A standard is] a technical specification or other document, available to the public, drawn up with the cooperation and consensus or general approval of all interests affected by it, based on the consolidated results of science, technology, and experience, aimed at the promotion of optimum community benefits, and approved by a body recognized in the national, regional, or international level" (Kemmler, 1984: 10).

These definitions all refer to the process used to set standards and the authority granted to them, but they are quite different in orientation. The first definition refers to the ideal situation. It sets out the optimum conditions for the development of standards: an orderly process, related to scientific activity, developed with the cooperation of everyone involved, with economic efficiency, functionality and safety as the primary characteristics of the desired result. The second definition has an equally prescriptive tone, but its purpose is to emphasize the need for standards developed by organizations such as ISO to be adopted by the regulatory authorities in various countries. The third definition is also prescriptive, but it concentrates upon the process by which standards are set, and introduces the notion of public involvement and community benefits. Taken together, these definitions provide an outline of the ideal standards-setting process: an organized effort, carried out by a duly authorized body, operating in the public interest with scope for public participation, producing guidelines that are adopted by various classes of users, including governments that may regulate their use as regulations. Not surprisingly, the reality seldom matches the ideal. Politics, market conditions and strategies, national interests and organizational politics often undermine the efforts of the most committed and worthy standards-setting organizations.

The Standards Council of Canada defines standards in a similarly prescriptive manner, and it considers consensus to be an important part of standards setting. The Standards Council discusses four progressive steps resulting in the adoption of its consensus standards. First, the Council defines standard as the "approved rules for an orderly approach to a specific activity." Then it notes that "in standardization practice a consensus is achieved when substantial agreement is reached by concerned interests involved in the preparation of a standard. Consensus implies much more than the concept of a simple majority, but " 'not necessarily unanimity.' " A consensus standard is, then, "a standard which is prepared by individuals who provide a balanced representation of interests relevant to the subject in hand and approved by consensus." The Council emphasizes that the result of this process can be officially described as "a consensus standard approved by the Standards Council of Canada" (Standards Council of Canada, 1974). In the case of the Council, as with the ISO, their definition of standards, while prescriptive in tone, also relates to the formal steps taken to arrive at standards.

A fourth method of classification picks up the emphasis on the eventual status of the standards, and relates it to their status as legal documents. As noted above, standards can be called rules, regulations, protocols, criteria, or guidelines. In spite of this, standards are often confused with regulations. In some cases it is true that regulations also define a standard, but most frequently, these accrue under the terms of broad enabling legislation. This is the case most often in areas of high public concern. Castrilli and Lax make this point in their study of standards setting in the Canadian environmental protection arena (Swaigen, 1981: 334).

Misunderstandings are compounded in that voluntary consensus standards are, from time to time, referenced in legislation and regulations. An example of a referenced standard used for regulatory purposes would be the Canadian Standards Association (CSA) Electrical Code, which is developed and kept up-to-date by a non-governmental agency. It has been incorporated into the legislation in every province in Canada. It is, however, not unknown for governments to develop such standards themselves, independent of the recognized, private standards-writing organizations.

In making distinctions between standards and regulations, "intent" becomes the operative factor. The intent of regulation is imposition of order; this may be done for a variety of reasons, some of which may well not take the interests of all parties into consideration. The intent of standards writing, by contrast, is simply to create a common point of reference for producer and user groups. Both standards and regulations are coercive in orientation, but regulations are, of course, considerably more coercive than standards. Indeed, participation in the standards process may be designed to prevent the development of a standard because a common point of reference is undesirable to some and, in turn, many standards never become regulations because the affected parties (who may have participated in standards development) successfully lobby against any further coercion.

Donald Lecraw (Economic Council of Canada, 1981) has written at some length on the ways in which standards are referenced in Canadian legislation and, thereby, made mandatory and used as a means of regulation. Lecraw specifies four forms in which standards can be referenced.

1. Open reference—The date of the standard remains unreferenced, allowing for revisions by the standards writing organization to be incorporated as they occur.
2. Dated reference—Refers to a specific version of a standard. Revisions are not automatically recognized.
3. Standard written directly into regulation—Operates in the same way as the dated reference except that the text of the standard is included in the regulation.
4. Standard written "as is" into legislation—The text of the standard appears in the legislation itself.

Lecraw lists two further forms of referencing standards which step away from acceptance of the consensus principle.

1. Modification of consensus standard written into legislation or regulation.
2. Government-developed standard written into legislation or regulation.

The government-developed standard is a form that Lecraw includes in a category he calls the bureaucratic standard. The form is not, however, restricted to use by government; Lecraw defines a bureaucratic standard as "one that has been formulated by an individual organization (e.g., a firm, government department, or government agency) or group of organizations outside the consensus system."

A word must be added in order to separate two concepts with respect to mandatory standards. Standards which are referenced in legislation become mandatory because of their legal force. Standards which are developed beyond the consensus process by private concerns may become mandatory because of the market advantage which the standard gives to the individual firm or group that developed the standard. Lecraw cites the example of computer language standards which were, until recently, controlled by IBM Corp. He refers to this type of proprietary standard as a "kept" standard, having the sole aim of protecting a market segment for a single producer.

In order to appreciate Lecraw's points, it is important to remember that standards-writing organizations can be either public or private, even though their common purpose is to seek to represent the interests of all parties affected by each standard they write. Canada has five recognized standards-writing organizations, but of the five standards-writing organizations accredited by the Standards Council of Canada, only two are government agencies. The term voluntary consensus standard is commonly used to refer to any standard set by a standards-writing organization and developed in such a way as to incorporate input from, and afford due process to, each affected party. There are two voluntary aspects to consider. First, the individuals involved in writing a standard within the private standards-writing organizations are, for the most part, volunteers, usually engineers or other experts in a particular field who perform standards-related work as an adjunct to their normal professional activities. The second important aspect of the voluntary consensus standard relates to the method of compliance envisioned, at least until the standard is referenced or incorporated into legislation.

Returning to the different classification systems for dealing with standards, a fifth system approaches standards with reference to their impact upon industrial activity. This is the most politically controversial approach, as might be expected, since decisions about the type of standard to be used are also decisions about how the standards will be applied and enforced in specific instances, either by regulatory agencies, by the courts, or by industry consensus.

Broadly speaking, using the method of defining standards based on their impact, there are three classes of standards: descriptive, prescriptive, and performance standards. Prescriptive standards are like rules, set in advance, broadly declared and known to all before any activity is commenced. These are the standards applied to such things as the acceptable level of heat produced by an iron, the zoning of a neighbourhood, the required amount of Canadian content on Canadian television, and the uniform size of coaxial cable for particular purposes, and so on.

The most commonly used prescriptive standards are environmental and product standards. These are the standards applied to the height of smokestacks for industries locating in urban areas, and to the wiring used in house construction. These standards are set in advance of the construction of any particular house or smokestack, and they apply without discretion to all wiring or smokestack construction, regardless of the circumstances of the particular case.

The second broad class is that of the descriptive standard, which is a seemingly simple statement of the optimal condition of the object. Hemenway interprets prescriptive and descriptive standards more simply as "standards of quality" and "standards of uniformity" respectively (Hemenway, 1975). The metric system is a descriptive standard. Similarly, the size of bags of sugar or bales of wire, the dimensions of various screws, the labelling of food and beverages, and the designation of warnings on potentially dangerous products are examples of descriptive standards.

The term descriptive standard should used advisedly. Descriptive standards are no less problematic than prescriptive or performance standards, regardless of their appearance. It will be useful to illustrate some of the controversial effects of descriptive standards, in order to show how controversy might result from their instigation. For example, it is easy to understand how some companies might find it cheaper than others to make bales or screws to a particular size or uniformity. Such companies will support standards development, while other companies—less likely to benefit—will fight it. Or consider a worker in his tiny backyard metal works in a Third World country. Such a worker is unlikely to be able to meet the most seemingly innocuous descriptive standard for his product since it requires high levels of skill, technology, and resources to produce product uniformity. Indeed, should his country adopt the international standards, even for products manufactured domestically, this worker will likely be priced out of the market. In a different vein, consider the seemingly straightforward descriptive standards that govern product labelling, and particularly warnings, which often become the subject of litigation. These examples illustrate how critical even descriptive standards are to the management of technology.

The third class of standards is the performance standard. The orientation of performance standards is to the effects created by potentially dangerous situations. By and large, they take into account the conditions experienced by the industries generating the danger. Again, some examples will help differentiate this type of standard.

Pollution standards are often performance standards. What is of interest is not the equipment used (smokestacks) to deal with pollutants, but rather the effects or performance of the industry with respect to pollution. In order to gauge whether the standard has been met, the amount of waste, or airborne contamination, or fish kill is measured. If the standard has been exceeded, it means that the levels of waste, contamination, or dead fish exceeds the standard. In performance standards, then, the method by which the standard is achieved is of no particular consequence. It does not matter, for example, whether a company builds a higher smokestack, installs a particular type of filter or routes its waste one way or another. What matters is the end product of its actions, the level of pollution. This is what is meant by performance.

The distinction between descriptive, prescriptive, and performance standards is a very important and difficult one. Although descriptive standards are seemingly innocent of political implications, they provide a common point of reference which may not be desirable to all, and their existence makes it difficult for other standards—other descriptions and other points of reference—to be considered or accepted. Thus, it will often be the case that there is significant political resistance from one sector or some groups within society against the development and formalization of descriptive standards.

Prescriptive standards are the ones most easily confused with regulations. As is the case with regulations, with prescriptive standards, the rules are clear. They are set in advance of actions. They provide easy reference points, and are unlikely to be misunderstood by groups acting in good faith. They are, by definition, fair, in the sense of being applied uniformly and without exception to all cases. These positive attributes notwithstanding, prescriptive standards are often contested, particularly but not exclusively by industry. The complaints about prescriptive standards concern their lack of flexibility, their "straitjacket" enforceability and their potential disassociation with the actual levels of harm that they are designed to prevent. In the worst case scenario—which is all too common—prescriptive standards (as regulations) accomplish few of the public interest goals they were originally designed to meet, but act as barriers to entry for new firms in the marketplace.

Performance standards have equivalent drawbacks, although such diverse groups as supporters of deregulation and some public advocate groups tend to favour them. In theory, performance standards allow for the exigencies of individual circumstance. They focus attention on the end result, the objective to be met by the standard. At the same time, however, performance standards depend upon the application of proper monitoring and supervisory procedures, upon the existence of suitable analytic techniques for measuring harm, upon an active, well-funded enforcement facility, and, of course, on adequate assessment procedures to be used in each case. Since most of the prerequisites for the proper application of performance standards are seldom met, their obvious benefits are easily offset by their negative attributes (Legget, 1970: 28; Salter, 1988: 32-33, 180-182).

Finally, in yet another classification system for standards, Cerni has divided written standards—irrespective of the classes given above—into three working types.

1. "Basic" or "fundamental standards"—These are standards that "establish basic principles for any industrial development." Included are standards of measurement and reference.
2. "Product standards"—"… addresses performance and output requirements relating to actual product use…. The product standard is primarily an external standard … not an aim in itself."
3. "Integrated standards"—"… born of two recent phenomena: the need to match newly developed 'high technology' with newly developed frameworks … and the overlapping of technologies formerly seen as separate" (Cerni, 1983: 11).

This last method of classifying standards is perhaps most useful in the management of technology, because it draws attention to the new standards development in the high-technology industries, a development that focuses on systems rather than products.

These many, diverse methods of classifying standards reflect both the ubiquitous nature of standards and the complexity of the phenomenon. No one method will suffice to capture all aspects of standards setting, or of the impact of standards on industries, technology, and innovation. Indeed, it may be most useful to focus on standards setting as a realm of activity which has many different levels and dimensions. This realm is at once international and national in scope. It involves major producers and users of industrial products and activities, but also government representatives and members of the public. It involves a wide variety of organizations. It creates standards which are different in kind, in application, in form, and in effect. All of these aspects of standards setting are interconnected, and all related very directly to the management of technology.

That said, the problem of coming to terms with standards can be simplified for the purpose of research, because many of the same people and organizations are involved at all the various levels and in all the various activities of standards setting. Indeed, the same individuals are involved in standards setting for a variety of different types of products and activities, and across several sectors of the environment. What appears, at first glance, to be an almost endless number of activities and organizations connected to standards setting can, in fact, be reduced to a relatively small number of key organizations, activities, and people who, by virtue of their work in standards setting, play a critical, but almost invisible role in the management of innovation, technology, and industrial activity more generally.

The various classification systems have been provided here because they each illustrate aspects of standards setting, and in doing so, they each indicate the some dimensions of the management of technology and of the political ramifications of standards setting. By now, it should be evident that the decision to proceed with standards development is the critical decision to be made from the point of management. By and large, the type of standard envisioned will determine the attitude of management towards participation in the standards process. As well, decisions about the legal status of standards and their applicability affect all members of industry, regardless of size. At the very least, attention must be paid by management to standards development, since the results—whether standards or the lack of standards—affect product development and its potential for commercialization and export. In turn, the distinction between descriptive, performance, and prescriptive standards is an essential one, for it determines the type of regulatory regime that may follow from the acceptance and implementation of standards. And the distinction among the various type of organizations involved is important when firms, governments, or public interest groups are deciding where their input will be most effective, and how they will respond to the resulting standard or lack of standards.

Standards Writing in Canada

Standards activities in Canada began in 1919 with the establishment of the Canadian Engineering Standards Association (CESA) by a group of Montreal engineers. The organization was solely concerned with engineering standards. The need for the development of national standards in the consumer area was first identified in the 1930s by the Royal Commission on Price Spreads under the Chairmanship of Vancouver member of Parliament, H. H. Stevens. By 1944, the CESA had changed its name to the Canadian Standards Association (CSA) and had begun to look into consumer product standards.

In 1948, the Canadian Government Procurement Standards Committee —which had been formed in 1938 to develop standards for materials and services for government purchase—was renamed the Canadian Government Specifications Board (CGSB). In 1979, the name was changed again to the Canadian General Standards Board (retaining the CGSB acronym). By 1979, some 50 percent of the CGSB's standards work was in areas unrelated to government procurement.

Hemenway (1979) has noted that the often cited extremes of the Canadian geography and demography—large area, small population, and harsh climate—have resulted in a unique set of requirements for national standards. He also notes the effects of the constitutional divisions between the federal and provincial governments, our relatively less stringent anti-trust position, and the requirement that standards setting be undertaken in two languages.

Responding to a CSA request for resources with which to carry out international standardization activities, in 1970 the federal government initiated a study into the entire area. The result was the establishment of the Standards Council of Canada by Act of Parliament. Before this time, the CSA had participated directly in the activities of the International Organization for Standardization and the International Electrotechnical Commission, the two principal international organizations affiliated with the United Nations and dealing with technical and manufacturing standards. The Standards Council was envisioned as the forum in which national standards could be adopted, referenced, and carried effectively into the international arena.

The creation of the Standards Council of Canada was not without its detractors. Lecraw and Hemenway suggest that there was no consensus among those performing standards work that a separate body, much less a government one, was required in order to expand standards-setting activity effectively. In the first place, under the Standards Council of Canada Act, the Standards Council of Canada would have little real authority over the standards-writing organizations, either as to their composition or operation. The Standards Council of Canada was mandated simply to "foster and promote" standards activity. One real power of the Standards Council of Canada, however, lies in its authority under the Act to accredit standards writing organizations, testing organizations, and certification organizations, and its responsibility for coordinating Canada's international standards profile. In Hemenway's estimation, the Standards Council of Canada's accreditation requirements for these organizations are not very exacting. The real power, he asserts, comes from the fact that the necessity for accreditation effectively restricts the number of organizations in the country performing standards-related work.

The creation of the Standards Council of Canada has resulted in another identifiable entity, officially called the National Standards System. In addition to the Standards Council of Canada itself, there are five components to the National Standards System:

1. **Accredited Standards Writing Organizations**—At the present time there are five of these: the Canadian Standards Association (CSA), the Canadian General Standards Board (CGSB), the Canadian Gas Association (CGA), the Underwriters Laboratories of Canada (ULC), and the Bureau de normalization du Quebec (BNQ).

2. **Accredited Certification Organizations** (COs)—Although all of the accredited standards-writing organizations, with the exception of the BNQ, carry out certification procedures, only the CSA and ULC have been accredited by the Standards Council of Canada. There is an additional accredited certification organization, Warnock-Hersey, which does not write standards.

3. **Accredited Testing Organizations** —There are presently in excess of twenty accredited testing organizations in Canada, including the CSA.

4. **The Canadian National Committee on ISO** (CNC/ISO) —This is the organization that coordinates and administers Canadian representation on the technical committees of the International Organization for Standardization (ISO).

5. **The Canadian National Committee of the IEC** (CNC/IEC) —This organization coordinates and administers Canadian representation on the technical committees of the International Electrotechnical Commission

The ultimate responsibility of the Standards Council of Canada is to approve standards as National Standards of Canada. Accredited standards-writing organizations may submit any standard to the Standards Council of Canada for consideration. Provided that the standard meets a series of criteria set by the Standards Council of Canada, the standard will be promulgated as a National Standard of Canada. Of principal interest among the criteria are the provisions that the standard be written in both official languages, that it use the metric system where possible, that it not duplicate any existing National Standards, and that it offer no problems with respect to restraint of trade and international standards.

Of the five accredited standards-writing organizations in Canada, three (the CSA, ULC and CGA) are privately operated. The CGSB is a federal government service responsible to the Minister of Supply and Services, although, in practice, the organization is interdepartmental. The BNQ is offered as a service by the Trade and Commerce Ministry in the Province of Quebec. Technically, the BNQ does not meet the criteria to be a part of the National Standards System as it is not national in the scope of its activities. However, the imperative to prepare national standards in both official languages makes the participation of the BNQ in the National Standards System both necessary and desirable.

Accredited Canadian standards-writing organizations must submit to any inspection called for by the Standards Council of Canada with respect to the membership of any standards-setting committee. This is to ensure that all interested parties are represented at this level. There is no allocative power within the National Standards System to determine the areas in which each of the standards-writing organizations will work. In practice, however, the standards-writing organizations have acquired areas of expertise and specialization and tend to determine their own agendas. Occasionally, there are requests for particular standards-writing organizations to originate standards in new areas. Such an initiative was taken by the federal government in 1983, when the CSA was asked to cooperate in the development of telecommunications standards, following the recommendations of the Lapp Reports (1982, 1983). The CSA responded by forming the Steering Committee on Telecommunications (SCOT) in 1983. The Department of Communications has since reinstated departmental participation in and control over standards setting.

Standards-writing organizations are financed through the membership fees of their corporate sustaining members, various government and private support initiatives for particular standards, through revenues from the sale of standards, and, in some cases, of certification seals.

All committees of the Canadian standards-writing organizations are comprised of volunteers.

In some cases—like those of the CSA and ULC—the standards-writing organization is also a testing and certification organization. The Standards Council of Canada criteria specify that the various tasks within the standards organization are represented by separate managements in order to prevent any conflict of interest. The role of the certification organization is to determine compliance with a standard based on test results. The role of the testing organization is to provide test results, but not to evaluate them. This separation is intended to preserve the integrity of all aspects of the standards process.

The process of standards writing through the five standards-writing organizations involves a number of steps.

1. The need for a standard must be identified and submitted to the standards-writing organization by a party with an interest in the standard.
2. The standards literature must be searched to ensure that no applicable standard is already in existence.
3. Financing of the standard must be obtained.
4. A committee must be formed which includes representatives from every group having an interest in the standard, or likely to be affected by it. A balance must be achieved between those members with an interest in the standard, and those with the technical expertise to actually prepare the specifications.
5. A consensus must be reached.
6. The standard must be drafted and published for comment.
7. Once comments have been received and any matters arising dealt with, the standard can be promulgated.
8. The option exists that the standard may be submitted to the Standards Council of Canada for approval as a National Standard of Canada, or, in turn, submitted via a National Committee to one of the international organizations for consideration as an international standard.

In assessing this standards-setting process, it is important to keep in mind that other organizations use different versions of it, and that many government departments and agencies also set standards by their own methods. The government's standards-setting process varies according to the department or agency involved. In general, however, for government-generated standards, expert committees are used to provide advice, consultation with producers and users is undertaken, and a period of time for notice and comment is provided. In some cases, there are also means for consumer or public participation, and in a few cases, public hearings are used.

The matter of consumer representation in standards setting is gaining increasing emphasis. In standard setting, traditionally, the term "consumer" is used to distinguish a class of product user not primarily interested in deploying the product in a manner so as to generate further commercial activity, but rather in the course of satisfying personal needs. Standards organizations are not consumer organizations, even though the Consumer's Association of Canada is often represented on standards committees. That said, the CSA has an active program of consumer involvement, and consumer members of committees are full members, designated either as user-interest or general-interest participants. The general CSA guidelines as to whether consumer representation is in order include such matters as the orientation of the product (consumer, industrial, etc.), and the perceived level of general interest, as in the case of hazardous substances.

Before the formation of the SCC, Canada had not participated in international standards-setting to any significant degree. In Hemenway's estimation, neither Canada nor the U.S. has held a profile in international standards setting commensurate with their respective economic positions in the world. It is in the international arena that the potential benefits of the Standards Council of Canada can be seen. In 1970, Canada was not represented in a single ISO technical or policy committee. By 1979, there was Canadian participation in over thirty such committees. However, it is difficult to assess whether this increase in participation was a direct result of the activities of the Council, or merely an indication of the increasingly international nature of standards.

In international standards setting, a further term is added, harmonization. Harmonization means simply the coordination of standards so that a standard developed in one locale can be made compatible with one developed in another locale. In the process of international standards setting, it becomes crucial to the economic health of a nation's technological capacity that national and international standards are harmonized within the country's standards system in such a way as to balance acceptance of international standards with the aggressive marketing abroad of domestic standards.

Hemenway suggests that as of 1979 the Canadian position was one of "we can meet your requirements" (1979: 44). There was relatively little emphasis on trying to promote Canadian-developed standards internationally. There is evidence, however, that the pace of Canadian international involvement is picking up, particularly in the communication technology standards sector. Canada is an active member of the International Consultative Committee for Telegraph and Telephone (CCITT), and the International Consultative Committee for Radio (CCIR). Both of these organizations are standards-developing arms of the International Telecommunications Union (ITU). In addition, Canada has played an important role in the ISO initiative to develop the Open Systems Interconnection (OSI), an emerging world standard in computer networking. Adoption of the OSI system is now Canadian government policy, with full deployment expected by the early 1990s.

Issues in the Research

As mentioned above, the literature on standards development is sparse, in spite of the importance of standards in the management of technology. The following issues have attracted some attention:

Rationales for standards

In spite of the relative popularity of standardization activity at the present time, and irrespective of the existence of well established mechanisms for the development of voluntary consensus standards, there remains considerable debate as to the functions and effects of standards in the marketplace and in the management of technology. Some rationales for standards are obvious—it is desirable to have common standards of measurement, for example. The rise of industrial economies has extended the reasons for standards setting to include the technical compatibility and interchangeability that standards make possible. Yet standard setting is by no means universally accepted as beneficial, and a large component of the existing literature on standards is devoted to a discussion of their value and problems. For example, liberal economists have had a traditional distrust of standardization, because it was originally viewed as market manipulation (Lecraw, 1981).

The growing complexity of industrial society and the increasing perception of the importance of the management of technology have largely removed any negative attitudes to standardization. In Lecraw's view, a chief factor in the acceptance of standards is one of information. The complexity of industrial production has made it impossible for the user of the products, including consumer goods, to acquire necessary information about the product without standards. In other words, it has been suggested that market failure (lack of access to information) has become the rule and, in this context, standards are seen as a valuable tool for correcting market failure, because standards communicate information minima about product characteristics.

In dealing with the benefits and dangers of standards, Kindleberger (1983) begins with the definition of "public goods," which he sees as goods available for use by all, regardless of their value to any single economic entity. He applies this definition of public goods to standards activity. He then distinguishes public goods from collective goods, which are good primarily of benefit to particular groups. Applying Kindleberger's approach to standards, the possibility exists that a collective good could sway the standards process in such a way that the standards desired by producer groups become the standards mandated by the government. Kindleberger cites the "appellations controlees" of the French wine industry by way of example. In this example, he argues that the government mandatory standards, which actually served the interests of the producer groups, were presented as if they were the result of a democratic process and, as a consequence, as public goods.

Despite the relative acceptance of standardization activity at the present time, and irrespective of the mechanisms which exist for the development of voluntary consensus standards, there remains considerable debate as to the functions and effects of standards in the market and in the public perception. Cerni (1984: 12) identifies several traditionally accepted benefits of standards:

(a) to increase efficiency and productivity in industry because of larger scale, low-cost production of interchangeable, uniform parts;

(b) to foster competition by allowing smaller firms to market products, readily acceptable by the consumer, without the need for a massive advertising budget;

(c) to disseminate information and provide technology transfer;

(d) to expand international trade because of feasible exchange of products among countries;

(e) to conserve resources;

(f) to improve health and safety.

Cerni notes that "standards constitute a vast store of expert technological information. Widespread implementation permits quality control. "In communications, standards permit worldwide voice ... and ... computer connectivity." Cerni stresses the two traditional function of standards: standards facilitate the exchange of technical information, and they widen the international communications network. These benefits do not accrue solely from voluntary consensus standards, however. Further to his observations about market failure, Lecraw (1981: 53) states that "when the price of the product in the competitive market system does not reflect the true costs to society for producing or consuming the product," the government may correct the situation by the use of some form of mandatory standard. Examples cited include pollution standards, gas mileage standards, and health and safety standards, all of which are government or mandatory standards rather than voluntary consensus standards.

Cost and competitiveness

Some industrial and political sectors will oppose a standard, be it a consensus or a mandatory one, as being an instrument designed to abrogate a posture of market privilege, or conversely, to restrict entry into an economic sector. Consensus standards, moreover, being the product of a highly "diplomatic" process, are, by nature, compromises possessing all the attendant difficulties.

The writing of consensus standards and the operation of the resulting necessary certification procedures for products is costly from two perspectives. Both procedures are time consuming, thus delaying the deployment of new products in some instances. Second, the cost of preparing the standard can be considerable and must largely be funded by the stakeholders in the standard. Moreover, the exact costs of preparing consensus standards are not accurately measurable owing to the fact that most of the work is carried out on a "volunteer" basis (Lecraw, 1981). On the other hand, Hemenway is of the opinion that the use of standards, once developed, need not result in high economic costs. The costs must be considered in light of the fact that the use of standards, once developed, can result in substantially lower costs for the majority of producers (Hemenway, 1975).

The development of a proprietary or "kept" standard suggests immediate disincentives towards competition. Indeed, the traditional suspicion of standards by economists was born of this type of standardization activity. However, the public availability of standards, whether mandatory or voluntary, has the potential to increase competition. Firms not having the potential to manufacture every component of a product, or without the capacity to develop proprietary standards of quality and performance in isolation, have markedly increased opportunities owing to the "interchangeability" factor and the informational component of standards. In conjunction, the evolution of a non-proprietary standard may weaken the relative market position of a firm that had previously defined the standard in its own products.

Veall (1985) has raised the question about the effect of standardization on the variety of goods. He theorizes that in a case where all economies of scale have been lost due to production of an overly large number of similar products, a limited case can be made for government to impose a standard as an instrument of competition policy. Gouldson (1988) reports on an effect of the certification process on competitiveness. Goods requiring government approval can loose their potential market position because of delays in certification procedures, and the fact that several certifications are often required to enable a product to be marketed internationally. In Canada, this has resulted in the formation of the Standards Approval Group, a private firm which provides test documentation to a number of national and international certification bodies on a "one-stop" basis for electrical and electronic goods.

Approaches to standards writing

Verman (1973) has observed that standards set by consensus "acquire an authority" greater than that accorded by a simple majority vote. Proponents of the consensus process in standards setting recognize the costs involved in this time-consuming method, but argue that the resulting standard is more acceptable to the users (who, after all, had development input). Olley suggests further that consensus standards are cost effective "because the resultant standards are pre-tested for workability and reasonability, thus minimizing the costs of false starts, fundamental re-doing of the standards, and impediments to initiative by other members of the community" (Olley, 1985). Lecraw (1981) notes that the consensus process is far less likely to produce unnecessary standards than is the bureaucratic process. Cerni (1984) observes complications in the international consensus process. She notes how in rapidly developing technological areas, such as computing and telecommunications, the international standards-setting process has become "proactive" rather than "reactive"; the result has been that standards are appearing "prior to implementation or experimentation," and with potentially negative effects.

Bureaucratic standards, be they of government or private sector origin, have the advantage that they can be developed swiftly and cheaply, at least in the short run. Two pitfalls of the bureaucratic process are that the sum of available information may not be utilized, and that the interests of every group affected by the standard may not be taken into account (Lecraw, 1981). In some cases, immediate concerns, like those over health and safety, make the imposition of a bureaucratic standard imperative. Also, the bureaucratic alternative must exist for those instances where a standard is urgently necessary, but no agreement through the consensus method has been forthcoming.

Standards and innovation

Farrell and Saloner (1985) discuss the relationship of standards and innovation in terms of the standard itself; a definition is sought concerning the extent to which the adoption of a standard will inhibit the development of new standards. Farrell and Saloner conclude that a new standard will be adopted only after a complete exchange of information among the users of an existing standard has led to the unanimous conclusion that a change is desirable.

Cerni identifies the main problem to be that the wide use of standards may serve to "inhibit innovation" and to restrict customer choices However, Cerni's idea of the "integrated system standard" is highly significant with respect to innovation. Her remarks are worth quoting in full.

> The integrated systems approach to standards not only helps establish a standards direction that is consistent with the overall objectives of an industry, but allows for multiple development efforts to be integrated into a cohesive structure. A total system understanding ensures the practicality and feasibility of a particular standard, determines that a standard from one part of the system does not have a detrimental effect on any other segment of the system, helps insure that restrictions are not put on internal systems design options, and helps avoid inhibitions to innovation. [1984: 12]

Recent international standards developments such as the Integrated Services Digital Network (ISDN) in data transmission, and the Open Systems Interconnection (OSI) in computing, illustrate the use of standards according to Cerni's model. In each case, the objective is to impose a universal standard by which evolving technologies may interact with one another and continue to develop.

Lecraw puts forward the position that the needs of innovation can be reconciled to the use of standards. Once again, he sees a particular advantage in the informational component of a standard; in this instance, the result is seen to be that standards provide an instrument for developing user confidence in new products. However, Lecraw also notes that technical progress may be impeded through the specification of particular materials in an existing standard. Also (mirroring the observations of Farrell and Saloner), he notes the tendency for inertia to develop in producers and users alike once a standard has been adopted.

Standards and the consumer

Many standards are developed in response to consumer requirements, and it is possible for the consumer to have input into the development of these standards. Olley (1979) identifies two key standards issues of importance to the consumer which have not, as yet, been allotted the deserved amount of attention by the standards-writing bodies, or which have proven difficult to define. These are service standards and performance standards.

Service standards exist in the professions (medicine, law, etc.) under which the customer is assured a minimum service level. Olley cites the example of the Office des Professions du Quebec, in which there is lay input into that province's professional structures, as an example of how ways can be found for the consumer to participate in service standards development. When applied to products, service standards take on the appearance of performance standards. Olley identifies the issue in terms of consumer expectations for maintenance, energy use, availability of spare parts, and so on. He also refers to an initiative at the CSA to develop such standards for electrical products.

The issue of mandatory (especially bureaucratic) standards versus voluntary ones looms large in the consumer area. The concept of the standard as a "public good" also makes a reappearance. Many standards issues are related to concerns about public safety; as such, there is a measure of expectation that governments have the responsibility of ensuring that standards are referenced in legislation to ensure that they are being met. In his discussion of the rationales for mandatory bureaucratic standards, Lecraw (1981) presents several public and private alternatives to standards which are of relevance to consumer matters. A government may elect to correct for market failure in the identification of goods considered to have a "negative" societal effect by means of public education campaigns or through financial intervention in the form of selective taxation. The tobacco and alcoholic beverage sector has been handled in this way. Alternatively, a producer may offer consumer information in the form of product guarantees or service warranties.

Standards and international relations

Rhonda Crane (1979) has documented an interesting standards case in the international arena which serves to highlight the connections between standards activities and international politics. The case in question is that of the French initiative in the 1960s to impose the French developed SECAM colour television system as the European standard.

Crane relates how the "championing" of a standard by a government can result, virtually, in a geo-political incident. A national standard is, "inter alia", an expression of national technological prowess. The aggressive promotion of the SECAM standard resulted in a system of political and cultural alliances which were substantially based on the compatibility of the communications technology.

The SECAM affair was played out in the forum of the International Telecommunications Union (ITU). Unlike other international standards-setting bodies (the ISO and IEC, for example), the ITU is a treaty organization, the participants being national governments on a "one nation-one vote" basis. The final decision on the European colour TV system turned out to be a political one, based on perceptions of national, social, technological, and industrial interests. The result was contrary to the expressed objective of adopting a common standard. The political nature of the process is best exemplified by the fact that France was able to exploit superpower tensions to form a SECAM alliance with the U.S.S.R. Finally, the SECAM affair illustrates that technological superiority alone will not always win out in an international standards-selection initiative. Ironically, the French system was superior in many respects, but its political baggage resulted in it being rejected as the European standard.

Trade policy and industrial development

A special concern about standards has long been their potential for use in restraint of trade. The Tokyo round of the General Agreement on Tariffs and Trade (GATT), saw the adoption of an "Agreement on Technical Barriers to Trade." The Agreement is also known as the "GATT Standards Code," and it came into force in January of 1980 (see Nusbaumer, 1984). Standards, if used to restrain trade, would fall into the category of non-tariff barriers. Middleton (1980) outlines two types of barriers; those arising from technical incompatibility, and those arising from the certification process.

With respect to the role of developing countries in standards issues, Middleton notes that the GATT Standards Code presents a contradiction. On the one hand, the Code contains provisions for the exchange of technical information that would greatly benefit developing economies. On the other hand, there are also provisions that would seem not to encourage developing countries to bring their domestic standards systems into line with accepted international practice.

Research Questions to be Pursued

The survey of Canadian and international standards practices and issues illustrates that the scope for research in the area is great, and the field largely unexplored. Even the basic information has not yet been gathered or analyzed. Furthermore, the research areas are highly interdisciplinary, ranging from technical analysis to social and economic concerns. The situation of Canadian research on standards is reflective of a worldwide shortage of literature on these same issues.

The exceptions are in the areas of information and communications technology, and in environmental protection. The Department of Communications (DOC) commissioned two studies (Lapp, 1982, 1983) into the role of the DOC in setting standards for information and communications systems. A further study, this time about the Canadian role in the ITU, was also prepared for the DOC (Mosco, 1986). The study deals partly with standards. The issue of telecommunications standards could provide an ideal laboratory for the study of the standards process. The issue is new—in Canada, dating mainly from the CRTC decisions, beginning in the 1970s, allowing interconnection of competitor equipment with the regulated telecommunications monopolies—and the processes are highly indicative of the emerging emphasis on international standards development.

In the area of occupational and environmental standards, a recent study (Salter, 1988) provides the background information about standards in the context of a more general discussion about the relationship between science and public policy. Evident from this study is the fact that, although environmental and occupational standards are thought of as government-generated standards, the vast majority of such standards are developed outside government departments, by organizations about which little is yet known.

Probably the largest single standards issue in the Canadian context was (and is) the matter of metric conversion. A standard of measurement represents a very fundamental kind of standard; it has an effect on the entire standards structure. Writing for the information of an American government department, Hemenway found much of interest in the Canadian process of metric conversion, noting that the process would induce an "intense examination of standards." To date, this "intense examination" has not been undertaken except as concerns review of the technical content of Canadian standards by the standards-writing organizations.

The three general studies of standards activities in Canada—Legget, Lecraw, and Hemenway—date from the 1970s, and are not always reflective of the current scale of standards activities. The Hemenway study was commissioned by the U.S. Department of Commerce to provide comparative information for the U.S. National Bureau of Standards. The remainder of the literature from Canadian sources is in the form of occasional papers and news items.

As technical, economic, and commercial matters are the ones most obviously affected by standardization activities, it is hardly surprising that the principal scholars to examine the area have been economists and engineers. Cerni, however, echoing Verman's assertion that standardization is a discipline in itself, makes the following statement: "The standardization technique, the set system of rules by which standards are developed, has evolved over a century and can now be considered a discipline in its own right, to be adhered to by participants, and to be studied and learned by newcomers" (1974: 14). Cerni sees the standardization system as highly interrelated with most other activities in an industrial society—the economic, social, legislative, judicial, educational, and ecological systems, to name a few. The potential scope of standards studies is much larger than the existing social science literature would indicate.

Perhaps the area of greatest potential interest to social scientists is the process by which standards are set. As Salter (1988) asserts, standards, in spite of their technical guise, are not free of social values. The consensus principle, for example, under which all accredited standards-writing organizations operate in Canada, is open to all manner of questions. How are the needs for standards identified? Which values influence the selection of committee members? What are the dynamics of a group which puts together those having great economic and political power (like industrial interests) with those having less power (homemakers, or social action groups)?

Other areas for study include certification and accreditation. Hemenway, for example, is concerned with the need for an economic analysis of accreditation and its public policy implications. The matter could be extended to include the role of accreditation in forming public perceptions about standards and the way in which they are set. Is public confidence in standards enhanced through accreditation, and, if so, is this enhancement justified?

There is also a need for study of individual standards, both national and international, from a variety of economic and social perspectives: for example, a study of metric conversion, and the effects this decision has had on the standards system in general, and on public perceptions about standards. Also, it is important to examine the influences of metrification on innovation in Canada. This work would be enriched by comparative studies of standards systems in different countries.

From a policy perspective, an assessment of the need for the development of a national standards policy would be useful. This might focus on the interplay between technical and economic or political information and the respective roles of technical staff and volunteer members on standards-writing organization committees; the relationship of standards and government regulation; questions concerning due process and the fair treatment of interest groups in standards setting, the federal-provincial relationship and its effect on standards activities; and the effect of the Free Trade Agreement on the standards environment in Canada.

Finally, there are a number of issues that have attracted international attention, not the least of which concerns the "proactive/reactive" debate in the setting of international standards. At the heart of this debate is the question of how standards and technological innovation are, and should be, related, and more particularly, whether standards setting can be used as a means of stimulating technological innovation.

Chapter Nine

Problem Areas in the Management of Technology II: Technology Assessment

Uschi Koebberling

Introduction

A major reason for the considerable literature on technology is a growing concern over the threats of technology to economic and social structures. However, despite the growing interest, until recently technology itself has rarely been subjected to analytical inquiry. This is the principal objective of technology assessment.

In Canada, the role of technology assessment in managing technology is just beginning to emerge. The need to develop an institutional and methodological framework for technology assessment was recognized by institutions such as the Federal Environmental Review Office (FEARO) and the Minister of State for Science and Technology (MOSST). What is currently available is mostly part of environmental and/or social impact assessments of particular technologies in specific contexts.

The most advanced sub-field of studies of technology can be found in the discipline of history, yet there it has remained within the conceptual and methodological framework of an academic field, with little relevance to policy. Social scientists of many persuasions, particularly economists, have examined the development of technology with the aim of optimizing the economic process. This has also stimulated analysis of the forces operating on industry and society due to what are seen by some as the "imperatives of technology." Johnston (1984: 101) characterizes the state of studies on technology as "immature" concerning the objects of inquiry, the methods used to analyze them, and the results of research.

In the twenty years since the introduction of the concept of technology assessment, the United States has become the leading country in its institutional and methodological developments. Several OECD countries have also been active in discussing institutional arrangements and methodological questions. Interest in technology assessment has increased enormously, as can be seen from the growth in literature, conferences, and associations (see, for example, references in Porter et al., 1980). However, Canada has basically been absent in this discussion, and the Canadian literature and research is consequently skimpy.

Because of the small body of material developed in Canada on technology assessment, reference is also made to developments in the U.S. and OECD countries to outline the current state of the discussion. This chapter of the report on managing technology analyses a number of issues. First, it identifies the objectives, approaches, and directions in the assessment of technology. Second, it looks at technology assessment in Canada. Third, it examines some methodologies and analytical techniques used in technology assessment, and goes on to examine some of the key issues and problems of performing technology assessment. (In this context, it is important to look at public participation and political usage.) Finally, it identifies selected research questions and priorities for future work.

Objectives, Approaches and Directions in the Assessment of Technology

The term "technology assessment" was coined in 1967, and is generally attributed to U.S. Congressman Emilio Q. Daddario, who first called for a new form of policy research to help policymakers deal with the various pervasive effects of technology on society. A leading review study by Armstrong and Harman (1977) identified five elements that appear to be central to most technology assessments. First, there is the assumption that it is possible and desirable to manage technology objectively toward goals that contribute to societal benefit. Second, the prime objective of technology assessment is to inform policy decisions by providing information on the potential advantages and disadvantages to various societal groups of likely technological developments and alternatives. Third, the claim is made that technology assessment is inherently and necessarily a multidisciplinary field. Fourth, it is noted that technology assessment entails projecting into the future and addressing the uncertainties associated with such projections. Finally, it is stressed that the term technology includes both "hard" and "soft" technologies.

The OECD undertook a series of studies on the assessment of technology which included a review of the existing literature and the experiences in OECD countries. The U.S. National Science Foundation (NSF), the body with the longest and broadest experience in technology assessment studies, considers that the primary objectives of technology assessment are as follows:

1. To identify and analyze relevant economic, social, technological change;
2. To analyze the ability of existing institutions to accommodate institutional change;
3. To explicate the different points of view of interested parties;
4. To compare the alternative policy and technological choices available to decision makers; and
5. To identify and analyze the uncertainties and risks associated with alternative policy choices (OECD 1978).

Technology assessment has acquired a uniquely American character, a situation which needs to be kept in mind when addressing the Canadian context. In the U.S., there is a substantial literature regarding the institutional arrangements of technology assessment, particularly the Office of Technology Assessment (OTA) (see, for example, Porter et al., 1980; Boroush et al., 1980; Unesco, 1984; Hetman, 1983; Coates, 1983; O'Brien et al., 1982). These studies indicate that there is a considerable difference in technology assessment done by or for the Office of Technology Assessment, which serves the Congress; the agencies of the executive branch of the federal government; the National Science Foundation; state governments; special national commissions; and industry. These differences derive primarily from differences in the power, scope, and responsibilities of the decision-makers whom the assessments are intended to serve, and the timing and other constraints on decision making. They outweigh those differences stemming from variations of finding levels, subject matter or performers of the assessment (e.g., university groups, research organizations, in-house staff, or consultants).

Since 1972 the OECD has undertaken a series of studies on technology assessment (OECD, 1983). These indicate that sufficient attention has been paid to the methods of technology assessment and to the clarification of its importance for decision-makers. OECD therefore emphasizes the need to shift the focus to policy issues and the role and place of the assessment function within the decision-making structures.

There have been a number of attempts in other nations to establish technology support organizations that serve the national legislatures. Yet these efforts have failed. Coates and Fabian (1982), Wood (in Boroush et al., 1980), the OECD (1978, 1983), Dickson (1986), Tisdell (1981), and Hetman (1982) provide an overview of institutional developments and methodological issues in European countries, Japan, and Canada. Coates and Fabian list four general forms outside the legislative framework:

1. In some countries, technology assessment is incorporated into one or more pre-existing government offices;
2. A special government office or committee may be established;
3. Government offices contract out for technology assessment; and
4. Ad hoc technology assessment is carried out by a government body, such as a royal commission especially established to conduct the technology assessment.

The shortcomings of technology assessment within government offices are precisely the problems that have constrained the use, and usefulness, of technology assessment in executive mission agencies in the U.S. Experiences with special government offices of technology assessment and with futures studies are limited. But special ad hoc assessments, particularly using the structure of royal commissions, have been proven effective to collect and analyze all the relevant data on a complex technological issue, and to present it to the citizens and the government for an informed decision.

In a number of countries, technology assessment activities are being conducted outside of government offices and commissions. They are centred in universities, professional groups, research institutes, industries, or industrial groups. Some of these groups are actively engaged in seeking government involvement in technology assessment, while others are adapting the methodologies and philosophies of technology assessment to their own uses. Coates and Fabian (1982) particularly refer to successful examples of technology assessment by industry in Japan, at times in cooperation with the Japanese government. Technology assessment there is evolving into a corporate rather than a governmental process, with consequences yet to be determined. Generally, the promotion of the welfare of the parent company is broadly assumed to be consonant with the public interest.

The OECD review of assessment studies suggests a gradual shift from cost-benefit analysis to a form of policy analysis. Technology assessment is viewed as a specific process, searching for positive outcomes and controlling negative impacts, rather than as an analytical tool. Technology assessment thus tends to be less controversial because attitudes have converged on the need for a "foresight function" (OECD, 1983: 13). The review also recognizes the limited effective association of technology assessment with policymaking. "The major stumbling block seems to be the absence of a means of illuminating future trends in a manner relevant for formulation of feasible public policies" (OECD, 1983: 13).

Technology Assessment in Canada

The Canadian literature on technology assessment is small and primarily found as part of the discussion of environmental and social impact assessment (Marshall (interview), Demirdache, 1980, Coates and Fabian, 1982).

Demirdache (1980), writing at the time as a member of the Ministry of State for Science and Technology (MOSST), and Coates and Fabian (1982) are among the few who deal specifically with technology assessment in Canada, though the OECD studies also refer briefly to Canadian experiences. Demirdache describes the institutional structure of government technology assessment. Decisions concerning large technological projects are made by the ministers in Cabinet. These decisions are largely based on information from the departments involved, and each federal department is expected to conduct its own technology assessments in accordance with its particular needs and responsibilities. This approach serves a useful function, but it has a number of shortcomings. First, if no department has a mandate to oversee a particular technology or its impacts, a technology assessment is unlikely to take place. Second, if a number of departments have different or overlapping interests in a technological development, they may each assess it independently and produce conflicting recommendations or implementation guidelines. Third, any department, in strict pursuit of its mandate, may promote a technology that, when assessed under wider terms, is found to be detrimental to the public good; inherently, conflict of interest precludes effective assessment. And finally, the technology under consideration may be so pervasive that no government—federal, provincial or municipal—has authority to act (Demirdache, 1980).

Canada, however, has a science advisory structure that can be tapped for technical information and various forms of technology assessment.

The main bodies, as discussed by Coates and Fabian (1982) include the National Research Council (NRC), the new Ministry of State for Science and Technology, and the Science Council.

MOSST has been most active in the assessment of technologies, and has completed studies on the implications of urban growth, the changing age structure of the population, and the development of a "conserver society" rather than a "consumer society." NRC provides technical data to government and industry and facilitates the movement of R&D data to the industrial sector. The Science Council sees two aspects of particular importance: the assessment of technology itself, and the process operating within the social system that conducts the assessment. Demirdache (1980) considers the advice of the Council helpful to the government in reviewing the issues and possible solutions.

With special regard to the Canadian Arctic, the Science Council was instrumental in bringing about the ad hoc comprehensive technology assessment of oil and gas development in the western Arctic, the MacKenzie Valley Pipeline Inquiry, commonly called the "Berger Inquiry" (1978). The Berger report paid much more attention to such values as wilderness, native peoples, and social impacts than any previous study required to deal with social and environmental impacts of development on the Canadian Northland.

Some of the most significant studies in technology assessment and long-range planning are being carried out by organizations exclusively devoted to policy analysis, such as the Institute for Research on Public Policy.

Of particular importance in the social impact assessment field, as developed out of environmental impact assessment, are the two institutions of the Federal Environmental Impact Assessment and Review Process (EARP) and the Federal Environmental Assessment and Review Office (FEARO). Environmental and social impact assessment is the most visible and formalized process of project/technology approval established by the federal government for controlling technological development. There are a number of studies on the environmental and social impact assessment process in Canada and its strengths and shortcomings as, for example, the writings of Rees (1979, 1980, 1981), Boothroyd and Rees (1984), Land and Armour (1981), Beanlands and Duinker (1983), Sadler (1980, 1985, 1986), MacLaren and Whitney (1985), CEARC (1985), and Rosenberg (1981). Yet these deal not specifically with technology assessment (except Rees' response to Demirdache, Rees, 1980), but rather with the methodology and institutional structure of environmental and social impact assessment. Technology assessment, as part of environmental impact assessment, is thus indirectly addressed, although many of the issues discussed in environmental impact assessment are similarly applicable for technology assessment.

EARP in Canada, as Rees (1979, 1980, 1981) points out, has no legal basis and is founded squarely on the principle of self-assessment by the initiating agency. Although significant strides in improving the process have been made recently, EARP suffers from all the weaknesses of self-assessment mentioned by Demirdache (1980) for government in-house technology assessment. Rees (1980) points out that there is no incentive for the proponent of a particular technology or project to undertake a thorough self-defeating analysis of alternate means of achieving objectives or the "no-go" option. Hence, credible analysis of these alternatives is rarely part of environmental impact assessment.

Analytical Techniques and Methodologies

Most studies on technology assessment/social impact assessment include a presentation of techniques and types of assessment used (Boroush et al., 1980; OECD, 1983; Porter et al., 1980; Unesco, 1984; Demirdache, 1980). A substantial range of techniques has been adapted from other fields for use in the various stages of assessment. They range from extremely sophisticated quantitative approaches to qualitative or subjective procedures. Porter et al., provide an overview of techniques, characteristics, uses and references. The literature also indicates, however, that even though there is a large variety of available techniques, most have been ignored by technology assessment practitioners (Unesco, 1984).

There have been some attempts, including some from within the Canadian impact assessment community, to develop more integrated and systematic approaches to technology assessment (Cornford, 1987; McLaren and Whitney, 1985). Cornford lists as key requirements:

1. Consultation and public participation as an integral part of planning, impact assessment and management decision-making;
2. Technical rigour; and
3. Appropriate institutional arrangements, i.e. technical inputs through a policy-planning framework and an implementation and management system that will permit monitoring and evaluation of actual, as opposed, to predicted impacts.

He then develops a methodological and institutional model, outlining the steps of an integrated research, planning, and implementation strategy.

There have been several proposed structures for technology assessment, listing what are considered the key stages in the technology assessment process. Many of these have evolved out of environmental and social impact assessment. As mentioned earlier, in Canada no special methodology and institutional structure for technology assessment has been developed. It is part of the environmental and social impact assessment process. Demirdache outlines the ideal structure for technology assessment undertaken in Canada.

However, as Rees (1980) points out, this model or structure rarely works in practice, because it does not account for the political and economic interests and pressure groups at work. He argues that the identification of potential impacts is nearly impossible, because the most important impacts or effects may be unpredictable or unknowable before the fact, (i.e. new phenomena deriving from the interactions of known and unknown components of the system impacted). He questions the reasoning underlying the search for mitigation and minimizing the scale of disaster: "That is, let us experiment boldly with acceptable risks and inconsequential failure" (Rees, 1980: 205).

Cornford (1987) and MacLaren and Whitney (1985) discuss new directions of environmental impact assessment in the Canadian context. They emphasize the need for integrated planning and assessment strategies that address policy and planning, the project assessment, and implementation. Such strategies must also have technical rigour, include consultation, and demonstrate institutional integrity.

Several analyses of environmental and social impact assessment have been published over the past six years (e.g., Beanlands and Duinker, 1983; Rosenberg et al., 1981; Boothroyd and Rees, 1984) that also affect technology assessment. They indicate a historical evolution of four periods: pre-1970, early 1970s, and the late 1970s to the present.

The pre-1970 period was characterized by a limited use of analytical techniques, and research was largely confined to economic and engineering feasibility studies. Narrow emphasis was placed on efficiency criteria. Safety of life and property were usually viewed in relation to conventional technology. There was no real opportunity for public review. Emphasis was also placed on multiple-objective cost-benefit analysis, and on the systematic accounting of gains and losses and their distribution, which were seen to be reinforced through planning, programming, and budgeting review. Environmental and social consequences were not incorporated.

In the early 1970s, environmental impact assessment primarily focused on description and prediction of ecological and land-use change. Formal opportunities for public scrutiny and review were established, and emphasis was placed on accountability and control of project design and mitigation.

In the late 1970s, multi-dimensional environmental impact assessment was introduced, incorporating social impact assessments of changes in community infrastructures, services, and life-styles. Public participation became an integral part of project planning. Increased emphasis was placed on justification for technology or project development in review processes. For example, emphasis was placed on doing risk analyses of unproven technologies in frontier areas.

From the 1970s onward, increased attention has been given to establishing better links between the project-impact assessment and policy-planning, and implementation-monitoring phases of decision-making. There has been an evaluation of fairness and efficiency of public processes, and the search has begun for more interactive, less protracted forms of consultation based on facilitated negotiation (Cornford, 1987: 381). Numerous other calls have been made for a more systematic approach (see Beanlands and Duinker, 1983; Sadler, 1986; MacLaren and Whitney, 1985).

Key Issues and Problems

Many studies on technology assessment, particularly those from the U.S. (see Porter et al., 1980), pay a lot of attention to techniques, although "the majority of assessors found the techniques excessively formal and not suited to the work they wanted to do" (Porter, 1980: 81). The paradigm used in structural modelling in technology assessment is technically oriented, and it has gone unchallenged because it has become the sine qua non of scientific management. Hoos (1979) reports that since the late 1970s there has been a move towards appreciating limitations to economic rationality.

Assessments are often based on a simplistic model of rationality in policymaking which is inadequate because of both a disproportionate emphasis on formal, quantitative analytical techniques considered more scientific than qualitative information, and the difficulties of anticipating and considering all alternatives or all information. Assessments are mostly limited to individual technologies or projects involving particular technologies (e.g., oil-sand development). Critiques of this practice point out that technology assessment in its institutionalized form does not evaluate technology in its collective sense, as part of the present industrial order (Carpenter, 1980; Rees, 1980). This direction of the impact assessment community argues that a fundamental change of social impact assessment is necessary, that fine-tuning is insufficient, and that it needs to be replaced by a principal emphasis on human needs and values (Tester, 1987; Carpenter, 1987). The Berger Inquiry (Berger, 1977) is one of the few exceptions to this narrow approach.

Rees (1980) points out that the original intent of aiding decision-makers has degenerated to an uncritical descriptive analysis of alternative consequences. Every effort is made to find policies to mitigate adverse effects while enhancing positive aspects of the particular technology. The criteria used in these assessments are inevitably themselves technical with some acknowledgement of other quantifiable variables, such as economic feasibility.

Closely related to the technical emphasis is the question of the ideological dimensions of technology assessment. The assessment of social impacts is based on either a technical or socio-political paradigm. The technical paradigm focuses on the production of social impact assessments that are objective and, to the extent possible, scientific and quantified. A basic assumption is that better information results in better (informed) decisions (MacLaren and Whitney, 1985; CEARC, 1986).

The socio-political paradigm focuses on the processes by which social impacts are assessed; hence, an association with community development and public participation. A basic assumption of this paradigm is that an open participatory process results in better decisions (Lang and Armour, 1981; CEARC, 1985; Cornford, 1987). To date, researchers have been unable to suitably meld these technical and socio-political perspectives and effectively satisfy both points of view by integrating both quantitative and qualitative variables (Sadler, 1985, Cornford, 1987). The areas chosen for technology assessment, most often as part of a social impact assessment, continue to reveal a narrow perspective. Technology assessment is seen almost exclusively, as Rees (1980) points out, as a relatively limited technical exercise. Authors within this understanding of technology assessment seem

> ... to accept the current mode of technological development and implementation as inevitable. The best we can hope for through technology assessment is to improve our current 'satisficing' in decision making and learn to duck when things go awry. [Rees, 1980: 206]

Little consideration has been given to understanding the institutional and structural factors underlying technology assessment, and the values that are fundamentally responsible for developing particular technologies. Hoos (1979) argues that the methodology systematically excludes institutional arrangements, social impacts, and societal implications.

Public Participation and Political Usage

The role of public participation in technology assessment has generally been recognized. Although there have been efforts to incorporate such public inputs into all stages of the technology assessment (environmental and social impact assessment) process, typically, these have been limited to initiating contacts with representatives of concerned public interest and stakeholder groups (see Unesco, 1984; Priscoli and Homenuck, 1986). The increased interest in public participation in technology assessment is seen as a general long-term development in public policy and discussed primarily in the context of environmental and social impact assessment mandated projects (see the literature on environmental and social impact assessment). A number of calls have been made for more relevant yet disciplined consultative procedures (e.g., Sadler, 1980; Rees, 1981; Berger, 1976; Priscoli and Homenuck, 1986).

So far it is mainly the U.S. experience that has been surveyed and examined regarding the utilization of results of technology assessment. The findings (e.g., Armstrong & Harman, 1977) indicate that technology assessment has greater conceptual than instrumental usefulness. A review by the OECD in 1983 also shows that the policy analysis part of impact assessments has not much facilitated or simplified the decision-making process. Its main contribution has been a more systematic structuring of uncertainty and an awakening of awareness of often neglected or unnoticed impact areas. Most of the officials interviewed felt that the vague and inconclusive treatment of social impacts on the one hand, and the naive and unrealistic treatment of policy issues on the other, constituted barriers to the utilization of technology assessment in the decision-making process (OECD, 1983:58). Other conclusions are, for example, that findings of the technology assessment have rarely been taken into account when felt to be incompatible with institutional self-interest, or that lack of use was due to poor timing (OECD, 1983:58).

Environmental impact assessment is a special case because these assessments are mandated by law as part of the formal decision-making process. Consequently, research in the U.S., and also in Canada, has focused on this area. The discussion of environmental and social impact assessment in Canada through EARP and FEARO stresses the need for more effective institutional arrangements in relating components of the process of environmental and social impact assessment to each other, as well as to the larger structure of project and policy decision-making (e.g., Rees, 1981; Sadler, 1985; Cornford, 1987).

Substantive Areas of Impact

Impact assessments of new technologies spread over a wide field. There is no systematic review of the research that has been done. The assessment of economic implications usually addresses macro-economic concerns and input-output related issues, based on a cost-benefit analysis framework. As part of environmental and social impact assessment/technology assessment, economic impacts are related to the national industrial strategy in the various economic sectors. This area has been well developed in the U.S. and has become a vital and highly sophisticated part of technology assessment/environmental impact assessment (see Porter et al., 1980). Yet the methodology raises a number of concerns, such as the impossibility of quantifying all effects, the difficulties in measuring costs and benefits over time, the need to weigh intangibles, and the methodological intricacies of many economic techniques.

A major assessment theme is the difficulty for the Canadian economy of adjusting to technological change (McCallum, 1985; Campbell, 1985/86). This is then linked to Canadian science and technology and R&D policy. The presentations at the conference "Prospects for Man: Science, Technology and the Economy" (1984) provide an example of the character of this discussion. For example, Swan (1984) outlines the contribution of technology to social well-being and comfort. His discussion of the slowdown in the growth of living standards emphasizes the need for government policies to support technological advance. Soete (1984) similarly stresses the "economic crisis" brought about by new technologies, and the need for government support to reverse the slowdown in productivity gains and living standards.

Education and skill development are seen as essential to cope with technological change and to exploit the benefits (e.g., Alecxe & Parsons, 1986; Barrett, 1985). A main argument in this literature is that the Canadian education system has not kept pace to absorb the impact of high-technology. Strategies that would reflect the educational requirements and the options for management, labour, and the public are still lacking (e.g., Alecxe, 1986). It is also considered necessary to train future managers and technical entrepreneurs in the process and management of technological innovation. The case study by Clarke and Reavley (1987) shows how the industrial strategy of high-technology development is challenging universities to broaden the range of intellectual skills taught, to develop a greater awareness of the problems that must be overcome, and to explore how they are responding or could respond to industry's needs.

Although communication and information technologies have profound impacts on society, Coates (1983) claims a "paucity of assessment results" in the U.S., in part due to the fact that no major federal line agency has communication and information technology development as its primary responsibility. Both the American and Canadian literature refers to the challenge and difficulty of conducting impact assessments of communication and information technologies. The most important impacts usually do not stem directly from the physical characteristics of the technology, but are related to the capabilities offered and the ways in which the technology will be used. These are manifested in terms of changes in behaviour, institutional structures and functions, in efficiency and productivity, and in power relationships. These impacts are much subtler, more complex, and much more difficult to display than changes in the flow of dollars, materials, energy, or finished goods. The meaning of social impacts is usually narrowly defined and interpreted as impacts on employment and related socio-economic concerns.

A substantial part of the Canadian literature is further characterized by an uncritical approach which focuses on benefits that are, or could be, realized, and on potential problems that will arise if no policy is put into place to mitigate negative effects. Structural aspects, including possible alternatives, development goals and social values, are neglected (e.g., Thompson, 1980; Godfrey and Parkhill, 1980; Solntseff, 1980; Serafini and Andrieu, 1981). Leiss (1974) has critically reviewed the assumptions underlying the literature on "technological" and "information society."

Other research (not reviewed in this section) outlines the enormous potential social problems resulting from technological change, particularly those arising from the massive displacement of jobs. These studies refer to the institutional changes only on a general level, however. Recommendations rarely address the likelihood of implementing particular strategies. Generally the literature is characterized by a short-term and narrow approach. Consequently there is a recognized need for comprehensive research (Peterson, 1980). Rosenberg's (1986) analysis is one of the few comprehensive studies undertaken in Canada. It provides a detailed discussion of the impacts of computers, analyzing a variety of technical applications and their impacts in a range of social areas (work, health, privacy, centralization, responsibility, human self-image, ethics and professionalism, and national interests).

The concept of alternative technology is the basis for a third direction in the literature. These studies emphasize social development goals and stress the need for alternative approaches that will allow the affected community to accept or reject technologies (Olsen, 1983).

The problematic issues referred to in the communication and information technologies assessment studies can be summarized under several themes. The first of these is: **information capability vs. information access.** This theme refers to the policy question emerging from the new communication and information technologies. Of particular importance is the question of the degree to which the potential of these new technologies can be achieved and equal access to information guaranteed with or without regulatory controls.

The federal government's involvement in the development of Telidon led to an extensive assessment of videotext in the early 1980s. The Department of Communications contracted research on a variety of issues, such as market penetration, impacts on education, libraries, small businesses, agriculture and handicapped people. It also undertook intensive research concerning the technical specifics, including the human response to various kinds of visual representation. The discussion was characterized by optimistic projections of usage, enthusiasm about future applications, and the importance for Canada (Serafini and Andrieu, 1981; Department of Communications Telidon reports; Cameron, 1982; Booth, 1985; Kurchak, 1981). Only some of these studies expressed concerns about access and privacy, urging public awareness and participation in social policy issues (e.g., Cameron, 1982; Booth, 1985).

A similarly optimistic approach has been taken in assessments of new broadcasting developments. Many of the studies on interactive broadcasting (Pergler, 1980), direct broadcast satellites (Department of Communications, 1983; Telesat, 1981; Ministry of Transportation and Communication, 1985) and mobile satellites (Department of Communications, 1984), produced by, or contracted for the Department of Communications, focus on potential benefits, economic feasibility, user rates, market penetration, and possible regulatory implications. In particular, the early projects with direct broadcasting through Hermes and Anik B have led to extensive assessments (Bischof, 1981; Royal Society of Canada, 1977). Reference is made to the need for equal access, yet how this can be implemented is rarely addressed. For example, Pergler (1980) outlines the many potential benefits and the potential threats and recommends on a general level that steps must be taken to ensure a wise usage.

Melody (1982), Mansell (1985) and McNulty (1988) point out that the impact of new technologies on different sectors of society, the reasons for not realizing potential benefits, and the assessment of alternative technologies are systematically neglected. Rather, the discussion is characterized by a "technology-push" approach. Mansell (1985) has critically reviewed the narrow approach of many of these studies, the underlying assumptions and the failure to analyze structural arrangements.

The question of deregulation of telecommunication carriers in the U.S. has also led to an assessment in Canada (e.g., McPhail and McPhail, 1985; Mosco, 1986). In recent years, the technology-push character of these developments, the moderate or slow user response, and the unrealistic optimism have been recognized (Booth, 1985).

A few authors refer to the differences among user capabilities and the institutional structures of access to the market of information that may lead to changes in social stratification, based on the degree of information-richness or information-poverty (Einsiedel, 1984; Melody, 1983, 1985).

The second theme is: **information access versus information protection.** As access to communication and information technology expands, the potential for problems with regard to privacy of data and information also arises. This is discussed in several studies. Many of these studies (Cordell, 1985; Levy, 1985; Mann, 1987; Science Council, 1985; Brown and Billingsley, 1980) emphasize the impacts on law and regulation posed by the proliferation of easily accessible information and the need to protect privacy. A few studies focus on audio-visual services (video, broadcasting), stressing not only the implications for the Canadian economy and sovereignty but also the impacts on Canada's cultural identity and freedom (e.g., Meisel, 1985; Task Force on Broadcasting Policy, 1986; McNulty, 1986). In particular, the activities leading to the proposal of a new Broadcasting Act have led to a variety of reports and studies that address the impacts of new broadcasting developments on information capabilities and access (see Task Force Report and commissioned studies listed therein).

A third theme is: **information capabilities and institutional changes.** The new capabilities for using information in new ways opens up the potential for change in a number of established institutions. Cultural, political, and economic issues become increasingly intertwined, which needs to be recognized in policy analysis and policy strategies. Policy papers and studies often refer to the institutional arrangements and the need for increased or decreased regulation. The question of deregulation caused considerable debate concerning the impacts on regulation and national political, economic and cultural goals. Yet the structural institutional change and its implications on the different sectors of society is usually neglected. A few authors focus on these impacts.

Melody (1983, 1984, 1985) analyzes the institutional changes related to new communication and information technologies, the increase in technical efficiency and market extension, but also the impacts on competition, access, availability of services, costs, and the like. He outlines how the conception of the public interest within a nation changes and how national interests identify with the corporate interest of the dominant home-based transnational corporations. These changes also affect international trade relations.

The Task Force on Broadcasting Policy (1986), McNulty (1986), and Meisel (1986) reviewed the implications in terms of limited benefits, particularly cultural benefits for Canadian society. They indicated that opportunities have been missed and benefits foregone due to the specific structural arrangements of Canadian broadcasting.

Of particular importance is the emphasis on: **the human consequences for the new communication technologies.** The widespread use of telematics could considerably reduce the need for face-to-face communication, and the effect on human communication could be significant, although subtle. However, investigation in the Canadian context is still lacking. For example, the behavioural research of Telidon applications was narrowly defined, focusing on what technical arrangement will likely result in maximum user-acceptance. Other studies are too broad to be of much use (Godfrey and Parkhill, 1980; Serafini and Andrieu, 1981; Vanier Institute, 1982). The report of the Vanier Institute, for example, outlines the applications of microcomputers and the implications in terms of learning, value systems, personal initiatives and interaction. Conclusions are general, arguing that people need not be passive recipients but can use the new technologies to serve human needs and aspirations.

Most recently, attention has been drawn to a new theme: **the biotechnical and biomedical context.** Biotechnology and biomedical ethics have rapidly developed over the last decade, as reflected in the rapid growth of the literature, including journals and bibliographies. The discussion is dominated by the U.S.; however, there are several studies that address the issue in a Canadian context. In 1982-83 "Science and Technology" featured a special series over several issues that addressed the impact of biotechnology on (mostly American) societal institutions.

The series of articles indicates that the nascent biotechnology industry is challenging traditional government-university-industry relationships, raising questions among the partners that are likely to effect basic changes in those research relationships. They also show that one of biotechnology's major accomplishments will be the custom design of proteins and enzymes, which will have major political, economic and ethical implications that need to be assessed in terms of potential and actual risks and benefits. This leads to questions of the impact of government regulations and priorities on scientific and technological innovation, and the government's capacity to assess risk and manage it (see Chapter Ten on risk analysis).

Hoffmaster (1980) has reviewed the literature, including the Canadian contributions to the field. He finds a theoretical confusion, due to the interdisciplinary nature of the research, the failure to integrate conceptual and normative issues, the variety of normative approaches adopted, the failure to distinguish the principal questions pursued, and the general poverty of modern moral philosophy. In an appendix he provides a detailed bibliography of Canadian works in biomedical ethics. He stresses that research in this area must be interdisciplinary and that the results must be communicated to those affected by the ethical issues.

The workshop "Biotechnology in Canada" (Slotin, 1980) is an example of Canadian research in this field. It addresses industrial opportunities for applying biotechnology, the international context, as well as more ethics-related questions. The workshop makes evident that Canada lags behind in its development of biotechnology and needs an appropriate science and technology policy that addresses the needs for manpower, venture capital, information systems, and improved government, industry, and university relations.

The Institute for Research on Public Policy has also been actively involved in the debate. It has sponsored and participated in workshops and has produced in-house analyses (e.g., Roy and de Wachter, 1986). Roy and de Wachter outline the four issues considered crucial for managing biotechnology: value conflicts, the question of concentration of power, public participation, and pros and cons of university and industry cooperation. The question of power is generally a major concern expressed in the literature. Emphasis is consequently placed on the importance of policy regulation and intervention (Roy and de Wachter, 1986; O'Neill, 1986).

Finally, a consistent theme has been: **the environmental context.** Most of the impact studies within the environmental context are part of the mandated social and environmental impact assessment studies. As the above discussion on technology assessment in Canada indicates, the impact assessment of technologies is thereby focused on a specific technology for a particular project at a particular time, such as oil and gas development in the Beaufort Sea. The lack of technology assessment as such within environmental impact assessment has already been discussed above.

Three priorities for further work can be identified:

Technology assessment

Within environmental and social impact assessment, technology assessment has not emerged as a special issue of concern, although the need is recognized. The research needs to move away from a specific technological or problem management mission and to become interdisciplinary, integrative, and holistic. Within the framework of environmental impact, social impact and technology assessment, the following issues need to be pursued further.

First, the orientation of technology assessment, either as technical planning or as political community development activity, needs to be determined. Under what conditions and for what types of projects is each appropriate? What research methods and techniques should best be employed? How can the two approaches be integrated?

Second, the content boundaries of technology assessment need to be determined. How encompassing should the definition of social impacts · be? What is the appropriate social unit of analysis (individual level, sectors of society)? Should the basic need for the technology be considered? What is the relevant time frame of impacts (short-term, long-term)? What guidelines should be applied for the impact assessment? Finally, what is the role of those most likely to be impacted upon in deciding the appropriate boundaries for each assessment?

Third, the relationship of impact prediction and impact monitoring needs to be identified. To what extent can social impacts be predicted, and what methods of prediction are most appropriate? How can affected groups participate more effectively in impact monitoring? What frameworks and techniques exist for undertaking post-impact analysis and how well have they worked?

Fourth, the institutional arrangements and administrative procedures for undertaking technology assessment studies, post-project evaluation, mitigation, and monitoring should be examined. What are the appropriate procedural and policy arrangements to produce the most competent and comprehensive technology assessment studies? What internal procedures and policies have different institutions developed to review technology assessment and social impact studies, to determine deficiencies or adequacy, and to decide on study recommendations? What forms of auditing are best to increase technical and administrative performance in the planning and implementation process?

Fifth, attention should directed to the question of significance: who decides what constitutes significant positive and negative social impacts, and on what basis? What methods can be used to place values on impacts (see CEARC, 1985, 1986)?

Finally, CEARC (1985) has also indicated that two areas of concern are particularly pressing and need to be pursued: research on institutional arrangements for social impact assessment, and research on improved impact prediction, monitoring, and management capabilities.

This literature review has made it evident that broader questions of social development goals need to be addressed, such as societal values, development goals, and conflicts of interest. The potential and scope of alternative technologies should be examined, as should the "no-go" option, to see what practical — as opposed to rhetorical—potential they have. Attention should be paid to the integration of the technical and political and community-oriented paradigms, the political usage of results, and the interrelation of political, economic, social, and cultural issues.

Communication and information technologies

The discussion of the literature on technology assessment indicates the importance of communication and information technologies, but also the current lack of analysis of them. In particular, research needs to be directed to the institutional arrangement and institutional changes wrought by the new communication and information technologies, including an evaluation of the incentive structures used to promote and realize benefits. In this context, it will be important to determine the impacts of the new communication and information technologies on different sectors of society in order to determine their benefits and beneficiaries, their unintended effects, and their long-term and short-term impact. More attention needs to be paid to the problem of technology-push versus technology-pull, and the role played by technology initiatives in economic and social development. Finally, in studying communication and information technologies, it is important not to neglect the human element: social values, communication, and behaviour patterns, etc.

Biotechnology

Although there is a separate literature on biotechnology not surveyed for this study on managing technology, there are important areas of overlap. The literature review conducted on managing technology points to several areas which require further research: the normative theories of public policy, the institutional aspects of biomedical research, the role of technology in society, the impacts on different sectors of society, and the beneficiaries of developments. Research in particular areas such as human reproduction and technology, or behaviour control and modification and technology, may well be part of the management of technology as more broadly understood (see Hoffmaster, 1980).

Chapter Ten

Problem Areas in the Management of Technology III: Managing the Risks and the Consequences of Innovation

William Leiss

Introduction

In a number of important senses, managing the process of technological innovation in modern industrial societies is nothing but the assessment, communication, and management of risks. Indeed, Fischoff et al. (1984) argue that "risk is the focal topic in the management of many activities and technologies." Through an understanding of the nature and consequences of risks, governments, businesses and the public seek to monitor and control those industrial products and practices that are potentially harmful to human health, the well-being of other species, and ecosystem functions. These attempts are classified under a variety of headings, the most commonly used of which are risk assessment or risk analysis, risk perception and acceptable risk, risk communication, and risk management.

Managing the risks associated with technological innovations in practice means making difficult choices on highly complex matters. Industries, regulatory authorities, and citizens must determine levels of acceptable risk for environmental and heath hazards, for instance those caused by toxic chemicals; these determinations involve very difficult operations, such as choosing appropriate extrapolation models for estimating human health risks on the basis of animal test data. All these parties must also make choices about how to balance estimated health and environmental risks against the estimated economic and social benefits to be derived from using toxic chemicals, in full knowledge of the likelihood that new information accumulated in the future will show that certain earlier choices were incorrect.

For members of the public, managing the process of technological innovation means making choices about the truly bewildering array of risks present in industrial societies, both voluntary (such as smoking or skiing) and involuntary (such as airborne lead or occupational hazards). This means, among many other things, deciding how to regulate one's exposure to voluntary risks, deciding how to rank risks in relation to each other, and deciding how much governments should regulate hazardous products and processes, and how much they should spend on reducing risks associated with them.

The inherent element of uncertainty in risk assessment shows itself in a public forum most clearly when risk controversies are hauled into courtrooms. Limitations in the current state of scientific understanding, lack of essential data, and ongoing debates over appropriate analytical models and methodologies mean that litigants encounter almost insurmountable hurdles when they are forced to prove causation where toxicological, epidemiological, or other test results are concerned. For example, litigants are often unable to prove which of a number of possible wrongdoers is responsible for the injury that is alleged, or which specific hazardous substance or environmental pathway resulted in the injury itself. It has been suggested that courts may have to modify traditional burden of proof and onus of responsibility rules in order to achieve more socially desirable results in the areas of environmental protection and compensation for injured parties (Versteeg, 1988).

Managing Risks—An Overview

Governments and industries have developed a set of administrative procedures for making their own choices about how to manage the risks associated with technologies. There is a range of risk management approaches that have been worked out in Canadian practice. They are: cost-effectiveness analysis (CEA), risk-benefit analysis (RBA), cost-benefit analysis (CBA), and socio-economic impact analysis (SEIA). The following discussion of these approaches draws heavily upon a paper by P. Victor (1985).

Cost-effectiveness analysis is the most restricted of the four. Cost-effectiveness analysis takes a predetermined goal as its objective (e.g., a 50 percent reduction in the level of allowable applicator exposure to a pesticide), and seeks the means of achieving that objective with the least monetary cost. In the example given, this might be achieved through better protective gear, changes in the formula mix, or a different method of application. In a cost-effectiveness analysis the costs of each of these ways of meeting the risk management objective would be estimated, so that the least-cost means could be identified. These costs normally would include costs to the farmer, to the pesticide producer, and to the taxpayer (for administration of the regulation).

The main difference between a cost-effectiveness and a risk-benefit analysis, using this illustration, is that with risk-benefit there is no predetermined health or other objective specified. Instead, it is the relationship between potential risks to health on the one hand, and the anticipated (net) benefits derived from the use of the product on the other, that must be weighed against each other. Net benefit is the benefit to the consumer from the use of the pesticide minus the sum of the costs, as above. In a completed risk-benefit analysis, the health and environmental risks are sometimes stated as the probability of the occurrence of some incremental adverse impact—for example, three cases of a certain type of cancer per one million lifetime exposures that would be avoided if the product were not used. Net benefits can be expressed entirely in monetary terms, but qualitative judgments are also made.

The overall evaluation of this information is a two-step consideration: first, whether the levels of risks indicated fall within the guidelines for acceptable risks to health established by the relevant scientific authorities (this is the domain of risk assessment specialists). Second, if the first criterion is met, whether the risks appear to "outweigh" the benefits, or vice versa, including an explanation of why that judgement should be accepted (this is the domain of the risk managers).

Approaching the same issue with cost-benefit analysis, health effects would be incorporated directly into the evaluation of the benefits and costs, and not be kept separate as in a risk-benefit analysis. If a new pesticide posed a certain type of additional health risk to applicators, then the estimated monetary cost for incremental medical expenditures would be added to any other costs of using it. Alternatively, the new pesticide might be a substitute for a more hazardous chemical already in use, in which case the reduction in projected health costs would be counted as a benefit. Cost-benefit requires that all costs and benefits of all relevant alternatives (including health effects) be evaluated in monetary units.

Benefits are estimated in terms of a person's willingness to pay for them, whether or not they actually have to make the payment (if relevant data is lacking, various techniques are used to arrive at these estimates). Costs are figured in terms of a person's likely demands to be compensated for encountering additional health risks. The basic objective of cost-benefit analysis is to simulate the workings of a perfectly competitive market situation, and to ask how the market would decide an issue (in this case, whether to register a new pesticide) if there were perfect competition and all effects were taken into account.

There are quite a number of problems associated with the attempts to use both cost-benefit and risk-benefit analysis methods, as noted by Stanbury and Vertinsky (1988): "When health, safety and environmental regulations are subject to cost-benefit analysis, another layer of complexity is added to the treatment of uncertainty and risk.... Regulations aimed at reducing risk to life, health and the environment are problematic as they often involve a high level of emotion, value judgements and a great deal of uncertainty." Stanbury and Vertinsky comment on three major sources of this uncertainty: the exogenous variability in nature, ignorance, and the cost of information. In addition, sometimes the cost-benefit analysis does not clarify the differences in results which may follow from choosing two different ways of assessing probabilities (statistical probability, which expresses the relative frequencies of occurrence, and subjective probability, which is a measure of confidence or likelihood). Nevertheless, if these approaches are used with care, they can make a useful contribution to risk management decisions.

A socio-economic impact analysis (SEIA) is the most comprehensive of the four techniques, in that it seeks to incorporate the widest range of probable impacts. Thus, whereas a cost-benefit analysis will be concerned with only one type of market-based effects (so-called "allocative effects," those concerned with changes in production and consumption), a socio-economic impact assessment takes into account so-called "non-allocative effects" as well: changes in international trade, rate of inflation, employment, regional impacts, and so forth. Although few regulatory decisions in themselves will have significant non-allocative impacts, this cannot be ruled out entirely. For example, there are a number of agricultural chemical products with significant extent of use or market predominance for a specific commodity, and major regulatory actions affecting them could bring into play the kinds of effects for which a socio-economic impact assessment might be appropriate.

The Risk Approach—Overview

One of the most significant developments during the last ten years has been the widespread acceptance of the distinction between risk assessment and risk management. In this perspective, risk assessment is intended to be an "objective" characterization (normally in quantitative terms) of the types and severity of potential harm, to be arrived at by using the most up-to-date research methods that have the confidence of the scientific community. Thus hazards should be identified, for example, in controlled laboratory experiments or in environmental monitoring with the aid of well-established scientific protocols, and the results of such investigations should be available for review by the researchers' peers. No important health concern may be overlooked: these include (but are not limited to) cancer, reproductive effects, inherited characteristics and genetic alterations, occupational exposure, and so forth.

There is an ongoing methodological debate concerning the adequacy of the types of extrapolations that are made from animal test data to presumed human health effects; the techniques and mathematical models used in such extrapolations are continuously being refined and discussed in peer-review journals. The overriding criterion for acceptability of results is whether the procedures of risk assessment do or do not meet the current standards of good scientific practice. There are also heated debates about the nature of the "value-based" assumptions within risk assessments and the uses of scientific findings in regulatory decision-making (Salter, 1988).

Risk management takes risk assessment (including its scientific basis) as one of its principal decision inputs, but also includes a host of other considerations—political, economic, and social. Some considerations are amenable to reasonably precise measurement in quantitative terms, but many are not. For example, the economic benefits that are expected to be derived from the use of a pesticide may be estimated in terms of improved crop yield (both quantity and quality), and then in terms of monetary gain to producers and the economy as a whole. However, field conditions are not laboratory situations; a wide variety of unforeseen or uncontrollable variables can affect the realization of forecast benefits, without—it should be said—necessarily calling into question the usefulness of benefits estimates.

Risk management decisions are often heavily influenced by factors arising out of political and social processes that have nothing to do with either scientific or quantitative analysis. Examples include the situation in which political or legal authorities in one jurisdiction, responding to political pressures, will ban (or permit) use of a chemical that is permitted (or banned) elsewhere, although both sets of authorities are operating in the context of the same database and risk assessment. Another example involves differences in conceptions of acceptable risk and perceived risk in various societies, or even in different regions and subpopulations within a society.

There continues to be lively debate on what are or should be the most important factors in a risk management process, and how both qualitative and quantitative measures should be used. However, there is a strong consensus of opinion on what the essential feature of the process is—namely, the effort to make explicit the nature and quality of the information base, together with the operative presuppositions and values, that form the basis for decisions. And among the chief presuppositions that are usually made in Canada today, two stand out as especially important: first, that risk is acceptable only in the light of demonstrable benefits; and second, that there must be a continuous striving to reduce the level of risk associated with hazardous materials or practices.

Another dimension entirely is represented by risk perception and the conception of acceptable risk. In the final analysis regulatory, legislative, and legal authorities all must respond to the way in which the citizens in each country understand the nature and variety of risks in the environment, how they "rank" each type of risk in relation to others, and how they expect public authorities to conduct the risk management process. This understanding is conveyed through responses to electoral platforms, lobbying by pressure groups, reactions to media coverage, and in many other ways. There is no doubt that the prevailing public idea of acceptable risk does affect the outcomes of risk management processes. Disagreements between "expert" and "public" evaluations in risk assessments present a great obstacle to attempts to arrive at a reasoned consensus on the management of risks in contemporary industrial societies.

Dilemmas of risk perception are relevant to the growing interest in "risk communication." By the latter term is meant the flow of information and risk evaluations back and forth among academic experts, regulatory practitioners, interest groups, and the general public. The sharp disagreements that can occur among members of these constituencies over the best ways to assess or manage risks are based sometimes on disagreements over principles or approaches, sometimes on differences in the information base available to various parties, and sometimes on a failure to consider carefully each other's position. At least some portion of those disagreements can be expected to disappear when due attention is paid to the need for better risk communication.

Risk Assessment

Before we proceed to the description of risk categories given here, it should be noted that there are some major disagreements and ongoing debates among specialists in the field about basic definitions and correct terminology. The leading organization in this field, the U. S. Society for Risk Analysis, has had various "committees on definitions" operating for many years, and those committees have been unable to forge a consensus to date on some basic terms, including the term "risk" itself. Although the following account is based on well-established usages, the reader should keep in mind that some authorities prefer alternative formulations. The definitions quoted below are from the recently issued "Handbook" compiled by Health and Welfare Canada's Environmental Health Directorate (1988).

Risk has been defined as "a measure of both the hazard to health from exposure to a substance and the probability of its occurrence." Thus risk is a function of both the nature of a particular hazard arising from a product, process or natural occurrence, on the one hand, and the probability (for a person or non-human species) of encountering that hazard and suffering an adverse effect, on the other. The identification of a potential hazard and the nature and severity of the possible health risks attendant upon it is the entry-point for the risk assessment process. Probability is a function of exposure in the first instance, although it is also dependent on the intensity of exposure as well as on the susceptibility of particular organisms to specific chemicals. Both acute and chronic effects are investigated through studies in toxicology, epidemiology, and molecular chemistry.

Thus risk is a function of hazard plus exposure. Hazard has been defined as "the adverse impact on health that can result from exposure to a substance"; exposure has been defined as "contact between a substance and an individual or a population." (Note that we may refer to hazards to the environment as well, that is, to ecosystems and to plant and animal species.) The threat posed by a hazard depends not only on the severity of its effect but also on whether or not the effect is reversible. A good deal of the dispute over terminology here has to do with whether the substance itself, or its adverse impact, is regarded as the hazard.

Risk assessment or risk analysis attempts to provide scientific estimates of health and environmental risks, and to identify sources of uncertainty inherent in scientific data. A comprehensive summary of approaches in this area prepared by the United States National Science Foundation (1985) presents the components of risk assessment as follows:

1. Risk-Source Characterization: A description of the characteristics of the risk source that have a potential for creating risk (e.g., types, amounts, timing, and probabilities of release of toxic substances, energies, etc.).
2. Exposure Assessment: Measurement or estimation of the intensity, frequency, and duration of human or other exposures to the risk agents produced by a source of risk.

3. Dose-Response Assessment: Characterization of the relationship between the dose of the risk agent received and the health and other consequences to exposed populations.
4. Risk Estimation: The process of integrating a risk-source characterization with an exposure assessment with a dose-response assessment to produce overall summary measures of the level of the health, safety, or environmental risk being assessed.

The resulting risk analysis and assessment is supposed to display the nature and significance of each of the components, as well as that of the overall judgement; methods used to make dose-response extrapolations; the assumptions used in arriving at estimates of effects and degrees of uncertainties in those estimates; and the distribution of risk across various sectors of the population. The risk assessment judgement sometimes presents the probability of the increased risk of cancer or other adverse health effect, based on all assumptions made in the analysis, for each exposed individual and for each intended use of the product, summed up as total risk.

Risk Perception and Acceptable Risk

Perceived risk has been defined as "an impression or intuitive judgement about the nature and magnitude of a health risk. Perceptions of risk involve the judgements people make when they are asked to characterize and evaluate hazardous substances and activities." These judgements about hazards are often contrasted with those made by experts who have professional training in engineering or natural science disciplines, and who use quantitative methods for assessing and comparing risks.

A recent paper has described well the importance of perceived risk:

The objective, quantitative nature of risk analysis, however, does not take into account how the public views risk. In contrast to risk analysis, risk perception is a process in which individuals subjectively or intuitively comprehend, estimate, and evaluate the probabilities and consequences of risks. As risk analysis fails to consider the subjective elements of risk perception, it is important for decision makers to be aware of public concern for health risks in order that risk management decisions properly reflect such concern and ultimately receive public acceptance....

In recent years the issue of perceived risk has perhaps become the talisman of the misunderstood. The gap between factual reality and the perceived view is taken by community leaders, be they politicians, industrialists or bureaucrats, to be due to a lack of understanding on the part of the public. This leads to the obvious corollary that education will remedy the situation. Such a solution is however likely to raise more issues than it answers, and ultimately prove facile, for public policy can be strongly influenced by the social and cultural values and human emotions which shape public perception of risk. Thus, the proponents of nuclear energy and hazardous waste dumps have learned to their cost that the public is not easily reassured by the parade of exceedingly low estimates of risk associated with such hazards. [Krewski, Somers & Birkwood, 1987]

Risk perception research has been heavily influenced by psychological studies in the areas of "heuristics and judgements under uncertainty." These studies have shown that most people experience difficulties in understanding probabilistic expressions, and also that people tend to overestimate the frequency of rare events and underestimate the frequency of common events. Perceptions of risk are also known to change markedly over time as new information becomes available. These characteristics, as well as others associated with them in the processes of everyday decision-making, frequently lead individuals to deny uncertainty, misjudge risks, and maintain unwarranted confidence in judgements of fact. In general, our information processing is hindered by biases and limitations which affect our subjective evaluation of probabilities.

Certain characteristics of risk are also known to influence risk perception. For example, individuals tend voluntarily to accept higher risk levels for themselves than for society as a whole, frequently because they feel that the benefits are worthwhile and that they have autonomy over their lives. In general, three main factors have been shown to influence perceived risk: the degree to which the hazard is understood, the degree to which it involves feelings of dread, and the size of the population at risk.

We all tend to simplify complex and uncertain information, relying on rules of thumb and tradition to shape our perceptions. Further, there are difficulties in detecting omissions in information received, in evaluating opinions, and in detecting inconsistencies in debates about risk. Despite these difficulties in assessing risk, people may utilize existing information to form strong views about risks. Such perceptions are often resistant to change: new evidence which is consistent with initial perceptions is accepted, while that which is contrary is dismissed.

People do not perceive all lives to be of equal value, nor do they perceive all forms of death as equal. Frequently, non-fatal health impairment such as permanent brain damage is seen as more serious than death itself. In the public's view, the significance of the probability of an event tends to decrease as conceivable consequences increase, until what is possible becomes more important than what is probable.

Risk Acceptability

In an attempt to develop risk policies that are satisfactory to the public, decision-makers have frequently adopted the notion of acceptable risk. This concept is based on the assumption that there exists a small but nonzero probability of an untoward event occurring, below which the population at risk is willing to accept the risk. The level of acceptable risk has been widely debated as a means of establishing guidelines for exposure to trace levels of carcinogenic agents present in the environment. While regulatory authorities are reluctant to establish a precise level of risk they would support as tolerable, lifetime risks on the order of one in a million seem to have been implicit in many regulatory actions to date.

"Zero risk" is often the cry of those who believe they have been exposed involuntarily (and unfairly) to a suspected hazard, but it cannot be a management objective, certainly not where "all" industrially generated hazards are concerned, since implementing it would entail eliminating entirely the industrial processes which give rise to the hazards. (Of course, it may very well be the case that a particular group of individuals has been unfairly treated under particular circumstances.)

The increasing sophistication of analytical methodology has resulted in the detection of environmental contaminants in ever-decreasing levels of concentration, with concentrations at the parts per trillion level and below now being measured. The level of risk associated with such trace levels of environmental toxicants may be infinitesimally small in many cases. One may thus question the advisability of controlling man-made hazards with such vigour that the resulting level of risk is insignificant in relation to risks from common natural hazards or voluntary human activities. For these reasons, it is important to consider what level of risk should be considered as socially acceptable.

Covello et al. (1987) suggest that an understanding of risk perception is crucial because it contributes, through both societal and political processes, to societal decisions about risk acceptability. Although risk perception does have a place in risk management decision-making, it cannot replace risk analysis. Governments, which are mandated to make decisions on public health issues, are compelled by the sheer numbers of risks that must be managed to take a broad perspective on the totality of risks and the means of reducing them. Policies that are directed primarily at alleviating public anxieties, particularly in response to well-publicized accidents, can result in large expenditures having low relative effectiveness. Conversely, serious risks may also be neglected due to public indifference or lack of awareness.

The importance of an understanding of the public perception of risk for risk management decision-making was emphasized recently by Vertinsky and Wehrung (1989). They note the following points: (1) risk perceptions can influence the public policy agenda concerning the allocation of resources and regulations to reduce risks; (2) risk perceptions can influence market processes, and when these perceptions reflect a lack of information, there is "market failure," i.e., a loss of social welfare; (3) risk perceptions can influence individual behaviour in ways that may generate additional exposure to risks; (4) risk perceptions can affect how new risk evidence is evaluated; (5) risk perceptions can affect views of the integrity of the regulatory process and trust in risk assessors.

If risk perceptions are to be considered in risk assessment and risk management, decision-makers have to determine how best to measure those perceptions, how to reconcile conflicting perceptions, and how to balance public perception, expert opinion and other inputs in the decision-making process.

Risk Communication

Communication of risk-related information is now recognized as a critical part of the risk management process. In particular, it is important that risk data be expressed in understandable terms, that uncertainties surrounding estimates of risk be understood, that perceived risks be taken into account, and that effective channels of communication be established among individual, advocacy group, government, and corporate actors involved in decisions about risks.

The term risk communication has come into use in recent years to describe this process, and has been formally defined by Covello et al. (1987) as "any purposeful exchange of information about health or environmental risks between interested parties." More specifically, they state that:

> ... risk communication is the act of conveying or transmitting information between interested parties about (a) levels of health or environmental risks; (b) the significance or meaning of health or environmental risks; or (c) decisions, actions, or policies aimed at

managing or controlling health or environmental risks. Interested parties include government agencies, corporations and industry groups, unions, the media, scientists, professional organizations, public interest groups, and individual citizens.

With this broad definition, risk communication encompasses most forms of communication within the process of risk assessment and risk management, including information flows between academic experts, regulatory authorities, special interest groups and the general public. However, it also focuses on the communicative processes through which individuals and institutional actors negotiate their interests and concerns about the assessment and management of risks in contemporary society. Thus, risk communication is what all participants in the risk assessment process engage in by virtue of their public involvement. This includes their attempts to inform, persuade, or warn others, to analyze problems and circulate findings on new knowledge, to change attitudes or behaviour, to set charges or rates for costs, or to carry out legally mandated responsibilities. One way of representing risk communication flows schematically is given in Figure 1.

In such situations, the risk communication process itself often becomes an explicit focus of controversy. Charges of media bias or sensationalism, of distorted or selective use of information by advocates, of hidden agendas or irrational standpoints, and of the inability or unwillingness of regulatory agencies to communicate vital information in a language the public can understand, are common. Such charges are traded frequently at public hearings, judicial proceedings, and conferences, expressing the general and pervasive sense of mistrust felt by many participants toward others. Of course, there are also genuine differences of principle, outlook, and values among the citizenry; disagreements will persist even with the most complete and dispassionate knowledge of others' views.

As a discipline, risk communication tries to achieve an adequate understanding of the processes in the risk area, an understanding that responds to its inherent complexity and array of participants. In terms of its practical orientation, risk communication seeks to improve the workings of these processes, and so to reduce the level of mistrust among participants. The ultimate objective is to assist in the formation of a reasonable consensus in contemporary society on how to assess and manage risk.

Covello et al. (1987) have utilized what may be called a "message transmission model" for delineating major issues in risk communication. This model categorizes those issues into four types: message, source, channel, and receiver.

Message problems include both deficiencies in the knowledge base and analytical techniques used by experts to assess risk, as well as difficulties in expressing inherently complex risk assessments in a way that the general public can understand. There are deficiencies in the current state of scientific understanding of risk and in the methods used for assessing risk. The difficulties experienced by the general public attempting to understand highly technical analyses represent a barrier to risk communication.

Source problems include such regular occurrences as disagreements among experts that fuel public uncertainty and concern. In many cases, resource limitations mean that these uncertainties cannot be reduced. There is also a lack of data addressing the specific fears and concerns of individuals and communities and a limited understanding on the part of many experts of the interests, concerns, fears, values, priorities, and preferences of individual citizens and public interest groups. Finally, the use by experts of bureaucratic, legalistic, and technical language can lead to a diminishment of their credibility and a lack of trust in the eyes of the general public.

Channel problems are, in this model, primarily a function of the role and practices of the mass media in risk communication. The main problems are thought to include selective or biased media reporting, premature disclosure of information, and oversimplifications, distortions, or inaccuracies in interpreting technical risk information.

Receiver problems include inaccurate perceptions of risk and, indeed, lack of sufficient interest in risk on the part of many citizens. Research in risk perception has shown a significant level of overconfidence in one's ability to avoid harm, as well as strong beliefs based on this overconfidence which are resistant to change; both of these factors make the task of risk communicators difficult to carry out. There are also unrealistic expectations about the effectiveness of regulatory action, demands of levels of scientific certainty that are impossible to achieve, and a reluctance to accept trade-offs.

In light of these problems, it has been suggested that the most promising approaches to better risk communication are to effect improvements in the following areas: information and education; behaviour change and protective action (to encourage risk-avoidance); disaster warnings and emergency information; and joint problem solving and conflict resolution, in which the public is actively involved in risk management decision-making.

The importance of improving risk communication, in relation to the overall processes of managing risks, should not be underestimated. The current limitations on the effective use of scientific risk assessments result in part from the inherent difficulties in communicating, from experts to lay audiences, research findings that are based on complex theories that necessarily incorporate probabilities, ranges of uncertainties, and choices of extrapolation models. Current limitations of public understanding occur because people's perceptions of risk are often inconsistent: this is because risk information by its very nature often frightens the public, because strongly held beliefs are hard to modify, and because views are easily influenced by the ways in which information is presented (see Figure 1).

The structure of risk communication flows is indicated in Figure 1 (Leiss and Krewski, in Leiss, 1989). The main actors in risk controversies are arranged in this model according to which "language" each normally uses in speaking about risk. Industry and university researchers, for example, are placed in the domain that is labelled "technical risk," reflecting the fact that they usually employ highly technical language (scientific risk assessments, including probabilistic calculations, within

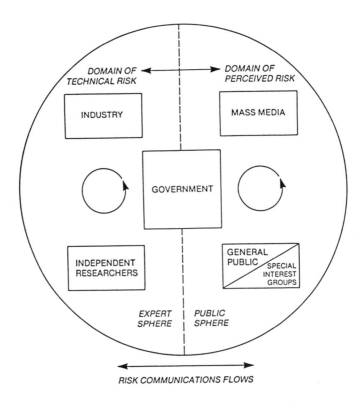

Figure 1

very specialized domains of scientific and engineering knowledge). The mass media, members of the public, and environmental groups normally employ the language of perceived risk, that is, ordinary non-specialist language. (However, it must be noted that this is a general rule, and that there are many exceptions to it; for example, environmental groups increasingly use the language of technical risk.) Governments occupy the position that straddles the dividing line, because governments are obliged to carry on the discourse about risk in both languages, depending on the audience. The model indicates that risk communication flows tend to be structured as a dialogue that moves back and forth across the line separating the two domains.

At this point, several steps may be taken to improve risk communication practices in the future. With respect to information presentation, there is a strong need for delivering quantitative risk estimates in intuitively meaningful terms that do not oversimplify problems of uncertainty. We need to know more about how to present the consequences of risk, as well as the probabilities of occurrence, in order to make the appropriate impact at the individual level at which people evaluate how they should respond personally to risk information. We need to know more about the bases of informed consent with respect to establishing an acceptable risk for the public, evaluating both the public's information needs on risk and also the adequacy of information presentations. More research should also be done on the ways in which messages about risk are received by the public, including tests for measuring the "comprehensibility" of different types of messages.

Risk Management

Risk management has been defined as "the selection and implementation of a strategy for control of a risk, followed by monitoring and evaluation of the effectiveness of that strategy." In one sense, risk management consists just in putting together the elements of risk already described into an "orderly" framework, so that a reasonable and responsible decision can be reached by an agency that has authority to manage risk.

Given the clear importance to society of managing risks responsibly and effectively, it is not surprising that efforts are being made now to bring some procedural discipline and commonality of language to this process. A working group, operating under procedures recognized by the Canadian Standards Association, has drafted a "protocol" or standard for risk assessment. When approved, this protocol will set out the steps that must be followed in order that a risk assessment performed by

Figure 2

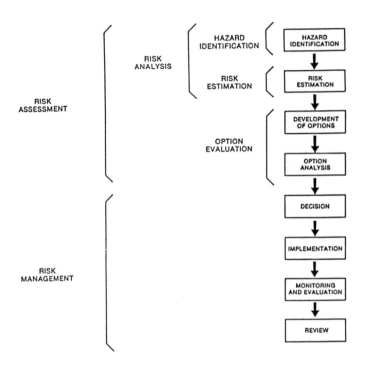

any agency will meet minimum criteria for such an exercise, criteria that are widely recognized by professionals in Canada and elsewhere.

Other practitioners have sought to characterize the risk management process as a step-by-step decision-making procedure, one which also meets certain minimum criteria for what will be considered within this process. One example is given in Figure 2 (Krewski and Birkwood, 1987, from which the following account of its individual steps is taken).

The first step in the process is hazard identification, which is based on case reports, epidemiological studies of human populations, and toxicological experiments conducted in the laboratory. Another possible approach for the identification of chemical risks is to compare the molecular structure and biological activity of the substance under study with that of known toxicants.

The next step is to obtain an estimate of the magnitude of the risk in question. This involves the statistical analysis of epidemiological and toxicological data to determine the level of risk associated with specific hazards, and to establish acceptable criteria for exposure to environmental hazards. This process is subject to considerable uncertainty and may require strong assumptions, as in the conversion of animal results to the human situation.

The first step towards selecting a strategy for dealing with a given environmental risk is the development of a number of alternative courses of action. Available options can range from advisory to economic to strict regulatory control. In order to ensure a consistent approach to risk management, the set of options selected for further evaluation should be compatible with existing environmental health program objectives and remain cognizant of any overall risk management policy guidelines (Figure 2).

The decision as to the most suitable course of action depends on a host of factors, including a balancing of health risks against health benefits in some cases. Consideration may also be given to the public's perception of risk, which may not coincide with the level of risk determined by scientific analysis. The technical feasibility of each proposed course of action should be demonstrated, including the ability to enforce any proposed regulations. Economic effects are often important in evaluating alternatives, both in terms of program-related costs and the impact on productive output. Socio-political factors involving equity considerations and repercussions at the international level should not be overlooked.

Implementation of the selected risk management strategy will usually require some commitment of resources and should be accommodated by attempts to communicate the nature of the chosen control mechanism to all affected parties. Once the control mechanism is in place, continued monitoring is recommended. Continual evaluation and review of new health risk information may suggest modification to the risk management strategy currently in place.

In some cases it would be better to display a separate pathway for consideration of benefits, parallel to that of hazard identification and risk assessment. It is important that net benefits from technological innovations be clearly recognized and assessed in risk management decision processes, because of the general rule that risks are acceptable only in the light of measurable benefits. Another important point with respect to the decision stages indicated in Figure 2, for example, is that risk and benefit assessments should be available as public documents for examination by all interested parties, and that the rationale underlying regulatory decisions should always be clearly explained.

A very important, and as yet insufficiently recognized, aspect of risk management is the role of peer review for risk assessment documents, especially in controversial cases. This can provide valuable criticism, expose new ideas and findings, maintain the quality of scientific information, and increase public confidence. Adequate peer review can ensure that the best data are being utilized, that any assumptions made are reasonable ones, that critical calculations are free from error, and that uncertainty is adequately recognized and taken into account. It is the responsibility of regulatory agencies, as overseers of the risk management process in society, to insist that peer review should be an integral part of scientific risk assessment.

It will be apparent by now that, among other things, the risk management process is a domain where two major institutional forces in modern society meet and interact: science and technology, on the one hand, and our economic and political institutions, on the other. We shall refer to these as the "science side" and the "policy side" of risk management (see generally Salter, 1988).

There have been some attempts to separate these two sides as a way of improving the management of risks in society. This is based on the belief that the scientific side (identified with risk assessment) could yield a perfectly neutral and objective assessment of hazard identification, risk estimation, and the specification of technical solutions to exposure, as well as comparisons of relative risks. In short, in principle, everyone who wished to take the trouble to understand the scientific basis of risk assessment, and who was starting from the same knowledge base, would agree on the nature of risks and their consequences. We may label this the "technical solution."

From the standpoint of the technical solution, the tasks of social institutions charged with the responsibility for managing risks (industry and governments) are seen as being largely as follows: (1) to set policies and adopt specific solutions in accordance with scientific findings, and (2) to challenge and overcome the "irrational" responses that are widespread in the public perception of risk. Risk communication, in this perspective, has the mission of translating the scientific understanding of risk into common-sense terms, and of transmitting this understanding effectively via the established media.

The best example is provided by the case of using nuclear reactors for electrical power generation. The engineering assessment of hazards and risks associated with this activity ranks it very low on the overall "table" of risks for individuals in contemporary society, and on this basis judges it to be a very attractive option for energy policy. On the other hand, this attitude meets strong resistance in the public generally, which consistently has perceived the risks in this case to be much more serious. This case illustrates well the weakness of the technical solution, for the great number of public information campaigns from industry and governments to date has failed to change the public's perception of risk from nuclear power generation.

By now most specialists in the field recognize the inherent weaknesses in the technical solution. In the first place, there is simply no basis for assuming that the scientific assessment of risk can be characterized as a "neutral" or purely objective process. There are too many unresolved (and perhaps unresolvable) uncertainties in risk estimation, requiring too many assumptions that rest on problematical grounds and are subject to challenge and to honest disagreement. As one source puts it:

> During the risk assessment process, analysts may overlook hazards, deem them unimportant, or ignore them because they are difficult to assess. Decisions are often influenced by judgements or policy due to gaps in scientific information. Assumptions must frequently be used in order to fill in gaps in the underlying scientific data base, and to allow for timely decision making. In order to maintain scientific credibility, the inferences and judgments used in such assumptions should be supported by scientific data and the assumptions and their likely impact on the risk assessment outcome be identified and communicated to the public." [Krewski and Birkwood, 1987]

Second, there are very considerable social and economic interests in the outcomes of managing risks, and each interested party can be expected to select for itself, out of the sea of uncertainties, those assumptions and methods of analysis that put the best face on the problem at hand.

These weaknesses have led to the increasing interest in another approach, which may be labelled the "process solution." This does not start from the science/policy contrast, but rather assumes that either or both scientific and policy considerations may emerge at any time, and in any setting, where risk management issues are at stake. The process solution is inherently focused on the nature and adequacy of risk communication flows as such (see Figure 1), rather than on evaluation of the situation from a presumed "neutral observer" standpoint (which, it is assumed, cannot exist).

The process solution accepts the fact that risk problems themselves are inherently complex and can only be described adequately, in the first instance, in scientific languages—using theories of the physical world, findings based on the technical instrumentation of laboratories, and probabilistic mathematics. But it gives equal weight to the fact that it is, in the last instance, the perception of risks by members of the public that is the decisive criterion for public policy decision-making. Thus it should be expected that, at different times and places, societies will manage the same types of risks—as assessed by the science of the day—quite differently.

In this perspective, the two sides of science and policy are (ideally) not two solitudes, but rather two continuously evolving sets of understanding of the world, understandings that are mediated by the dominant institutional structures of society. All participants in this process have an interest in encouraging the continued development of each side towards greater depth and sophistication.

Current Research Questions

For each of the main sub-areas discussed above, a number of current research questions can be listed. It should be noted, however, that this listing must be somewhat arbitrary, given the complex nature of this field; thus it should be regarded only as an illustrative listing.

Risk assessment

Some current research needs are: (a) continuing research on exposure models for human health risk assessment; (b) how to improve the "systemic" approaches to integrating risk assessments into risk management strategies—for example, the new workplace hazardous materials information system; (c) how to win acceptance of uniform standards of professional practice for risk assessment and risk management; (d) how to assess the public understanding and acceptability of risk thresholds (e.g., "de minimis" risk); how to set priorities for repairing the existing data gaps in the assessment of widely used toxic substances.

Risk communication

Further research is required in a number of areas, including: (a) how to convey technical information accurately, and in a comprehensible form, to non-specialist audiences; (b) how to assess and represent perceived risks to risk managers; (c) how to measure the effectiveness of risk communication programs; (d) how to assess the role of the mass media in risk communication; (e) how to design guidelines for defining the responsibilities of project proponents (both public and private sector) for adequate risk communication to the public; (f) how to measure the effectiveness of health hazard warnings.

Risk management

Some questions are: (a) how to assess the completeness and adequacy of decision-making steps; (b) how to implement adequate public notice and intervention rights in decision making; (c) how to communicate effectively the basis and rationale of decisions to affected parties; (d) how to refine cost-benefit and risk-benefit methodologies so as to incorporate perceptions and social values; (e) how to communicate the concept of risk-benefit trade-offs.

Risk perception

Some current issues are: (a) how to assess and improve the public understanding of risk comparisons; (b) how to improve methodologies for measuring the public understanding of uncertainties; (c) how to involve affected parties in the judgements about acceptable risk; (d) how to integrate risk perception assessments into risk management decision-making; (e) how to improve our understanding of the personal decision processes used by individuals to make choices about their exposure to voluntary and involuntary risks.

Partnerships, Centres and Models of Funding

Liora Salter

Introduction

It has become clear during the course of research on the management of technology that neither partnerships nor centres are well understood, either as concepts or as practical working entities. Yet in every discussion about the management of technology, the need for partnerships and centres is stressed. Since support for the concept of partnerships and centres is often more a matter of rhetoric than a commitment to any particular model of either, it will be useful to provide a description of various models of centres and partnerships.

Models of Partnership

The term partnership refers in this instance to the collaborative relationship between university researchers and other groups or organizations. Partnerships can exist between university researchers and government departments, among researchers in and outside of industry, or between the university and private organizations.

1. *The TIRF model*

Several people involved in the management of technology have suggested that the TIRF [Technology Impact Research Fund] model of partnership bears close examination and possible emulation. TIRF (now called TIP) is a program operating under the sponsorship of Labour Canada. It makes available funding for studies about the impact of technological change upon the workforce.

It was originally intended by Labour Canada that the TIRF funds would go to private (labour) organizations, rather than to private consultants or university researchers. In practice, however, these organizations have often approached university researchers to assist in carrying out the research, in part because such organizations seldom have the necessary trained staff to carry out the research themselves. In approaching university researchers, partnerships have been formed that draw upon the expertise of university researchers, while focusing this expertise on issues of direct concern to the sponsoring organization. The partnerships that have emerged are not formal ones, nor were they the original intent of the program. Nonetheless, they have resulted in a substantial body of significant research, and appear to have been highly productive and satisfactory to all concerned. They have resulted in the creation of a "de facto" network of university- and labour-organization-based researchers who share a common set of concerns and similar research experience.

2. *The research-bed model*

A second model of partnership was proposed in the context of interviews conducted for this study. This model is not a formal one, in the sense of being formally propounded or adopted by various groups. Nonetheless it has been used, with considerable success, particularly in the area of communications.

In this model, the partnership is formed when one organization—industry or government—provides a "research-bed" or laboratory for the research by another—usually a university. The non-university participant's contribution to the partnership is the site for the research and cooperation in its completion. This may involve researchers' access to management teams and interviews, or formally scheduled workshops related to the design and conduct of the research. The university participant's contribution to the research lies in carrying out a project, usually of an evaluative nature. For example, studies of the innovation process used by various companies could be conducted using a "research-bed" model. In this instance, university-based researchers would be allowed to observe all aspects of the management process, discuss their findings with those involved in innovation, and report upon the findings.

The advantage of the "research-bed" approach to partnership lies in the particular skills and resources that each of the participants brings to the research. The non-university participants contribute access to their activities and personnel. They continue to engage in their normal activities, and gain the benefit of research without any significant new resource allocation. The university participants draw upon the full range of their expertise, and contribute a prospective understanding of the situation they are examining, something beyond that normally garnered through contract research. The university researchers are also able to publish their findings and, in doing so, they enrich the literature.

3. The co-researchers model

In this model, researchers from different sectors—some or all of university, government, industry, and private organizations—jointly design and sponsor research. This type of partnership requires extensive commitment of time and resources from all partners, and a cost-sharing arrangement for research sponsorship.

In the co-researchers model, the various participants can share the same objectives or have quite different ones, as long as all objectives are accomplished by the proposed research. For example, a government department could determine that statistical research was required to establish a database on technology transfer in Canada and in export markets. Lacking both financial and personnel resources to carry out the research itself, this department could approach not only other government departments (as is common) but also potential university and industry participants. The impetus for the research in this example is the need for the database, which serves a different purpose for each participating group. The advantage in the co-researcher model is that partnership provides access to personnel and resources.

A second example was proposed during the course of this study with regard to an institute for science policy. The initiative was inspired by the success of the Science Policy Research Unit in England, and the proposal was to create a similar centre in Canada. In the Canadian case, however, two things were recognized. First, it was understood that several existing organizations—the Science Council, the International Research and Development Centre, etc.—would have to be involved, because these organizations have both a role and considerable expertise in science policy research. Second, it was recognized that no one sector could provide the resources necessary to support such an initiative. In this instance, the actual proposal is "on hold," but the interest from various potential partners is very high.

4. The sponsorship model

By far the most common form of partnership, in discussion and in practice, is the sponsorship model. In this model, the research is conducted exclusively by the university researchers (or private consultants), but it is performed under the sponsorship of a non-university partner.

Many examples of the sponsorship model of partnerships can be found. In some, what occurs is not intrinsically different from contract research. In these instances, the university researchers or consultants agree to carry out specific research (usually designed to produce recommendations) for a client, but the relationship is described as a partnership. In others, large grants are made available to a university research centre to support a research program which is designed in advance of the sponsorship. Again, in some instances, this situation is described as a partnership, although the primary form of cooperation is the transfer of resources. Finally, in some cases, the non-university sponsors contribute a "presence" within the research unit, rather than or in addition to money. They are advisors to the research, and may sit upon the adjudication committees for research funding allocation. This last case is most convincingly described as a partnership, but it need not involve a shared research agenda, nor any financial commitment of resources (other than "in kind" services) beyond those funds raised (usually from government) on the basis of the partnership.

Assessment of Partnerships

The success of partnerships involving social scientists may depend upon a new perspective and new policies being adopted by their granting council, SSHRCC. At the time of writing, SSHRCC did not fund policy research, and the SSHRCC matching grant program did not include partnerships with government departments and agencies. Neither the TIRF model, nor the "research-bed" approach, nor even the co-researchers model (when co-researchers are from government) have been easily funded, then, under the current funding programs of SSHRCC.

The rationale for SSHRCC's not having funded policy research has conventionally been that such research is of limited scholarly significance, since it is designed to produce recommendations for a contracting agency (or industry), and is therefore more properly the responsibility of government departments. With respect to contract research, this rationale withstands scrutiny. What the past approach of SSHRCC seemed to neglect, however, is the area of policy research which is prospective in orientation, or which contributes to the database necessary to support more scholarly research. The examples discussed with respect to the TIRF, co-researcher, and "research-bed" models are good ones to illustrate the point. The Labour Canada studies and the statistical research partnerships contribute to databases upon which more far-ranging and scholarly inquiries can be based. As well, access to "research-beds" in industry and government can seldom be arranged unless the non-university partners see in the research some means of achieving their more limited and pragmatic objectives. The past reluctance of SSHRCC to fund research that has, among other objectives, the goal of producing recommendations for public policy not only limited the potential for partnership research, but also may have been short-sighted. Without such collaborative research (which often cannot be funded adequately without SSHRCC support), the database is not created to sustain more conventional research, and certain other areas of more conventional social science research are precluded.

In addition, as those with experience in contract research know all too well, contract research is seldom adequate to advance the understanding of public policy. Contract research is rarely prospective in orientation. It is designed to meet short-term needs for information, when—particularly in the area of the management of technology—a longer-run study would benefit both policymakers and scholars alike. Too often, corners are cut in conducting contract research simply because the needs of the government or industry outweigh the prerequisites of scholarly research. Moreover, only a limited amount of contract research is either peer-reviewed or published, although it constitutes one of the main sources of information about society and its problems. Thus, it will be particularly useful if some means are found to combine the pragmatic short-term goals of policy research with the more scholarly and prospective approach of university-based research. This requires the development of criteria for a funding program within SSHRCC (and possibly NSERC) that does not eliminate policy research of a prospective nature, or partnerships with government and industry.

Close attention should also be paid to the TIRF model, for it is likely to be applicable in a number of areas where a non-university constituency defines the need for the research. It should be noted that the TIRF model is an unusual one for government departments, and that SSHRCC cannot reasonably expect that the success of the TIRF program will automatically be emulated. As a consequence, SSHRCC should engage in discussions with other government and non-governmental units to determine whether a TIRF approach, supported in this case by funding from

SSHRCC for social science researchers, could be developed in the area of managing technology. Such units might include women's organizations, science-policy organizations, standards-writing organizations, etc. Our research suggests that such an initiative would be strongly welcomed by each of these groups.

Finally, some cautionary words are appropriate with respect to the sponsorship model of partnerships. As has been suggested above, the descriptive rhetoric about partnerships does not always match the practical working relationships that exist. This is not to suggest that little benefit is derived from the sponsorship of research centres by industry, or industrial and governmental participation on research advisory committees for such centres; on the contrary, much has been gained in these relationships that could not otherwise have occurred. The point to be made is a simple one. The sponsorship arrangements only sometimes constitute genuine partnerships, involving detailed cooperation in research and/or the actual transfer of financial resources to the research units involved.

One should not underestimate the difficulty of achieving more genuine partnerships. The level of trust among the various sectors is not reassuringly high. One could legitimately describe the problem as a cultural gap, viewing government, private organizations, industry and the university each as its own culture. Moreover, those outside the university often fail to appreciate the nature of the contribution that can be made by scholarly research, while those inside the university fail to appreciate the need for bridging the gulf between their scholarly work and the pragmatic needs of non-university partners.

The problem of trust is not resolved when university researchers abandon their commitment to scholarly and prospective work. Neither industry, nor private organizations, nor government requires university researchers to operate their own "in-house" training programs, or to conduct research of a highly mission-oriented and short-term nature, except as these groups currently draw upon the expertise of contract researchers. Without abandoning their commitment to scholarship, however, university-based researchers can act as facilitators to the sharing of information (as is done in the educational program of MTI, for example), or can extend the resources available to non-university partners in new directions.

There appear to be three prerequisites for successful participation of university-based researchers in partnerships with non-university partners. First, the individuals involved should be those who are deeply-rooted in their own cultures, successful by the standards applied in government, business or the academic communities from which they come.

Second, successful partnerships demand special skills and expertise. Too little attention has been given to the need for experience and expertise in partnership relationships in order to achieve their success. Finally, it appears that successful partnerships require the participation of individuals who occupy positions in their own organizations or communities that give them considerable scope for defining their own jobs and resources such that they can work in changing and unpredictable environments. These individuals also require the authority to speak for their organizations.

Centres and Networks

Just as there are a variety of partnership arrangements that might be applied in research on managing technology, so too there are several approaches to centres or networks. As generic concepts, both "centre" and "network" refer to focused and concerted efforts to develop research on particular topics by drawing upon the best expertise available. This definition leaves aside the question of whether partnerships are an intrinsic element in centres or networks, although the current conventional wisdom associates the two. There are a variety of different models, or institutional arrangements, which are called "centres" and "networks," and it is not always possible to use the labels "centres" and "networks" to distinguish among them. For this reason, the models will be described with no particular reference to whether each is a "centre" or a "network."

1. The strategics approach

The strategics approach has been to designate an area of research for special attention and funding from the appropriate granting council. The process of choosing which areas to designate involves extensive consultations (and often workshops) with individual researchers in the field, partly to determine the criteria to be applied in the granting program. In addition, individuals with special expertise in the designated research area are chosen to sit on the adjudication committee.

Integral to the concept of strategics (and different, therefore, from other approaches to centres or networks) is the idea that the granting council is passive with respect to the research to be carried out. Individual researchers, or groups of researchers, are responsible for developing their own applications and submitting them, in the same manner as research grants generally, to the granting council. Beyond the initial statements of intent and the adjudication criteria, the granting councils play no role in the design or development of a research program in the strategic areas.

2. The negotiated grants approach

The negotiated grants approach represents a direct contrast to the strategic granting program. Unlike the strategics approach, no designation is made by the granting agency of the areas of research to be funded, and the normal adjudication process of the council is applied. At the same time, however, the negotiated grants represent programs of concerted research. A number of separate studies are carried out, under the direction of what might be called a project research manager, and it is expected that these separate studies, taken together, will generate a coherent body of knowledge on a particular topic. The granting council becomes involved in the design of the research as a consequence of its approving the general outlines of the research program to be undertaken and its project research management. It is also involved at several stages during the conduct of the research in approving research plans and evaluating the progress of the researchers.

3. The "national network of centres" approach

The national network of centres approach bears some resemblance to strategics, in as much as the granting council (possibly through consultations) provides the description of the program and the criteria to be applied in adjudicating applications. These criteria represent strategic choices about the research that needs to be done to accomplish a national interest objective. Unlike the strategics model, however, particular topics for research are not identified in advance other than through the general criteria. Similarly, unlike the strategics program, the national network of centres model does not permit individual researchers to apply, except as such researchers are members of existing research centres. The number of potential national networks of centres is potentially very great, since almost every serious researcher in Canada could conceivably be tied into a "centre" and/or "network" by virtue of his or her existing contacts with other researchers in the same area of expertise.

National networks of centres act as mini-granting councils once they have been funded. They adjudicate and sponsor research, provide support for graduate students, encourage visiting professorates, sponsor conferences and workshops and perhaps their own publishing program. The only limitation on the powers of these seeming mini-granting-councils is given in their original applications and in whatever evaluation process is applied over the several-year tenure of their grants.

4. A centres approach

There are significant differences between the national network of centres approach and the centres approach, although the terminology is often confusing. In the centres approach, the individual applicants need not be universities; they need not have a national or a national interest mandate; and they need not represent researchers in more than one university.

A "centre" in this model is nothing other than a group of researchers who formally designate themselves as a unit and achieve some official recognition of that unit. The official recognition usually takes the form of approval of the centre designation by a university governing body. The researchers within a centre may have wide-ranging interests, or be narrowly focused on a particular topic. They may represent the "best" in their field, or simply a group of individuals from one or more universities with interest in a particular topic. There may be an advisory body of other academics, or of non-academics. And there may or may not be formal or informal partnership arrangements (of any of the types described above). In other words, centres differ among themselves in all aspects but their formal designation and official recognition.

The reason for creating a centre is often a pragmatic one. Within the university, designation as a centre often aids its members in gaining institutional support for research and related activities. Centres also seem to have an easier time raising external funds to support research and other programs (teaching, conferences, speakers, and publications) than do individual researchers. Finally, some centres are created in response to (or at the initiative of) sponsoring groups, which provide the necessary resources to support, not only a program of research, but also the administration of the unit. In the latter instance, centres often resemble national networks of centres in as much as they function as mini-granting-councils. Particular centres have their own advisory (non-university) and adjudication committees, and their own formal program of "grants" to support individual research projects, speakers or visitors, graduate students, publications, etc.

5. The network model

The last model to be described does not result in a centre or grant applications for specific programs of research. In effect, this model is designed to provide the infrastructure support for researchers in particular (or strategic) topic areas. The network model involves a granting program designed to support communication, collaboration, and research in particularly designated areas.

The network model rests upon the assumption that individual researchers in separate universities seldom are organized, or have access to the level of resources necessary to create formal working relationships among themselves, or have adequate databases to support highly sophisticated research. The means to achieve a concerted research effort are simply not available. The network model uses a granting program to create a "centre" by providing the resources for linking researchers in designated areas of research, and for the amassing of adequate data to support large-scale research. The resulting network can legitimately be called a "centre," although it is not located at a single university or designated formally as such.

Assessment

As the description of the various models of centres and networks illustrate, there is a multiplicity of different research units that can and are being called "centres" or "networks." Thus, it is important to recognize that the organization of a centre or network, however pragmatically reasonable, runs contrary to the normal pattern of organization within academic communities. In the normal pattern, not only are people sharing similar research interests spread across a large country (with all of the costs that this communication and collaboration involves), but each university department or discipline is organized to represent the breadth of the field, rather than a focused research interest.

For example, even in a relatively specialized and applied discipline such as communication, each communication department will have individuals with different research and teaching interests, representing some portion of the span of research within the field as a whole. For pedagogical reasons, one would not wish it otherwise, but the effect of this situation is often to preclude the development of large clusters of researchers focusing on a single topic within any one university. In this situation, the relative size of Canadian universities, in comparison to their European and American counterparts, and the limitations upon university resources militate against the formation of centres.

The existence of centres in every university in Canada, in spite of these constraints, requires some further examination, then. In some cases, such centres are, in fact, quite small, representing the concerted effort of only a few people. In other cases, the research program conducted under the centre designation is in fact much more diverse than it appears to an outsider, but the centre designation gives it apparent coherence. In a few instances—far fewer than one might expect—centres do represent inter-university cooperation, particularly in such major metropolitan areas as Montreal.

And finally, in some cases, the existence of a centre is the product of external sponsorship which has permitted the university to place extra resources into a single research area.

In other words, if one considers centres to represent major concerted research efforts—usually in the form of large clusters of researchers working in a single location—it is likely that only by external funding will such centres be created. On the basis of our study, the phenomenon of externally funded research centres is a relatively new phenomenon in Canada (with such notable exceptions as IRPP [Institute for Research on Public Policy]).

It is too soon to judge the effect upon the university as a whole, and upon the disciplinary teaching programs, of the infusion of large amounts of money from external sponsors to support the personnel required for an extensive research program in a single area of specialization. Moreover, it is not clear whether the research emanating from such centres exceeds that which would be produced were the same funds to be distributed to researchers located at various universities, for nothing in the establishment of a centre guarantees that the most competent researchers in the country will chose to relocate their work in conjunction with the centre. And finally, in the network of centres approach, nothing yet guarantees that the grants will not be redistributed within the network in a manner that limits collaborative research and concerted efforts.

Selected Bibliography

Chapter Three

Etat des recherches en gestion de l'innovation technologique au Quebec francophone: La Politique scientifiques et technologique

Blais, Roger A., *University-Industry Partnership in Canadian R&D*, Compte-rendu du Colloque de l'Association des manufacturiers canadiens sur la recherche industrielle et universitaire, tenu à Toronto les 3 et 4 novembre 1979. Montréal: Ecole Polytechnique, 1980.

Boismenu, Gérard et Graciela Ducatenzeiler, "Le Canada dans la circulation internationale de la technologie," dans Duncan Cameron et Francois Houle, *Le Canada et la nouvelle division internationale du travail*. Ottawa: Editions de l'Université d'Ottawa, 1985.

———, *Technologie et politique au Canada: Bibliographie 1963-1983*. Montréal: ACFAS, 1984.

Boismenu, Gérard, Robert Dalpé et Graciela Ducatenzeiler, "Le transfert de technologie au Québec: importation et formes d'accès," dans Christian DeBresson, réd., *Le développement technologique au Canada*, (sous presse).

Bonin, Bernard, "Licensing Joint Venture and the Transfer of Technology: Some Canadian Experience," *Development and Peace*. Vol. 2, no. 1, 1981, pp 118-132.

———, "Grandes entreprises et diffusion internationale des innovations," dans Gilles-Y. Bertin, *La croissance de la grande firme multinationale*. Paris: CNRS, 1973.

————, "La firme plurinationale comme véhicule de transmission internationale de la technologie," *L'actualité économique* Vol. 47, 1971, pp 707-725.

————, *Licensing and Joint Ventures as Alternatives to Direct Investment*, A study prepared for the Task Force on Foreign Ownership and the Structure of Canadian Industry. Ottawa: Privy Council, 1967.

Bonin, Bernard et Claude Desranleau, *Innovation industrielle et analyse économique*. Montréal: Gaëtan Morin, 1988.

Bonin, Bernard et Robert Lacroix, "La science économique, l'invention, l'innovation et le progrès technique," dans Paul Bernard et Edouard Cloutier, réd., *Sciences sociales et transformations technologiques*. Québec: Conseil de la science et de la technologie, 1987, pp 195-234.

Bonin, Bernard et B. Perron, *Les mandats mondiaux de production et l'économie du Québec*. Montréal: Ecole des Hautes études commerciales, 1984.

Cambrosio, Alberto, Charles Davis, et Peter Keating, "Le Québec face aux biotechnologies," *Politique* no. 8, 1985, pp 77-101.

Cambrosio, Alberto, Camille Limoges et Denyse Pronovost, "Representing Biotechnology: an Ethnography of Quebec Science Policy," *Social Studies of Science* (sous presse).

Carter, Richard, "La technologie et le leadership gouvernemental" dans Jacques Dufresne et Jocelyn Jacques, réd., *Crise et leadership: les organisations en mutation*. Montréal: Boréal Express, 1983, pp 189-207.

Chaussé, Raymond, "Le virage technologique: l'innovation et la recherche," *Gestion* Vol. 8, 1983, pp 9-14.

Conseil de la Politique Scientifique, *Avis au Ministre délégué à la Science et à la Technologie relativement à la mise sur pied d'un" lieu permanent d'échange en R-D industrielle*. Québec: Gouvernement du Québec, 1982.

Conseil de la Science et de la Technologie, *Les avantages fiscaux associés aux activités de recherche et de développement*. Québec: Gouvernement du Québec, 1988a.

————, *La performance du Québec dans le cadre de la politique fédérale d'impartition*. Québec: Gouvernement du Québec, 1988b.

————, *Science et Technologie. Conjoncture 1988*. Québec: Gouvernement du Québec, 1988c.

————, *La politique des subventions de contrepartie et les universités du Québec*. Québec: Gouvernement du Québec, 1987.

————, *La collaboration université-entreprise et le financement de la recherche universitaire*. Québec: Gouvernement du Québec, 1986a.

————, *L'organisation de la politique scientifique et technologique*. Québec: Gouvernement du Québec, 1986b.

————, *Science et Technologie. Conjoncture 1985*. Québec: Gouvernement du Québec, 1986c.

————, "Le développement" *industriel des biotechnologies au Québec*. Québec: Gouvernement du Québec, 1985.

————, *Les politiques et programmes fédéraux en matière de développement technologique*. Québec: Gouvernement du Québec, 1984.

CRIQ, *Eléments de politique industrielle pour la définition des orientations du CRIQ.* Québec: Centre de recherche industrielle du Québec, 1975.

Dalpé, Robert, "Innovation and Technology Policy in a Small Open Economy: the Canadian Case," dans Christopher Freeman et Bengt-Ake Lundvall, réd., *Small Countries Facing the Technological Revolution.* London & New York: Pinter Publishers, 1988, pp 250-261.

————, *Politique d'achat et développement technologique.* Québec: Conseil de la Science et de la Technologie, 1987.

————, "Les politiques canadiennes de l'industrie aérospatiale," *Politique* no. 8, 1985, pp 103-129.

Davis, Charles et Raymond Duchesne, "Le cadre institutionnel de la recherche-développement au Québec. Les tendances et le problème de la relève," *Questions de culture* no. 11, 1986a, pp 17-36.

————, "De la culture scientifique à la maîtrise sociale des nouvelles technologies, 1960-1985," *Questions de culture* no. 10, 1986b, pp 123-150.

DeBresson, Christian, Brent Murray et Louise Brodeur, *L'Innovation au Québec.* Québec: Les publications du Québec, 1986.

Descarries-Bélanger, Francine et Louis Maheu, "Ecrits scientifiques et enjeux de l'institutionnalisation de l'activité scientifique au Québec," *Canadian Journal of Sociology* Vol. 13, no. 3, 1988, pp 235-260.

Doré, Roland, *Le défi technologique,* Rapport technique EP82-r-6. Montréal: Ecole Polytechnique, 1982.

Duchesne, Raymond, *La science et le pouvoir au Québec.* Québec: Editeur officiel, 1978.

Duquette, Michel, "Politiques canadiennes de l'énergie et libre échange—ou le sacrifice d'Iphigénie," *Etudes internationales* Vol. 19, no. 1, 1988, pp 5-32.

Faucher, Philippe, André Blais et Robert Young, "L'aide directe au secteur manufacturier, Québec-Ontario," *Revue d'études canadiennes* Vol. 18, no. 1, 1983, pp 54-78.

Forum Entreprises-Universités, *Du mécénat au partenariat: Le soutien des entreprises aux universités.* Montréal: Forum Entreprises-Universités, 1987.

————, *Investir plus sagement: collaboration entreprises-universités en recherche et développement.* Montréal: Forum Entreprises-Universités, 1985.

————, *Ensemble vers l'avenir: Collaboration entreprises universités au Canada.* Montréal: Forum Entreprises-Universités, 1984.

Gagnon, Gilles, "Le transfert international de technologie," *L'ingénieur* Vol. 69, no. 354, 1983, pp 5-9.

Gingras, Yves et Paul Dufour, "Development of Canadian Science and Technology Policy," *Science and Public Policy* 1988, pp 13-18.

Gingras, Yves et Jacques Rivard, "Energy R&D Policy in Canada," *Science and Public Policy* 1988, pp 35-42.

Hanel, Petr, *La technologie et les exportations canadiennes du matériel pour la filière bois-papier,* Rapport commandité par l'Institut de recherches politiques. Ottawa: 1983.

————, "Les entreprises innovatrices et leur performance à l'exportation," *L'actualité économique* 1982, pp 380-397.

————, "The Relationship Existing Between the R&D Activity of Canadian Manufacturing Industries and their Performance on the International Market" Rapport no. 40 de la série *Programme des études sur les innovations techniques*. Ottawa: Ministère de l'Industrie et du Commerce, 1976.

Hanel, Petr, Jean-François Anger et Michel Cloutier, *L'effet des dépenses en R-D sur la croissance de la productivité*. Québec: Ministère de l'Enseignement supérieur et de la Science, 1986.

Julien, Pierre-André, *Incidences de la politique scientifique fédérale sur l'économie québécoise*, Etude préparée pour le compte du Ministère d'Etat au Développement culturel, Québec, 1978.

Lacroix, Robert, "Un aspect de l'écart technologique," *Recherches économiques de Louvain* mai 1971, pp 21-35.

Lacroix, Robert et P. Scheuer, "L'effort de R-D, l'innovation et le commerce international," *Revue économique* janvier, 1977, pp 1009-1029.

Lacroix, Robert et Louise Séguin-Dulude, *Les disparités internationales et nationales dans les efforts de R-D: une explication de la situation canadienne et québécoise*. Québec: Fonds FCAR, 1983.

Lacroix, Robert et Fernand Martin, *Les conséquences de la décentralisation régionale des activités de R-D*. Québec: Conseil de la Science et de la Technologie, 1987.

Landry, Réjean, "Science politique et politiques technologiques" dans Paul Bernard et Edouard Cloutier, réd., *Sciences sociales et transformations technologiques*. Québec: Conseil de la science et de la technologie, 1987, pp 325-282.

————, "Les programmes d'aide à l'innovation des gouvernements canadien et québécois," dans Bernard Crousse, Jean-Louis Quermonne et Luc Rouban, réd., *Science politique et politique de la science*. Paris: Economica, 1986, pp 31-51.

————, "Impacts of the Institutional Arrangements on Technological Innovations," dans Michael T. Greven et Bernard Crousse, réd., *Political Science and Science Policy in an Age of Uncertainty*. New York & Frankfurt: Campus Press, 1985a, pp 185-216.

————, "Incidences du virage technologique sur les citoyennes et les citoyens: déficience des arrangements institutionnels du Québec," dans Marc-Adélard Tremblay, réd., *Nouvelles technologies et société*. Québec: Faculté des sciences sociales de l'Université Laval, 1985b, pp 122-134.

————, "La contribution de la science politique à l'étude de la politique scientifique," dans Vincent Lemieux et Gordon Mace, *La science politique dans les sociétés contemporaines*. Montréal: ACFAS, 1985c, pp 63-88.

————, *Les priorités de la politique scientifique et technologique du Québec*. Rapport. Québec: Conseil de la Science et de la Technologie, 1984.

————, "Le contrôle parlementaire des politiques scientifiques à l'Assemblée nationale du Québec," *Revue parlementaire canadienne* nos. 3-4, 1980- 1981, pp 2-6.

————, "La recherche universitaire et les politiques gouvernementales en matière de recherche," dans *La politique de la recherche scientifique*.

Commission d'études sur l'avenir de l'Université Laval. Sainte-Foy: Université Laval, 1978, pp 65-72.

Langevin, Pierre, "Le virage technologique: le financement des entreprises," *Gestion* février 1983, pp 4-8.

Leblanc, Daniel, *Rapport de synthèse du sous-système de la science et de la technologie: Projet Québec 1995.* Québec: OPDQ/Editeur officiel du Québec, 1978.

———, *Un modèle d'évaluation technologique pour un système productif.* Québec: OPDQ/Editeur officiel, 1977.

———, *Application du modèle de substitution technologique à la prévision des coefficients de production dans le tableau des échanges industriels du Québec.* Montréal: Centre de développement technologique de l'Ecole Polytechnique, 1976.

Leclerc, Michel, *Recherche fondamentale, innovation et changement technologique,* Document de problématique présenté au Groupe de travail sur la recherche fondamentale dans le cadre des travaux préparatoire à la politique scientifique et technologique nationale. Québec: Ministère de l'Enseignement supérieur et de la Science, 1987.

———, *Recherche et développement universitaire et structure de l'effort sectoriel de recherche au Québec.* Québec: ENAP, 1986.

Lefrançois, Pierre C., "Le transfert international de la technologie et la PME québécoise," *Gestion* février 1978, pp 22-30.

Limoges, Camille, "De la politique des sciences à la politique de l'innovation," dans Michel Leclerc, réd., *Les enjeux actuels des politiques scientifiques et technologiques.* Montréal: Presses de l'Université du Québec, 1989, sous presse.

———, *La détermination des priorités dans le cadre d'une politique de l'innovation: Prolégomènes.* Rapport préparé pour le Conseil de la Science et de la Technologie. Québec: Gouvernement du Québec, 1989.

Limoges, Camille, Alberto Cambrosio et Denyse Pronovost, "La politique scientifique comme représentation construite en contexte bureaucratique," *Recherches sociographiques.* 1989, sous presse.

Maheu, Louis, Francine Descarries-Bélanger, Marcel Fournier et Claudette Richard, "La science au Québec francophone: aperçus sur son institutionnalisation et sur les conditions d'accès à sa pratique," *Revue canadienne de sociologie et d'anthropologie* Vol. 21, no. 3, 1984, pp 247-274.

Martin, Fernand, "Progrès technologique et structure industrielle régionale," *Actualité économique* Vol. 58, no. 3, 1982, pp 321-334.

———, *Progrès technologique et structure industrielle régionale,* Cahier no. 81-25. Montréal: Département des sciences économiques, Université de Montréal, 1981.

Martin, Fernand, *Comparaison interrégionale de la diffusion des innovations au Canada.* Ottawa: Conseil économique du Canada, 1979.

Ministère d'Etat au Développement économique, *Le Virage Technologique. Bâtir le Québec-Phase 2. Programme d'action économique 1982-1986.* Québec: Gouvernement du Québec, 1982.

Ministère du Commerce extérieur et du Développement technologique, *La maîtrise de notre avenir technologique, Un défi à relever*. Québec: Gouvernement du Québec, 1988.

Ministère du Conseil exécutif, *A l'heure des biotechnologies: Programme d'intervention pour le développement de la recherche en biotechnologies au Québec.* Québec: Gouvernement du Québec, 1982.

Pascot, Daniel et Wilson L. Price, "Le virage technologique: à propos des ressources humaines," *Gestion* Vol. 8, 1983, pp 15-18.

Plante, Marie, "L'industrie canadienne de la technologie avancée," *L'investisseur étranger* Vol. 5, no. 2, 1982, pp 4-7.

Richard, Claudette, Louis Maheu, en collaboration avec Francine Descarries-Bélanger, "La science au Québec francophone: enjeux de son développement et analyse de sa structure de postes scientifiques en biologie et en psychologie," *Revue canadienne de sociologie et d'anthropologie* Vol. 24, no. 1, 1987, pp 58-80.

Séguin-Dulude, Louise, "Les flux technologiques interindustriels: une analyse exploratoire de la situation canadienne," *L'actualité économique* Vol. 58, 1982, pp 259-281.

———, "L'activité inventive des Canadiens: une image de nos forces et de nos faiblesses technologiques," *Revue internationale de gestion* Vol. 6, no. 2, 1981, pp 64-70.

———, "L'effort consacré à la recherche et au développement: un facteur explicatif de la structure et de l'évolution des exportations des pays industrialisés," *L'actualité économique* Vol. 54, 1978, pp 21-45.

———, *Essai comparé sur l'approvisionnement technologique d'un secteur de pointe et d'un secteur à maturité,* Cahiers du CETAI, no. 84-05. Montréal: Ecole des Hautes études commerciales, 1984.

———, *La statistique des brevets et des utilisations possibles à titre d'indicateur,* Etude réalisée pour Statistique Canada. Ottawa: 1983.

Valaskakis, Kimon, "Information Society Project" 4 vols. Ottawa: Supply and Services Canada, 1979.

Le management de la technologie au niveau de la firme

Bellon, Bertrand et Jorge Niosi, *L'industrie américaine, Fin de siècle*. Montréal: Boréal Express, 1987.

Blais, Roger, "La recherche, le développement et l'innovation," dans Roger Miller, réd., *La direction des entreprises: concepts et applications*. Montréal: McGraw Hill, 1985.

Bruneau, J.G. et Robert J. Ménard, *Etude des infrastructures de télécommunication: incidence technologique.* Québec: Ministère des Communications, 1983.

Cambrosio, Alberto, Michael Mackenzie et Peter Keating, "The Commercial Application of a Scientific Discovery: the Case of the Hybridoma Technique," *Research policy* Vol. 17, 1988, pp 155-170.

Chica, Joseph et Pierre-André Julien, "Les stratégies des PME et leur adaptation" *au changement,* Laboratoire en économie et gestion des systèmes de petites dimensions, Rapport no. 80-05. Trois-Rivières: Université du

Québec à Trois-Rivières, 1980.

Conférences socio-économiques du Québec, *L'informatisation des entreprises et des administrations publiques*, Rapport de la Conférence sur l'électronique et l'informatique. Québec: Gouvernement du Québec, 1985.

Côté, Marcel, *Entrepreneurship and Economic Development*. Montréal: SECOR, 1985.

———, "Les premières années d'une PME technologique de pointe," *L'ingénieur* Vol. 65, no. 332, 1979, pp 19-27.

Dalpé, Robert, "La stratégie technologique de Bombardier," *Recherches sociographiques* Vol. 25, 1984, pp 167-187.

DeBresson, Christian, réd., *Le développement technologique au Canada* (à paraître).

———, "A l'ombre de la dynamo technologique," *Politique* no. 10, 1987, pp 55-90.

———, "Industrial Patterns in Early and Late Adoption of New Products in Canada" dans Conseil des Sciences du Canada, *The adoption of foreign technology by Canadian industry*. Ottawa: Science Council of Canada, 1981.

DeBresson, Christian et Brent Murray, *Innovation in Canada*. Vancouver: CRUST, 1983.

DeBresson, Christian, Brent Murray et Louise Brodeur, *L'Innovation au Québec*. Québec: Les publications du Québec, 1986.

Etamad, Hamid et Louise Séguin-Dulude, *R and D and Patenting Characteristics of Canadian World Product Mandated Subsidiaries*, Cahier du CETAI, Rapport n 84-14. Montréal: Ecole des Hautes études commerciales, 1984.

Fortin, André, "L'informatique, un outil de gestion," dans Françoise Poirier, réd., *La micro-informatique dans le travail et "l'éducation*, Actes du colloque organisé par l'Association des femmes diplomées des universités, avec la participation de l'Université Laval. Québec: 1982.

Gasse, Yvon, "Le processus d'adoption des nouvelles technologies par les PME," dans Pierre-André Julien, André Joyal et Joseph Chica, réd., *La PME dans un monde en mutation*. Québec: Presses de l'Université du Québec, 1986.

———, "L'adoption des nouvelles technologies: un défi majeur pour les PME," *Gestion* Vol. 8, 1983, pp 27-34.

Godard, Mario, Andrew Hugessen et Dominique Mascolo, "Vers" *une productivité accrue: la technologie et les PME*. Montréal: Centre d'innovation industrielle, 1982.

Groleau, André, "Le plan directeur des systèmes d'information: élément-clé pour une gestion optimale," *Administration hospitalière et sociale* juillet-août 1986, pp 6-10.

Hurtubise, Rolland-A. et Jean-Pierre Pastinelli, *L'information et les technologies dans l'organisation: l'implication de la haute direction*. Montréal: Agence d'Arc, 1987.

Institut national de productivité, *Les impacts de l'informatisation des méthodes de gestion et de production dans les petites et moyennes imprimeries du Québec*. Montréal: Institut National de Productivité, 1983.

Julien, Pierre-André, "L'impact des nouvelles technologies sur l'économie québécoise," *Interface* Vol. 7, no. 6, 1986.

————, *Incertitude, PME et informatique.* Trois-Rivières: GREPME, 1985.

Julien, Pierre-André, Jean-Bernard Carrière, Louis Hébert, *La diffusion des nouvelles technologies dans trois secteurs industriels.* Québec: Conseil de la Science et de la Technologie, 1988.

————, *Les facteurs de diffusion et de pénétration des nouvelles technologies dans l'industrie des produits de plastique.* Trois-Rivières: GREPME, 1987.

Julien, Pierre-André et Hébert, Louis, "Le rythme de pénétration des nouvelles technologies dans les PME manufacturières," *Journal of Small Business and Entrepreneurship* Vol. 3, no. 4, 1986, pp 24-35.

Julien, Pierre-André et Morel, B., *La belle entreprise.* Montréal: Boréal Express, 1986.

Julien, Pierre-André et Jean-Claude Thibodeau, réd., *Impact des nouvelles technologies sur la structure économique du Québec.* INRS-Urbanisation, UQTR-GREPME et INRS-Energie. [20 monographies]

Lafontaine, Francine, Fernand Amesse, et Louise Séguin-Dulude, *Essai comparé sur l'approvisionnement technologique d'un secteur de pointe et d'un secteur à maturité,* Cahiers du CETAI, nos. 84-85. Montréal: Ecole des Hautes études commerciales, 1984.

Lamoureux, Daniel, *L'introduction de technologies nouvelles dans l'entreprise: facteurs et conséquences.* Montréal: Institut national de productivité, 1983.

Lavoie, Gilles, *Les impacts de l'informatisation des méthodes de gestion et de production dans les petites et moyennes imprimeries.* Montréal: Institut national de productivité, 1983.

Lefebvre, Louis A., Elisabeth Lefebvre et Jean Ducharme, *L'introduction et l'utilisation de l'informatique dans les petites entreprises: Etude des perceptions et des attentes de leurs dirigeants,* Rapport MCC-CCRIT-87-A01. Ottawa: Ministère des communications, Conseil canadien de la recherche sur l'informatisation du travail, 1987a.

————, *L'introduction et l'utilisation de l'informatique dans les petites entreprises: Etude des perceptions et des attentes de leurs dirigeants. Sommaire.* Ville de Laval: Centre canadien de recherche sur l'informatisation du travail, 1987b.

————, "L'entreprise québécoise prend le virage informatique," *Le Devoir: Spécial informatique* Montréal, le 21 mars, 1986a, pp 9-11.

————, "L'informatique dans la moyenne et grande entreprise au Québec," *Revue internationale de gestion* septembre, 1986b, pp 23-26.

————, "Le taux d'informatisation de la petite entreprise québécoise," *Revue internationale de gestion* Vol. 11, no. 3, 1986c, pp 27-32.

————, *L'introduction et l'utilisation de l'informatique dans les petites entreprises: étude des perceptions et des attentes de leurs dirigeants.* Montréal: Centre de recherche en gestion, Université du Québec à Monréal, 1986d.

————, "L'entreprise québecoise à l'heure de l'informatique," *Le Pentagone* Vol. 14, no. 5, 1985a, pp 18- 19.

————, "Les entreprises québécoises et l'informatique: situation actuelle et perspectives futures," *Revue internationale de gestion* Vol. 10, no. 4, 1985b.

Lefebvre, Louis-A. et Elisabeth Lefebvre, "L'entreprise innovatrice. Un regard vers demain," *L'actualité économique* Vol. 63, no. 1, 1987, pp 53-76.

L'Heureux, Richard, "Considérations sur les transferts technologiques et le rôle des sociétés-conseils," *L'Economiste* Vol. 4, no. 2, 1979, pp 38-41.

Longchamps, Gaétan et al., *L'introduction des nouvelles technologies dans les usines de transformation du poisson: le cas de Pêcheries Cartier,* Rapport déposé auprès de la Fédération du Commerce, CSN, s.d.

Martin, Fernand, *La localisation de l'industrie pharmaceutique au Canada,* Rapport à la Commission d'enquête sur l'industrie pharmaceutique. Ottawa: Approvisionnement et services, 1985.

————, "Progrès technologique et structure industrielle régionale," *Actualité économique* Vol. 58, no. 3, 1982, pp 321-334.

Miller, Roger, *La gestion de la technologie,* Montréal: Université du Québec à Montréal, 1988.

Miller, R., réd., *La direction des entreprises: concepts et applications.* Montréal: McGraw Hill, 1985.

————, "L'émergence des firmes de haute technologie," *Gestion* Vol. 8, 1983, pp 38-47.

————, "The Process of Emergence of High-Technology Firms." Cambridge, Mass.: Harvard University Consortium for Research on North America, 1983.

————, *La stratégie de la PME et la technologie.* Montréal: Centre d'innovation industrielle, 1982.

Miller, Roger et Marcel Côté, "Growing the Next Silicon Valley," *Harvard Business Review* Vol. 63, no. 4. 1985.

Miller, Roger et Roderick J. MacDonald, "La technologie et la stratégie de l'entreprise," *L'ingénieur* Vol. 71, 1985, pp 17-24.

Niosi, Jorge, *Canadian Multinationals.* Toronto: Between the Lines, 1985.

Paquette, Michel, "Les contrats de cession et de licence en droit des brevets d'invention," *Revue juridique Thémis* Vol. 10, no. 1, 1985, pp 107-136.

Pasquero, Jean, "L'entreprise technologique et le processus d'innovation," *L'ingénieur* Vol. 65, no. 332, 1979, pp 11-18.

Pichette, Serge, *Concepts et techniques de négociation lors de transferts de technologie: brevets d'invention et "know-how."* Montréal: Ecole des Hautes études commerciales, 1981a.

————, *La propriété industrielle: régime canadien et systèmes internationaux de protection.* Montréal: Ecole des Hautes études commerciales, 1981.

————, *Les perspectives de coopération industrielle entre le Canada et le Tiers-Monde. La coopération technique et les transferts de technologie.* Montréal: Ecole des Hautes études commerciales, 1979a.

————, *Problèmes juridiques de transfert de technologie.* Montréal: Ecole des Hautes études commerciales, 1979b.

————, *Le régime canadien de la propriété intellectuelle.* Montréal: Ecole des Hautes études commerciales, 1979c.

Primeau, Raymond, "Le secteur industriel québecois et la technologie," *L'ingénieur* Vol. 67, no. 342, 1981, pp 35-41.

Proulx, Gilles, *Le changement technologique dans votre entreprise.* Montréal:

Institut national de productivité, 1984.

Raymond, Louis, *Problématique des systèmes d'information en contexte de la PME*, Communication présentée au congrès de l'ASAC, Ottawa, Université d'Ottawa, 1982.

Raymond, Louis et Nadia Magnenat-Thalmann, *Information Systems in Small Business: are they Used in Managerial Decisions?* Rapport de recherche no. 81-05. Montréal: Ecole des Hautes études commerciales, 1981.

SECOR, *Etude des opportunités et de la stratégie de développement de l'industrie du logiciel au Québec*. Québec: Ministère des Communications, 1985.

Wybouw, George, Richard Kanaan, Sylvie Blais et al., *La bureautique et la productivité: revue de la littérature*, Rapport MDC-CCRIT-DLR-86/7-006. Ottawa: Ministère des Communications, Centre canadien sur l'informatisation du travail, 1986.

Impact sur le travail et les personnes

Allie, Emile, *L'impact des nouvelles technologies: la radio-diffusion et la téléphonie.* Trois-Rivières: GREPME, 1987a.

―――, *L'impact des nouvelles technologies: la construction.* Trois-Rivières: GREPME, 1987b.

Alsène, Eric, "Le changement technologique en entreprise," *Technologie de l'information et société* Vol. 1, no. 1, 1988, pp 91-108.

Ardouin, Pierre, *L'évolution de l'informatique et ses impacts sur le travail et les travailleurs*, Rapport de recherche no. RR8201. Ste-Foy: Université Laval, Département d'informatique, 1982.

Bégin, C., *Les attributs de l'organisation et de la gestion du travail et la sécurité dans les mines de métaux au Québec*, Rapport de recherche. Ste-Foy: Université Laval, GIROSST, 1987.

Benoit, Carmelle, "L'influence de la machine à traitement de textes sur l'emploi et le travail," *Cahiers de recherche sociologique* Vol. 3, no. 2, 1985, pp 99-115.

Benoit, Carmelle et Jacques Brutus, "L'impact de la machine-outil à commande numérique sur l'organisation du travail et les conditions de travail," *Le marché du travail* Vol. 8, no. 5, 1987, pp 62-68.

Benoit, Carmelle, *L'incidence de la machine à traitement de texte sur l'emploi et le travail*. Montréal: Ministère de la Main d'oeuvre et de la Sécurité du Revenu et Ministère du Travail, 1984.

Bernier, Colette, "Nouvelles technologies: requalification ou déqualification du travail? Bilan critique des études," *Interventions économiques* no. 12-13, 1984, pp 137-152.

Bernier, Colette et Catherine Cailloux-Teiger, *Nouvelles technologies: qualifications et formation. Les emplois de soutien dans le secteur de l'éducation.* Montréal: Institut de recherche appliquée sur le travail, 1988.

Bernier, Colette, *Nouvelles technologies et caractéristiques du travail: Bilan-synthèse des connaissances*. Montréal: Institut de recherche appliquée sur le travail et Institut national de productivité, 1983.

Billette, André, "Les systèmes flexibles de fabrication annoncent-ils la fin de la division parcellaire du travail?" *Sociologie et Sociétés* Vol. 16, no. 1, 1984, pp 149-150.

Billette, André et Jacques Piché, *Travailler comme des robots*. Montréal: Presses de l'Université du Québec, 1986.

————, "Problématique sur l'évolution de l'informatique et de l'organisation du travail" dans Claude Bariteau, Michel De Sève, Danielle Laberge et André Turmel, réd., *Le contrôle social en pièces détachées*. Montréal: ACFAS, 1985, pp 197-203.

————, *Travail et informatique, le cas des auxiliaires en saisie de données*. Sainte-Foy: Université Laval, Département de sociologie, 1985b.

Bisson, Louise, *Les effets des changements technologiques sur le travail des femmes*. Québec: Conseil du statut de la femme, 1986.

Blais, Linda, *Les impacts de la technologie de l'information*. Québec: Ministère des Communications, 1983.

Blondin, Andre, *Les répercussions socio-humaines de l'implantation d'un système de bureautique intégré*, Projet de recherche présenté à Travail Canada, Fonds de recherche sur les répercussions des changements technologiques. Québec: Ecole nationale d'administration publique, 1985.

Carpentier, Renée, *Les nouvelles technologies et le travail salarié des femmes*. Québec: Conseil du statut de la femme et Centrale de l'enseignement du Québec, 1983.

Centrale de l'enseignement du Québec, *Apprivoiser le changement*. Actes du colloque CEQ sur les nouvelles technologies, la division du travail, la formation et l'emploi, Québec, 1985.

Centrale des syndicats démocratiques, *Partenaires du virage technologique, un droit! un défi!* Québec: 1986.

————, *Technologies nouvelles*. Québec: 1983.

Chaumel, Jean-Louis, "Face aux changements technologiques sans précédent des années 80: l'ingénieur, son rôle, sa formation," *L'ingénieur* Vol. 66, no. 338, 1980, pp 3-6.

Clermont, Michel, *Informatique et emploi*. Québec: Ministère des Communications, 1983.

Conférences socio-économiques du Québec, *L'informatisation, l'emploi et le travail*, Rapport de la Conférence sur l'électronique et l'informatique. Québec: Gouvernement du Québec, 1985.

Conseil supérieur de l'Education, *Le perfectionnement de la main-d'oeuvre au Québec: Des enjeux pour le système d'éducation*. Québec: Gouvernement du Québec, 1987.

Cossette, Alfred, "Les emplois nouveaux: la micro-électronique et l'emploi," *Le marché du travail* Vol. 3, no. 3, 1982, pp 49-58.

Cossette, Alfred et Emmanuel Nyahoho, "L'incidence de la machine à traitement de texte sur l'emploi et le travail," *Le marché du travail* Vol. 5, no. 5, 1984, pp 67-74.

De Koninck, Diane, "Nouvelles technologies et nouveaux modèles de gestion dans l'industrie nord-américaine de l'automobile" dans Diane Tremblay, réd., *Diffusion des nouvelles technologies*. Montréal: Editions St-Martin., 1987,

Denis, Hélène et Eric Alsène, *Changement technologique et organisation dans une entreprise d'assemblage,* Rapport technique EPM/RT-88/19. Montréal: Ecole Polytechnique, 1988.

————, *Changement technologique et organisation dans une industrie de process,* Rapport technique EPM/RT-87-50. Montréal: Ecole Polytechnique, 1987.

De Sève, Monique, "Travail et nouvelles technologies dans la production télévisuelle," *Cahiers de recherche sociologique* Vol. 3, no. 2, 1985, pp 117-131.

Desjardins, André, *Les changements technologiques, Recueil de clauses-types.* Quebec: Centre de recherche et de statistiques sur le marché du travail, 1985.

Doray, Pierre, "Qualifications et contributions ouvrières: une critique de la qualification chez Braverman," dans Chris DeBresson, Margaret Lowe Benston and Jesse Vorst, *Work and New Technologies: Other Perspectives.* Toronto: Between the Lines, 1987, pp 110-122.

Doray, Pierre et Alberto Cambrosio, "Du robot à l'ordinique, en passant par la bureautique: espaces discursifs, découpages institutionnels," dans Khadya Toulah Fall et Georges Vigneau, réd., *L'informatique en perspective.* Montréal: Presses de l'Université du Québec, 1989, pp 73-88.

Doray, Pierre et Claude Dubar, "Structure de la formation post-scolaire: une comparaison entre la France et le Québec," *Education permanente,* 1988, pp 39-52.

Doray, Pierre et François Lapointe, *Adaptation de la main-d'oeuvre et changements technologiques,* Rapport préparé pour le Conseil de la science et de la technologie. Québec: 1988.

Dumas, Marie-Claire, *Les femmes et l'informatisation: Bilan et pistes pour un programme d'intervention,* Rapport MDC-CCRIT-DLR-85/6-032. Ottawa: Ministère des communications, Centre canadien de recherche sur l'informatisation du travail, 1985.

Fédération des travailleurs du Québec, *Pour un progrès sans victime,* Document de consultation, Montréal, 1985a.

Fédération des travailleurs du Québec, *Pour un progrès sans victime,* Rapport de sondage, Montréal, 1985b.

Frappier-DesRochers, Monique, " La microinformatique, son importance et l'emploi," dans Françoise Poirier, réd., *La microinformatique dans le travail et l'éducation.* Actes du Colloque organisé par l'Association des femmes diplomées des universités, avec la participation de l'Université Laval, Québec, 1982.

Frappier-DesRochers, Monique, *Rapport final du Bureau de coordination de la recherche sur les impacts de l'informatisation sur le travail et l'emploi.* Québec: Ministère de l'Enseignement supérieur et de la science, 1986.

Groupe de recherche et d'étude sur la technique et la société (GRETS), *Etude des modifications des programmes de formation entrainées dans les métiers de l'imprimerie par les changements de la technologie dans les années 80.* Montréal: Université du Québec à Montréal, 1981.

Groupe de recherche sur l'informatisation de la société (GRIS), *L'informatique et ses impacts socio-professionnels, le cas de la fonction publique,* 4 vols. Québec:

Université Laval, Faculté des sciences sociales, 1987.

Hébert, Louis, *L'impact des nouvelles technologies: les teneurs de livres et commis-comptables*. Trois-Rivières: GREPME, 1986.

———, *L'impact des nouvelles technologies: les téléphonistes et réceptionnistes*. Trois-Rivières: GREPME, 1986.

Hébert, Louis et Jean Lorrain, *Les sténodactylos*. Trois-Rivières: INRS-Urbanisation/GREPME-UQTR, 1987.

Hurtubise, Rolland-A., *La bureautique: éléments et impacts*. Montréal: Agence d'Arc, 1983.

———, "Les impacts possibles de la bureautique," *L'analyste* automne, 1987, pp 63-65.

Institut canadien d'éducation des adultes, *Négocier le virage technologique: Actes du colloque sur la télématique*. Montréal: Centrale de l'enseignement du Québec et Institut canadien d'éducation des adultes, 1983.

Institut de recherche en santé et sécurité du travail, *La rémunération au rendement et la sécurité du travail:recherche synthèse*. Montréal: Institut de recherche en santé et sécurité du travail, s.d.

———, *Rapport du groupe de travail sur les terminaux à écran de visualisation et la santé des travailleurs*. Montréal: Institut de recherche en santé et sécurité du travail, 1984.

Institut national de productivité, *Technologie et travail*, Rapport d'un colloque. Montréal: Institut national de productivité, 1983.

———, *Introduction de nouvelles technologies et effets sur l'emploi: un inventaire de stratégies nationales*. Montréal: Institut national de productivité, s.d.

Jacob, Réal, *L'impact des nouvelles technologies: le commerce de détail*. Trois-Rivières: GREPME, 1986.

———, "Les applications de la micro-électronique en contexte manufacturier et leur impact sur le travailleur: une question de qualité de vie," *La revue québécoise de psychologie* Vol. 4, no. 3, 1983, pp 74-94.

Jacob, Réal et Jean Lorrain, *Etude descriptive sur l'impact du traitement de texte sur la qualité de la vie au travail tel que perçu par le personnel de soutien administratif d'une organisation publique* Trois-Rivières: Université du Québec à Trois-Rivières, Laboratoire en économie et gestion des systèmes de petites dimensions, 1985.

Julien, Pierre-André, *Les institutions d'épargne et de crédit*. Trois-Rivières: INRS-Urbanisation/GREPME-UQTR, 1987a.

———, *L'impact des nouvelles technologies: les ingénieurs*. Trois-Rivières: GREPME, 1987b.

———, *L'impact des nouvelles technologies: l'enseignement et les bibliotheques*. Trois-Rivières: GREPME, 1986.

———, *L'impact des nouvelles technologies: l'hôtellerie et la restauration*. Trois-Rivières: GREPME, 1985a.

———, *L'impact des nouvelles technologies: les assurances*. Trois-Rivières: GREPME, 1985b.

———, "Nouvelles technologies, mutations socio-économiques et emplois," *Etudes d'économie politique* no. 1, 1984, pp 131-138.

————, "Travail et non-travail dans un Québec micro-informatisé," *Gestion* Vol. 8, no. 3, 1983, pp 35-40.

Julien, Pierrre-André et Louis Hébert, *L'impact des nouvelles technologies: la bureautique.* Trois-Rivières: GREPME, 1987.

Julien, Pierre-André et Samir Billi, *L'impact des nouvelles technologies: le commerce de gros.* Trois-Rivières: GREPME, 1987.

Julien, Pierre-André, Réal Jacob et Jean Lorrain, *L'impact des nouvelles technologies: la santé et les services sociaux.* Trois-Rivières: GREPME, 1985.

Julien, Pierre-André, Jean-Claude Thibodeau et Georges Mathews, "Les nouvelles technologies et l'emploi au Québec," *L'actualité économique* Vol. 60, no. 3, 1984.

Julien, Pierre-André, *Les nouvelles technologies et l'emploi au Québec,* Rapport préparé pour le compte du Bureau de la statistique du Québec. Trois-Rivières: GREPME, 1983.

Lacerte, Denis, *L'impact des nouvelles technologies: le transport.* Trois-Rivières: GREPME, 1985.

Lalonde, Francine et Richard Parent, "Les enjeux sociaux de l'informatisation," *Sociologie et sociétés* Vol. XVI, 1984, pp 59-69.

Larocque, Alain et al., *Technologies nouvelles et aspects psychologiques.* Québec: Presses de l'Université du Québec, 1987.

Lefebvre, Louis A., Elisabeth Lefebvre, Jean Ducharme et Dominique Colin, "L'impact de la technologie informatique sur la main d'oeuvre dans les organisations," *L'actualité économique* Vol. 62, 1986, pp 447-578.

Legendre, Camille, "Technologies et organisation: les voies de la liberté" dans Colette Bernier et al., réd., *Travailler au Québec: Actes du colloque de l'A.C.S.A.L.F.* Montréal: Editions Coopératives Albert Saint-Martin, 1981, pp 361-374.

Lescarbeault, Gérard, *Impact de la robotique sur les milieux de travail: économie, organisation du travail, effet sur la santé et la sécurité des travailleurs.* Montréal: Institut de recherche en santé et sécurité du travail, 1986.

Lorrain, Jean, *L'impact des nouvelles technologies: les comptables.* Trois-Rivières: GREPME, 1987.

Lyrette, Jacques, *Informatisation: le début d'une nouvelle ère dans le lieu de travail.* Ville de Laval: Centre canadien de recherche sur l'informatisation du travail, 1986.

Martineau, Yvon, *Fabrication de machines.* Trois-Rivières: INRS-Urbanisation/GREPME, 1987.

McNeil, Jeannine, "Concilier les objectifs d'efficacité et les besoins socio-économiques des travailleurs et travailleuses: défi de l'informatisation des organisations" *Les répercussions de l'informatisation en milieu de travail,* Actes du Symposium international à l'Hotel Quatre-Saisons, Montréal, 1985.

————, "La micro-électronique, l'emploi et la qualité de vie au travail," dans Françoise Poirier et al., réd., *La micro-informatique dans le travail et l'éducation,* Actes du Colloque organisé par l'Association des femmes diplomées des universités, avec la participation de l'Université Laval, Québec, 1982.

Ministère de l'Education, *Les carrières à l'aube des années 1990.* Québec:

Gouvernement du Québec, 1987.

Morin, Maria, "Adaptation aux changement apportés par la nouvelle technologie," dans Françoise Poirier, réd., *La micro-informatique dans le travail et l'éducation,* Actes du Colloque organisé par l'organisation des femmes diplomées des universités, avec la participation de l'université Laval, Québec, 1982.

Nyaoho, Emmanuel, "Impact des changements technologiques dans des secteurs d'activité économique du Québec et évolution structurelle de l'emploi," *Le marché du travail* Vol. 7, no. 5, 1986, pp 58-75.

———, *L'état des recherches sur les impacts socio-économiques des nouvelles technologies au Québec.* Québec: Ministère de la Main-d'oeuvre et de la Sécurité du Revenu, 1983.

Office des professions du Québec, *La révolution informatique et la pratique professionnelle.* Québec: Gouvernement du Québec, 1986.

Parent, Richard et Guy Frechet, *L'informatique chez les professionnels du gouvernement du Québec.* Québec: Université Laval, GRIS, 1985.

Paquin, Michel et Pierre Voyer, *Les impacts de le bureautique: un état de la question.* Montréal: Ecole nationale d'administration publique, 1987.

Pichette, Michel, "Quelques enjeux de la révolution de l'information et de la communication en éducation," *Sociologie et Sociétés* Vol. 16, no. 1, 1984, pp 115-123.

Pinard, Rollande et Thierry Rousseau, "Procès de travail et informatisation dans les assurances et les banques au Québec," *Cahiers de recherche sociologique* Vol. 3, no. 2, 1985, pp 25-55.

Raymond, Louis, "The Impact of Computer Training on the Attitudes and Usage Behavior of Small Business Management," *Journal of Small Business Management* Vol. 26, no. 3, 1988, pp 8-13.

Richard, Pierre, Thierry Rousseau, et Micheline Séguin, *Etude sur les modes d'introduction des changements technologiques dans l'industrie du bois au Québec.* Montréal: Fédération des travailleurs du Québec, 1987.

Rose-Lizée, R., "Technologie et travail à domicile dans l'industrie du vêtement," dans *Apprivoiser le changement,* Actes du colloque de la CEQ sur les nouvelles technologies, la division du travail, la formation et l'emploi. Québec: Centrale de l'enseignement du Québec, 1985, pp 84-95.

Roy, Denis, "Les attitudes des secrétaires face à la machine à traitement de textes," *Gestion* Vol. 8, 1983, pp 101-114.

Saint-Pierre, Céline, "Le tertiaire en mouvement: bureautique et organisation du travail. Itinéraire d'une recherche," dans Diane Tremblay, réd., *Diffusion des nouvelles technologies, stratégies d'entreprises et évaluation sociale.* Montréal: Editions Saint-Martin, 1987, pp 185-198.

———, "Enjeux et défis du virage technologique en milieux de travail," *Cahiers de recherche sociologiques* Vol. 3, no. 2, 1985a, pp 9-25.

———, "Informatisation et disciplinarisation du travail: du fouet au logiciel en passant par l'OST," dans Claude Bariteau, Michel De Sève, Danièle Laberge et André Turmel, réd., *Le contrôle social en pièces détachées.* Montréal: Les cahiers de l'Acfas, no. 30, 1985b, pp 33-47.

————, "Nouvelles technologies, nouvelles inégalités," Actes du colloque *Apprivoiser le changement*, Montréal: Centrale de l'enseignement du Québec, 1985c, pp 434-439.

————, "Les robots ne sont pas tous d'acier: l'impact de la micro-électronique sur l'organisation du travail dans le secteur tertiaire," *Sociologie et sociétés* Vol. 16, no. 1, 1984a, pp 71-80.

————, "Le secteur tertiaire à l'heure du virage technologique: restructuration du marché du travail et recomposition de la force de travail," dans *Les stratégies de reprise*. Montréal: Editions Saint-Martin, 1984b, pp 101-112.

————, "Micro-électronique et réorganisation du travail dans le secteur tertiaire," dans Françoise Poirier et al., réd., *La micro-informatique dans le travail et l'éducation*, Actes du Colloque organisé par l'Association des femmes diplomées des universités, avec la participation de l'Université Laval, Québec, 1982.

Teiger, Catherine et Colette Bernier, "Informatique et qualifications: les compétences masquées," dans Diane Tremblay, réd., *Diffusion des nouvelles technologies, stratégies d'entreprises et évaluation sociale*. Montréal: Editions Saint-Martin, 1987, pp 255-267.

Tremblay, Diane, "L'articulation travail-technique et les stratégies d'entreprises: réflexion fondée sur le cas des banques," dans Diane Tremblay, réd., *Diffusion des nouvelles technologies*. Montréal: Editions Saint-Martin, 1987, pp 67-85.

Vallée, Guylaine, *Les changements technologiques et le travail au Québec; un état de situation*. Québec: 1986.

La régulation de la technologie

Archer, André, *Situation et impacts des effets technologiques sur l'agriculture au Québec*. Trois-Rivières: GREPME, 1979.

Babin, Ronald, *L'option nucléaire*. Montréal: Boréal Express, 1984.

Bernard, Paul et Louis Maheu, "Les sciences sociales et les transformations technologiques: confrontation de perspectives," dans Paul Bernard et Edouard Cloutier, *Sciences sociales et transformations technologiques*. Québec: Conseil de la science et de la technologie, 1987, pp 9-30.

Bernier, Michel et al., *Les aspects culturels de la téléinformatique au Québec*, Rapport préparé pour le ministère des Affaires culturelles. Québec: Gouvernement du Québec, 1976.

Cambrosio, Alberto et François Blanchard, "Disaligning Macro, Meso and Micro Due Process: A Case Study of Office Automation in Quebec Colleges," dans R.B. Allen, réd., *Conference on Office Information Systems*. New York: Association for Computing Machinery, 1988, pp 118-125.

Cambrosio, Alberto et Camille Limoges, "La controverse, processus-clé de l'évaluation sociale des technologies," dans C. Limoges, réd., *Analyse évaluative et évaluation sociale des technologies*. Montréal: sous presse.

Carter, R., *La déréglementation des communications aux Etats-Unis: son impact effectif et potentiel sur la réglementation canadienne et québécoise*, Rapport préparé pour le Ministère des Communications. Québec: Gouvernmement du Québec, 1982.

Chabbal, Robert, Ugo Businaro, René Bryssinck, Michael Gibbons, Morten Knudsen, Camille Limoges, et Albrecht Matuschka, *Evaluation of the Community Programme on Forecasting and Assessment in the Field of Science and Technology-FAST (1983-1987)*. Bruxelles: Commission des Communautés économiques européennes, 1988.

Denis, Hélène, *La gestion de catastrophe: le cas d'un accident dans un entrepôt de BPC à Saint-Basile-le-Grand*, Rapport commandité par le Bureau de la Protection civile du Québec et présenté au Comité de protection civile provincial, Montréal, Ecole Polytechnique, 1989.

———, *Technologie et société. Essai d'analyse systémique*. Montréal: Editions de l'Ecole Polytechnique, 1987.

Grandbois, M., "Les récents développements de la jurisprudence québécoise: chronique de droit de l'environnement," *Revue du Barreau* Vol. 46, no. 4, 1986, pp 466-473.

———, "Le contrôle juridique des précipitations acides," *Cahiers de droit* Vol. 26, no. 3, 1985, pp 591-632.

Groupe de recherche en informatique et droit [GRID], *L'identité piratée*. Montréal: Société québécoise d'information juridique, 1986.

IRSST, *L'inégalité des risques affectant la sécurité des travailleurs par secteur d'activité économique*. Montréal: Institut de recherche en santé et sécurité du travail, s.d.

Kaufmann, "L'évaluation sociale des technologies: pour une éthique du risque," *Technologies de l'information et société* Vol. 1, no. 1, 1988, pp 41-56.

Knoppers, Jake V. T., *Sécurité des données en bureautique*, Rapport MCC-CCRIT-87-F-C03. Ville de Laval: Centre canadien de recherche sur l'informatisation du travail, 1987.

Lacroix, J-G et B. Lévesque, "Emergence et institutionnalisation de la recherche en communication au Québec," *Communication information* Vol. 7, no. 2, 1985, pp 7-23.

Lalonde, Francine et Richard Parent, "Les enjeux sociaux de l'informatisation," *Sociologie et Sociétés* Vol. 16, no. 1, 1984.

Lemasson, Jean-Pierre, J. Martin, P. Péladeau et René Laperrière, *Les renseignements personnels et l'ordinateur: Enquête sur la situation des bases de données à caractère personnel dans le secteur privé québécois*. Montréal: Société québécoise d'Information juridique, 1986.

Limoges, Camille, "Ethique médicale et évaluation sociale des technologies," dans Claire Ambroselli, réd., *Ethique médicale et droits de l'homme*. Paris: Actes Sud / Inserm, 1988a, pp 307-312.

———, "Analyse évaluative et évaluation sociale des technologies: une pragmatique sociale," dans Anita Caron et André Michaud, réd., *Recueil des activités CREST*. Montréal: Université du Québec à Montréal, 1988b, pp 259-279.

———, "De la technologie comme objet problématique à l'évaluation sociale des technologies" dans Diane Tremblay, réd., *Diffusion des nouvelles technologies. Stratégies d'entreprises et évaluation sociale*. Montréal: Editions

Saint-Martin, 1987, pp 169-184.

Limoges, Camille, Alberto Cambrosio, Eric Hoffman, Denyse Pronovost, Dominique Charron, Stéphane Castonguay et Eric Francoeur, "Controversies over Risks in Biotechnology (1973-1989): A Framework of Analysis," *Proceedings of the International Specialty Conference on Managing Environmental Risks,* 1989a, sous presse.

Limoges, Camille, Alberto Cambrosio, Frances Anderson, Denyse Pronovost, Dominique Charron, Eric Francoeur et Eric Hoffman, "A Public Assault on Biotechnology? Accounting for the Controversy over the Environmental Release of Genetically Engineered Organisms," dans Georges Ferné et Everett Mendelsohn, réd., *Science, Technology and Social Change. Questioning and Assessment.* New York: Reidel, 1989b, sous presse.

Maheu, Louis et Henri Beauchemin, "Les sociologies de la technologie: des trouvailles certaines et de nombreux problèmes," dans Paul Bernard et Edouard Cloutier, réd., *Sciences sociales et transformations technologiques.* Québec: Conseil de la Science et de la Technologie, 1987, pp 83-133.

Péladeau, Pierrôt, "L'informatique ordinatrice du droit et du procès d'information relatif aux personnes," *Technologies de l'information et société* Vol. 1, no. 3, 1989, pp 35-56.

Proulx, Serge, "L'appropriation de la culture informatique dans une société d'information," dans Serge Proulx, réd., *Vivre avec l'ordinateur: les usagers de la micro-informatique.* Montréal: Editions G. Vermette, 1988, pp 144-160.

Proulx, Serge, M. Levesque, D. Sanderson et M.-B. Tahon, *La Puce communautaire: Evaluation sociale d'une expérience d'éducation populaire avec l'informatique.* Québec: Ministère de l'Enseignement supérieur et de la Science, 1989.

Proulx, Serge et Marie-Blanche Tahon, "'La machine infernale': L'expression des peurs chez des usagers de la micro-informatique," *Technologies de l'information et société* Vol. 1, no. 3, 1989, pp 71-91.

———, "Micro: travailler tout le temps," *Terminal* no. 30, 1986, pp 7-15.

Tremblay, Gaétan, "Politiques canadiennes et québécoises concernant les nouvelles technologies de communication," *Bulletin de l'IDATE* no. 13, 1983, pp 30-37.

Tremblay, Gaétan et Michel Sénécal, "La science des communications et le phénomène technique," dans Paul Bernard et Edouard Cloutier, réd., *Sciences sociales et transformations technologiques.* Québec: Conseil de la Science et de la Technologie, 1987, pp 143-194.

Chapter Four

The Management of Innovation

Abbott, Mark, "The Need For Education in Management of Technology in Canada," *ASAC Proceedings,* Halifax: 1988a.

———, *Research and Education in Technology Management: Canada's Program,*

Paper presented to the First International Conference on Technology Management, Miami: 1988b.

———, "Managing Technology and Innovation," *Canadian Business Review,* Vol. 14, no. 3, 1987.

Badaway, Michael K., "Managing Human Resources," *Research Technology Management,* Vol. 31, no. 5, September-October 1988.

Barnhill, Al, Urs E. Gattiker and Daniel Lynn, "Marketing and Market Development Activities of High Technology Companies in Canada," *ASAC Proceedings,* Vol. 7, 1986.

Bart, Christopher K., "New Venture Units: Organizing for New Products," *NCMRD Working Paper Series,* no. 87-19, 1987a.

———, "Budgeting Gamesmanship: Survival Tactics in a Hostile Environment," *NCMRD Working Paper Series,* no. 87-20, 1987b.

Beatty, Carol A., *The Implementation of Technological Change.* Research and Current Issues Series no. 49, Industrial Relations Centre, Kingston: Queen's University, 1987.

———, "Promoting Productivity with CAD," *NCMRD Working Paper Series,* no. 86-05, 1986.

Beatty, Carol A. and John R.M. Gordon, "Organizational Barriers to the Implementation of CAD/CAM," *NCMRD Working Paper Series,* no. 87-17, 1987a.

———, "The High Priests of New Technology," *NCMRD Working Paper Series,* no. 87-25, 1987b.

Bennett, R.C. and Robert G. Cooper, "The Product Life Cycle Trap," *Business Horizons,* Vol. 27, September-October 1984.

Boag, David, "Marketing Control and Performance in Early-Growth Companies," *Journal of Business Venturing,* Vol. 2, 1987.

———, "The Design of Marketing Systems in Technology Intensive Manufacturing Companies," in Callahan and Haines.

Boag, David A. and Hugh J. Munro, "Analysis of Marketing Activities in High Technology Manufacturing Companies," *ASAC Proceedings,* Vol. 7, 1986.

Callahan, John R. and George H. Haines, *Managing High Technology, Vol. 1—Decisions for Success.* Ottawa: Research Center for High Technology Management, Carleton University, 1986.

Clark, Peter and Christian DeBresson, "Organizational Transitions and Sector Technology Life Cycle Models Applied to Car Firms: Rover (1896-1987)," *ASAC Proceedings,* Vol. 8, 1987.

Clarke, Thomas E. and Jean Reavley, "Problems Faced by R&D Managers in Canadian Federal Government Laboratories," *R&D Management,* Vol. 18, no. 1, 1988.

———, *Educating Technological Innovators and Technical Entrepreneurs at Canadian Universities.* Science Council of Canada Discussion Paper. Ottawa: Supply and Services Canada, 1987.

Conklin, David W. and France St-Hilaire, *Canadian High-Tech in a New World Economy: A Case Study of Information Technology.* Halifax: Institute for Research on Public Policy, 1988.

Cooper, Robert G., "The New Product Process: A Decision Guide for Management," *Journal of Marketing Management* Vol. 3, 1988.

———, *Winning at New Products*. Toronto: Holt, Rinehart and Winston of Canada Ltd., 1986.

———, "Overall Corporate Strategies for New Product Programs," *Industrial Marketing Management* Vol. 14, 1985a.

———, "Selecting Winning New Product Projects: Using the NewProd System," *Journal of Product Innovation Management* Vol. 2, 1985b.

———, "Industrial Firms' New Product Strategies," *Journal of Business Research* Vol. 13, 1985c.

———, "The Performance Impact of Product Innovation Strategies," *European Journal of Marketing* Vol. 18, 1985d.

———, "How New Product Strategies Impact on Performance," *Journal of Product Innovation Management* Vol. 1, 1984a.

———, "New Product Strategies: What Distinguishes the Top Performers," *Journal of Product Innovation Management* Vol. 2, 1984b.

Cooper, Robert G. and Elko J. Kleinschmidt, "New Products: What Separates Winners from Losers?" *Journal of Product Innovation Management* Vol. 4, 1987.

———, "An Investigation into the New Product Process: Steps, Deficiencies, and Impact," *Journal of Product Innovation Management* Vol. 3, 1986.

Cunningham, J.B. and T.H. White, eds., *QWL-Contemporary Cases*. Ottawa: Labour Canada, 1984.

Culver, David M., *Managing Technological Change*, Speech presented to the National Conference on Technology and Innovation. Toronto, 14 January 1988.

DeBresson, Christian and Joseph Lampel, "Beyond the Life Cycle. I. Organizational and Technological Design: An Alternative Perspective," *Journal of Product Innovation Management* Vol. 3, 1985a.

———, "Beyond the Life Cycle. II. An Illustration," *Journal of Product Innovation Management* Vol. 3, 1985b.

Dermer, Jerry, "Introduction." *Competitiveness Through Technology: What Business Needs From Government*. Lexington Mass. and Toronto: Lexington Books, 1986.

———, "Growing Canada's Threshold Technology-Producing Firms," *Business Quarterly* Vol. 49, 1984.

Doutriaux, Jerome, "Government Support of High Tech Entrepreneurial Firms at Start-up," *University of Ottawa Administration Working Paper*, no. 88-1, 1988a.

———, "Government Procurement and Research Contracts at Start-up and Success of Canadian High-Tech Entrepreneurial Firms," *University of Ottawa Administration Working Paper*, no. 88-22, 1988b.

Doutriaux, Jerome and Farhad Simyar, "Export Strategy and Success of High Tech Firms," *University of Ottawa Administration Working Paper*, no. 88-19, 1988.

Economic Council of Canada, *Innovation and Jobs in Canada*. Ottawa: Supply and Services Canada, 1987.

Ellis, Ned and David Waite, *Canadian Technological Output in a World Context,* in McFetridge.

Etemad, Hamid, "International Marketing at the Crossroads: The New Technologies and Strategies of the Past," *ASAC Proceedings,* Vol. 7, 1985.

Etemad, Hamid and Louise Seguin Delude, "The Development of Technology in the MNEs: A Cross-Country and Industry Study," in Safarian and Bertin, 1987.

———, "R&D And Patenting Patterns in 25 Large Multinational Enterprises," *ASAC Proceedings,* "International Business" Vol. 6, 1985.

Evans, M.G. and D.A. Ondrack, *The QWL Program at Petrochemicals Ltd.* Ottawa: Labour Canada, 1983.

Fauman, Bruce C. and Doyle W. Weiss, "What High Technology Managers Can Learn from the Soap Marketers," in Callahan and Haines, 1986.

Federowicz, Jan,, ed., *Proceedings of the Second National Workshop on Management and Technology.* Hamilton: Management of Technology Institute, 1988.

Frontini, Gian F. and Peter R. Richardson, "Design and Demonstration: The Key to Industrial Innovation," *Sloan Management Review* Vol. 25, 1984.

Globerman, Steven, *The Adoption of Computer Technology in Selected Canadian Service Industries,* Study prepared for the Economic Council of Canada. Ottawa: Supply and Services Canada, 1981.

Gotlieb, C.C., ed., *The Information Economy: Its Implications for Canada's Industrial Strategy.* Ottawa: Royal Society of Canada, 1984.

Hill, Neil and Tony Dimnik, "Cost Justifying New Technologies," *Business Quarterly* Vol. 50, 1985.

Killing, Peter J., *Strategies for Joint Venture Success.* New York: Praeger Publishers, 1983.

———, "Technology Acquisition: Licence Agreement or Joint Venture," *The Columbia Journal of World Business* Fall 1980.

Kleinschmidt, Elko J. and Peter M. Banting, "Product and R&D Characteristics in the Export Performance of Industrial Firms," *ASAC Proceedings,* Vol. 5, 1984.

Knight, Russell M., "Technological Innovation in Canada: A Comparison of Independent Entrepreneurs and Corporate Innovations," *NCMRD Working Paper Series* no. 87-18, 1988.

———, "Product Innovation by Smaller, High-Technology Firms in Canada," *Journal of Product Innovation Management* Vol. 3, 1986.

———, "Corporate Innovation and Entrepreneurship in Canada," *Business Quarterly* Vol. 50, 1985.

Kolodny, Harvey F., "Canadian Experience in Innovative Approaches to High Commitment Work Systems," in R. Shuler and S. Dolan, eds., *Canadian Readings in Personnel and Human Resources Management.* Toronto: West Publishing, 1987.

———, "Assembly Cells and Parallelization: Two Swedish Cases," in O. Brown Jr. and H.W. Henrick, eds., *Human Factors in Organizational Design and Management*—II, Amsterdam: Elsevier, 1986.

————, "Work Organization in Sweden: Some Impressions from 1982-83," *Human Systems Management* Vol. 5, 1985.

————, *Product Organization Structures Improve the Quality of Working Life.* Dearborn: Society of Manufacturing Engineers, 1984.

Kolodny, Harvey F. and Barbara Dresner, "Linking Arrangements and New Work Designs," *Organizational Dynamics* Winter 1986.

Kolodny, Harvey F. and Torbjorn Stjernberg, "The Change Process of Innovative Work Design and Redesign in Sweden, Canada, and the U.S.," *The Journal of Applied Behavioural Sciences* Vol. 22, no. 3, 1986.

Lefebvre, Louis A. and Elisabeth Lefebvre, "The Innovative Business Firm in Canada: An Empirical Study of CAD/CAM Firms," *International Labour Review* Vol. 127, no. 4, 1988.

Litvak, Isaiah A., *Canadian Trade Associations and the Promotion and Diffusion of Innovation,* TISP Research Report no. 100. Ottawa: DRIE, Office of Industrial Innovation, 1985.

Litvak, Isaiah A. and Christopher J. Maule, *Small-Medium Sized Canadian Firms and Their International Business and R&D Activities,* TISP Research Report no. 94. Ottawa: DRIE, Office of Industrial Innovation, 1984.

————, *Canadian Entrepreneurship and Innovation,* TISP Research Report no.86. Ottawa: DRIE, Office of Industrial Innovation, 1982.

————, *Entrepreneurial Success or Failure—Ten Years Later: A Study of 47 Technologically Oriented Enterprises,* TISP Research Report no. 80. Ottawa: DRIE, Office of Industrial Innovation, 1980.

Litvak, Isaiah A. and Timothy N. Warner, "Multinationals, Advanced Manufacturing Technologies, and Canadian Public Policy," *Business Quarterly* Vol. 50, Summer 1987.

————, "Advanced Technologies in the Canadian Secondary Manufacturing Sector," *NCMRD Working Paper Series,* no. 86-14, 1986.

Long, Richard J., *New Office Information Technology, Human and Managerial Implications.* London: Croom Helm, 1987.

————, "Introducing Employee Participation in Ownership and Decision Making," in Cunningham and White, 1984a.

————, "The Application of Microelectronics to the Office: Organizational and Human Implications," in Nigel Piercy, ed., *The Management Implications of New Information Technology.* London: Croom Helm, 1984b.

————, "Microelectronics and Quality of Working Life in the Office: A Canadian Perspective," in Malcolm Warner, ed., *Microprocessors, Manpower and Society.* Aldershot: Gower Press, 1984c.

Mansell, Jacquie, *Workplace Innovation in Canada: Reflections on the Past ... Prospects for the Future.* Ottawa: Supply and Services Canada, 1987.

Mansfield, Edwin, "Technological Change and the International Diffusion of Technology: A Survey of Findings," in McFetridge, 1985.

Martin, M.J.C. and P.J. Rosson, *Further Cases on the Management of Technological Innovation and Entrepreneurship,* TISP Research Report no. 108. Ottawa: DRIE, Office of Industrial Innovation, 1986.

MacCharles D.G., "International Knowledge Transfers and Competitiveness:

Canada as a Case Study," in Safarian and Bertin, 1987.

McFetridge, Donald G., "The Timing, Mode and Terms of Technology Transfer: Some Recent Findings," in Safarian and Bertin, 1987.

———, *Technological Change in Canadian Industry*. Toronto: University of Toronto Press, 1985.

McFetridge, Donald G. and R.J. Corvari, "Technology Diffusion: A Survey of Canadian Evidence and Public Policy Issues," in McFetridge, 1985.

McMullan, W. and Ken Melnyk, "University Innovation Centers and Academic Venture Formation," *R&D Management* Vol. 18, no. 1, January 1988.

Miller, Roger, Marcel Cote and James Mauldin, *Forging Our Future*, Discussion paper prepared for the National Conference on Technology and Innovation. Toronto: January 1988.

More, Roger A., "Generating Profit From New Technology: An Agenda For a Management Research Program," *Business Quarterly*, Summer 1987.

———, "Managing Supplier/User Interfacing in the Development Adoption of New Hardware/Software Systems," *NCMRD Working Paper Series*, no. 86-01, 1986a.

———, "The Impact of Organizational Buying Behaviour on Adoption Rate Forecasting for New Industrial Products," *NCMRD Working Paper Series*, no. 86-04, 1986b.

———, "Developer/Adaptor Relationships in New Industrial Product Situations," *Journal of Business Research* Vol. 13, 1986c.

———, "Developer/Adopter Relationships in the Adoption of CAD/CAM Systems: Implications for Operations Management," *International Journal of Operations and Production Management* Vol. 6, no. 4, 1986d.

———, "Generating Profit From New Technology: An Overview of Management Problems and Research Needs," *Business Quarterly* Vol. 50, 1985.

———, "Improving the Adoption Rate for High-Technology Industrial Products," *Journal of Product Innovation Management* Vol. 2, 1984a.

———, "Timing of Market Research in New Industrial Product Situations," *Journal of Marketing* Vol. 48, 1984b.

Munro, Hugh and Hamid Noori, "Canada and New Technology—Part 1: Canada's International Performance," *NCMRD Working Paper Series*, no. 87-10, 1987.

———, "Measuring Commitment to New Technology Adoption: Integrating Push and Pull Concepts," *NCMRD Working Paper Series*, no. 86-08, 1986.

National Advisory Board on Science and Technology, Industry Committee Report, Ottawa, 1988.

Newton, Keith, "The Interrelationship Between Technological and Organizational Change: An Exploratory Approach," in Gotlieb, 1984.

Nightingale, Donald, "Continous Renewal: Lessons From a QWL Project," in Cunningham and White, 1984.

———, *Workplace Democracy: An Inquiry into Employee Participation in Canadian Work Organizations*. Toronto: University of Toronto Press, 1982.

Nightingale, Don and Richard J. Long, *Quality of Working Life: Gain and Equity Sharing*. Ottawa: Labour Canada, 1984.

Noori, Hamid, "Economies of Integration," *NCMRD Working Paper Series*, no. 86-06, 1986a.

——, "Production Policy and the Acquisition of New Technology: Some Important Questions," *NCMRD Working Paper Series*, no. 86-07, 1986b.

Noori, Hamid and Hugh Munro, "Performance of Canadian Companies Due to Technology Adoption," *NCMRD Working Paper Series*, no. 88-19, 1988.

——, "Reflecting Corporate Strategy in the Decision to Automate: The Case of Canadian Manufacturing Companies," *Business Quarterly* Vol. 50, 1985.

Ondrack, D.A., *Innovation and Performance of Small and Medium Firms: A Reanalysis of Data on a Sample of Nineteen Small and Medium Firms in the Machinery Industry*, TISP Research Report no.74. Ottawa: DRIE, Office of Industrial Innovation, 1980.

——, *Foreign Ownership and Technological Innovation in Canada: A Study of the Industrial Machinery Sector of Industry*, TISP Research Report no.32. Ottawa: DRIE, Office of Industrial Innovation, 1975.

Ondrack, D.A. and M.G. Evans, "Job Enrichment and Job Satisfaction in Quality of Working Life and Nonquality of Working Life Sites," *Human Relations* Vol. 39, no. 9, 1986.

——, *QWL at Petrosar: A Case Study of a Greenfield Site*. Ottawa: Labour Canada, 1984.

Ontario Premier's Council, *Competing in the New Global Economy* Vol. 1, Toronto, 1988.

Pal, Siva P. and Shoukry D. Saleh, *Does CAM Technology have Different Implications for Production Unit Structures*, Paper presented at the IEEE Conference on Management and Technology, 1987.

Palda, Kristian S., *Technological Intensity: Concepts and Measurement*, TISP Research Report no.104. Ottawa: DRIE, Office of Industrial Innovation, 1985.

Palda, Kristian S. and B. Pazderka, *Approaches to an International Comparison of Canada's R&D Expenditures*. Study prepared for the Economic Council of Canada. Ottawa: Supply and Services Canada, 1982.

Poapst, James V., "Impact of Government Regulations and Programs on Institutional Debt Financing of Small High Technology Business," in Callahan and Haines, 1986.

Portis, Bernard, Neil Hill and Chris Naus, "Employee Participation in Technological Change," *NCMRD Working Paper Series*, no. 88-25, 1988.

Richardson, Peter R., "Winning Through Technology: A Strategic Approach," *Canadian Business Review* Vol. 13, Summer 1986.

——, "Managing Research and Development for Results," *Journal of Product Innovation Management* Vol. 2, 1985.

Roberts, Edward B., "Managing Invention and Innovation," *Research Technology Management* Vol. 31, no. 1, January-February 1988.

Rosson, Philip J. and Michael J.C. Martin, "Managing the High Technology Firm: Four Canadian Electronics Cases," in B.W. Mar, W.T. Newell and B.O. Saxberg, eds., *Managing High Technology*. Amsterdam: Elsevier, 1985.

Rugman, Alan, ed., *Multinationals and Technology Transfer: The Canadian Experience*. New York: Praeger, 1983.

Safarian, A.E. and Gilles Y. Bertin, eds., *Multinationals, Governments and International Technology Transfer*. London: Croom Helm, 1987.

Saleh, Shoukry D. and Siva P. Pal, "Robotics Technology and its Impact on Work Design and the QWL," *Industrial Management* Vol. 27, 1985.

Science Council of Canada, *Winning in a World Economy: University-Industry Interaction and Economic Renewal in Canada*. Report no. 39. Ottawa: Supply and Services Canada, 1988.

Schofield, Brian T. and Robert Thomson, *Technological Change and Innovation in Canada: A Call for Action*, Discussion paper prepared for the National Conference on Technology and Innovation. Toronto: January 1988.

Senker, Peter, *Towards the Automatic Factory? The Need for Training*. Bedford, England: IFS Publications, 1986.

Tucker, Brian and James C. Taylor, "Improving Quality of Worklife Through Socio-technical Design: Multiple-Craft Supervision in an Oil Refinery," in Cunningham and White, 1984.

Utterback, J.M. and W.J. Abernathy, "A Dynamic Model of Process and Product Innovation," *Omega* Vol. 3, no. 6, 1975.

van Beinum, Hans, Harvey F. Kolodny and Ann Armstrong, "QWL: A Paradigm in Transition," in Harvey F. Kolodny and Hans van Beinum, eds., *The Quality of Working Life and the 1980's*. New York: Praeger, 1983.

Chapter Five

Innovation and the Labour Process:

Armstrong, Pat, *Labour Pains: Women's Work in Crisis*. Toronto: Women's Press, 1984.

Benston, Margaret Lowe, Margaret White and Marcy Cohen, *Community-Based Research Around Technological Change*, in DeBresson et al., 1987.

Bernard, Elaine, *Technological Impact: The Hidden Bias in Machine Design*, Paper presented to the First National Conference for Women in Science and Technology, Vancouver, May 20-22, 1983.

———, "New Initiatives, New Technology, New Labour," in DeBresson et al., 1987.

Billette, A., M. Cantin and E. Labellois, *Phases in the Evolution of Computer Systems and Their Impact on the Organization of Work in General Insurance*, Quebec, 1986.

Bird, Patricia and Josephine Lee, *A High Traffic Area: Today's Automated Office*, Toronto, 1987.

Braverman, Harry, *Labor and Monopoly Capital: The Degradation of Work in the Twentieth Century*. New York: Monthly Review Press, 1974.

Clark, Susan, Jenny Blain, Margaret Dechman, Laraine Singler and Margaret Scott, *Microtechnology and the Nova Scotia Government Employees' Union*, Halifax, 1986.

Clark, Susan, Margaret Dechman and Laraine Singler, *Computerization in the Workplace*, Halifax, 1986.

Clark, Susan, Margaret Dechman and Laureen Snider, *Office Work: The Impact of Microtechnology*, Paper presented at the Information Technologies Inter-disciplinary Symposium, London, Ontario, June 15-16, 1988.

Clement, Andrew, "Office Automation and the Technical Control of Information Workers," in V. Mosco and J. Wasko, eds., *The Political Economy of Information*. Madison: University of Wisconsin Press, 1988.

Clement, Andrew and C.C. Gotlieb, "Evolution of an Organizational Interface: The New Business Department of a Large Insurance Firm," *ACM Transactions on Office Information Systems* Vol. 5, no. 4, October 1987.

Clement, Andrew, Ann Zelechow and Darrell Parsons, *Towards Self-Managed Automation in Small Offices*, North York, 1987.

Cohen, Marcy and Margaret White, *The Impact of Computerization on Temporary Office Workers: Some Empirical Evidence*, Vancouver, 1988.

————, *The Impact of Computerization on the Clerical Work Process: A Feminist Analysis*, Vancouver, 1986.

DeBresson, Christian with Jim Peterson, *Understanding Technological Change*. Montreal: Black Rose Books, 1987.

DeBresson, Christian, Margaret Lowe Benston and Jesse Vorst, *Work and New Technologies*. Toronto: Between the Lines, 1987.

Freedman, Jonathan L. and Norman W. Park, *Effects of Advanced Office Systems*, Toronto, 1986.

Gannagé, Charlene, *The Impact of Technological Change on the Toronto Ladies' Clothing Workers*, Toronto, 1987.

Gattiker, Urs E., "Computer End-Users: The Impact of Their Beliefs on Subjective Career Success," in Urs E. Gattiker and Laurie Larwood, eds., *Managing Technological Development: Strategic and Human Resources Issues*. New York: Walter de Gruyter, 1988.

Gattiker, Urs E., B.A. Gutek and D.E. Berger, "Office Technology and Employee Attitudes," *Social Science Computer Review* (forthcoming).

Gattiker, Urs E. and Todd W. Nelligan, "Computerized Offices in Canada and the United States: Investigating Disposed Similarities and Differences," *Journal of Organizational Behaviour* Vol. 9, 1988.

Grant, Rebecca A., "Computerized Performance Monitoring and Control Systems—Use in the Service Sector: A Review of the Literature," *ASAC Proceedings* Vol. 7, 1986.

Hansen, Ken, "The Focus of Union Research on Technological Change," in DeBresson et al., 1987.

————, *New Work Organized on Post-Taylorist Principles: Case Study Evidence and Conceptual Conclusions*, Paper presented to a Conference on Technology and the Labour Force, Ottawa, July 16-17, 1987.

Hansen, Ken and Elaine Bernard, *Technological Impact Research Project: A Case Study Approach*, Vancouver, 1986.

————, *Management Resistance to Change—Case Studies in the Introduction of Computer Information Systems*, Vancouver, 1986.

———, *Technological Change and Work Organization in Process Industries,* Vancouver, 1987.

Higgins, C.A., R.H. Irving and S.M. Rinaldi, "Small Business and Office Automation," *Canadian Journal of Administrative Sciences* Vol. 2, no. 2, 1985.

Higgins, C.A., R.H. Irving and R.A. Grant, *The Impact of Computerized Performance Monitoring and Control Systems: Perceptions of the Canadian Service Sector Worker,* London Ontario, 1987.

Hirschhorn, Larry, "The Soul of a New Worker," *Working Papers,* Vol. 9, no. 1, January-February 1982.

———, *Beyond Mechanization.* Cambridge, Mass: MIT Press, 1984.

Magun, Sunder, "The Effects of Technological Changes on the Labour Market in Canada," *Relations industrielles* Vol. 40, no. 4, 1986.

Marsden, Lorna, *Technological Change in Ontario: The Questions of Innovation and Control in the Small Office,* SCIT Paper no. 13, Kingston, 1987.

Martin, D'Arcy, "Canaries and Cargo Cults: Worker-Oriented Research in the Silicon Age," in DeBresson et al., 1987.

McDermott, Patricia, *The Differential Impact of Computerization on Office Workers: A Qualitative Investigation of 'Screen Based' and 'Screen Assisted' VDT Users,* Toronto, 1987.

Menzies, Heather, *Women and the Chip.* Montreal: Institute for Research on Public Policy, 1981.

Meurer, Susan, David Sobel and David Wolfe, *Challenging Technology's Myths: The Impact of Technological Change on Secondary Manufacturing in Metro Toronto,* Toronto, 1987.

Mosco, Vincent and Elia Zureik, *Computers and the Workplace: Technological Change in the Telephone Industry,* Kingston, Ontario, 1987.

Neis, Barbara, Susan Williams, Joel Rogers and Gregory S. Kealey, *The Social Impact of Technological Change in Newfoundland's Deepsea Fishery,* St. John's, Nfld, 1986.

Novek, Joel and Garry Russel, *Grain Handling in the Information Age,* Winnipeg, 1987.

Parker, Mike and Jane Slaughter, "Management by Stress," *Technology Review* Vol. 91, no. 7, October 1988.

Peitchinis, Stephen G., "The Attitude of Trade Unions Towards Technological Changes," *Relations industrielles* Vol. 38, no. 1, 1983.

———, *Computer Technology and Employment, Retrospect and Prospect.* London St. Martin's Press, 1984.

Robertson, David and Jeff Wareham, *Technological Change in the Auto Industry,* Willowdale, 1987.

———, *Computer Automation and Technological Change: Northern Telecom,* Willowdale, 1988.

Stoffman, L.D., U. Wallersteiner and R. Gordon, *Integrating Ergonomics into the Design of Laser/Scanner Checkout Systems,* Vancouver, B.C, 1986.

Storey, Robert, *The Impact of Technological Change on Job Structures, Employment Levels and Industrial Relations in the Steel Industry,* Hamilton, Ont, 1987.

Swimmer, Gene, Madelaine McNicholl and Janice Manchee, *Computers and*

CRs: The Impact of New Technologies on Federal Public Service Clerks, Ottawa, 1987.

Taylor, Don, Bradley Dow, Paul Brennan and Ken Waldie, *Negotiating Technological Change: The Case of the Canadian Pulp and Paper Industry*, Montreal, 1987.

Taylor, James R., "Organizational Adaptation: The Learning Problem," in *1985 Office Automation Conference Digest*. Reston, Virginia: AFIPS Press, 1985.

————, "The Computerization Crisis: End of a Dream or Threshold of Opportunity?" in *International Symposium on the Impact of New Information Technologies on the Workplace* Montreal: Institute for Research on Public Policy, 1986.

Vancouver Typographical Union, Summary TIRF Report, Vancouver, 1987.

Wells, Don, *Soft Sell: Quality of Working Life Programs and the Productivity Race*. Ottawa: Canadian Center for Policy Alternatives, 1986.

————, *Empty Promises: Quality of Working Life Programs and the Labor Movement*. New York: Monthly Review Press, 1987.

Wolfe, David and David Sobel, *The Impact of Technological Change on Secondary Manufacturing Industry in Metropolitan Toronto*, Paper presented to a Conference on Technology and the Labour Force, Ottawa, July 16-17, 1987.

Innovation and Industrial Relations:

Craig, Alton W.J., *Technological Change, Labour Relations Policy, Administrative Tribunals and the Incidence of Technological Change Provisions in Major Collective Agreements*, University of Ottawa Administration Working Paper no. 87-24, 1987.

Drache, Daniel and Harry J. Glasbeek, "The New Fordism in Canada: Capital's Offensive, Labour's Opportunity," *Osgoode Hall Law Journal* Vol. 27, no. 3 1989.

————, "A New Trade Union Strategy," *Policy Options* September 1988.

Gunderson, M. and N.M. Meltz, "Recent Developments in the Canadian Industrial Relations System," *Bulletin of Comparative Labour Relations* Vol. 16, 1987.

Jain, H.C., "Microelectronics Technology and Industrial Relations," *Relations industrielles* Vol. 38, no. 4, 1983.

Knight, Thomas R. and David C. McPhillips, *Recent Trends in Collective Bargaining over Technological Change*, Proceedings of the 23rd. Annual Meeting of the Canadian Industrial Relations Association, Winnipeg, Manitoba, 1986.

Mahon, Rianne, "From Fordism to ?: New Technology, Labour Markets and Unions," *Economic and Industrial Democracy* Vol. 8, 1987.

McDermott, Patricia, "Canadian Labour Law and Technological Change: An Overview," in Robert Argue, Charlene Gannagé, and D.W. Livingstone, eds., *Working People and Hard Times*. Toronto: Garamond Press, 1987.

Peirce, Jonathan C., *Collective Bargaining Over Technological Change in Canada: A Quantitative and Historical Analysis*, Discussion Paper no. 338, Economic Council of Canada, 1987.

Innovation, Training and Skill Development:

Adams, R.J., *Skills Development for Working Canadians—Towards a National Strategy*, Background Paper no. 2, Skill Development Leave Task Force. Ottawa: Employment and Immigration Canada, 1983.

Davies, James C., "Training and Skill Development," in Riddell, 1986.

Dodge, David, "Changing Skill Requirements and Training Needs Arising from Technological Change," in C.C. Gotlieb, ed., *The Information Economy: Its Implications for Canada's Industrial Strategy*. Ottawa: Royal Society of Canada, 1984.

Gaskell, Jane S., "Gender and Skill," in David W. Livingstone et al., ed., *Critical Pedagogy and Cultural Power*. Toronto: Garamond Press, 1987.

Globerman, Steven, "Formal Education and the Adaptability of Workers and Managers to Technological Change," in Riddell, 1986.

Jackson, Nancy S., "Skill Training in Transition: Implications for Women," in Jane S. Gaskell and Arlene Tigar McLaren, eds., *Women and Education: A Canadian Perspective*. Calgary: Detselig Enterprises, 1987.

Morrison, Ian and Kjell Rubenson, *Recurrent Education in an Information Economy: A Status Report on Adult Training in Canada*. Toronto: Canadian Association for Adult Education, 1987.

Muszynski, Leon and David A. Wolfe, "New Technology and Training: Lessons from Abroad," *Canadian Public Policy* Vol. 15, no. 3, September 1989.

Paquet, Pierre, *Employer-Employee Interests in Job Training*, Background Paper no. 25, Skill Development Leave Task Force. Ottawa: Employment and Immigration Canada, 1983.

Riddell, W. Craig, *Adapting to Change: Labour Market Adjustment in Canada*. Toronto: University of Toronto Press, 1986.

Rubenson, Kjell, *Barriers to Participation in Adult Education*, Background Paper no. 4, Skill Development Leave Task Force. Ottawa: Employment and Immigration Canada, 1983.

Sobel, David and Susan Meurer, *A Shameful Silence: Older Workers, New Technology and Re-training*, Toronto, 1988.

Chapter Six

Industrial Policy

Adams, F. Gerard and Lawrence R. Klein, "Economic Evaluation of Industrial Policies for Growth and Competitiveness: An Overview," in F. Gerard Adams and Lawrence R. Klein, eds., *Industrial Policies for Growth and Competitiveness*. Lexington, Mass: D.C. Heath, 1983.

Atkinson M.M. and W.D. Coleman, *The State, Business and Industrial Change in Canada*. Toronto: University of Toronto Press, 1989.

Averch, H.A., *A Strategic Analysis of Science and Technology Policy*. Baltimore and London: The John Hopkins University Press, 1985.

Belanger, Gerard, "Dans un systeme federale le gouvernement central doit-il essayer d'imposer l'harmonisation fiscale?," *Actualite economique* Vol. 58,

1982, pp 493-512.

Bernstein, Jeffery I., "Research and Development, Patents, and Grant and Tax Policies in Canada," in *Technological Change in Canadian Industry*, Volume 3 of the research studies prepared for the Royal Commission on the Economic Union and Development Prospects for Canada. Toronto: University of Toronto Press, 1985.

Blais, Andre, "Industrial Policy in Advanced Capitalist Democracies," *Industrial Policy*, Volume 44 of the research studies prepared for the Royal Commission on the Economic Union and Development Prospects for Canada. Toronto: University of Toronto Press, 1986.

Bozeman, B. and A. N. Link, "Public Support for Private R&D: The Case of the Research Tax Credit," *Journal of Policy Analysis and Management* no. 4, 1985.

————, *Investments in Technology*. New York: Praeger, 1983.

Brenner, Reuven and Leon Courville, "Industrial Strategy: Inferring What it Really Is," in *Economics of Industrial Policy and Strategy*, Vol. 5 of the research studies prepared for the Royal Commission on the Economic Union and Development Prospects for Canada. Toronto: University of Toronto Press, 1985.

Davenport, P., C. Green, W.J. Milne, R. Saunders, and W. Watson, *Industrial Policy in Ontario and Quebec*. Toronto: Ontario Economic Council, 1982.

Economic Council of Canada, *Looking Outward: A New Trade Strategy for Canada*. Ottawa: Information Canada, 1975.

Economic Council of Canada, *Living Together: A Study of Regional Disparities*. Ottawa: Supply and Services Canada, 1977.

Economic Council of Canada, *The Bottom Line: Technology, Trade and Income Growth*. Ottawa: Supply and Services Canada, 1983.

Hager, Wolfgang, "Industrial Policy, Trade Policy and European Social Democracy," in John Pinder, ed., *National Industrial Strategies and the World Economy*. London: Croom Helm, 1982.

Harris, Richard G., with David Cox, *Trade, Industrial Policy and Canadian Manufacturing*. Toronto: Ontario Economic Council, 1984.

Krugman, Paul, "The U.S. Response to Foreign Targetting," *Brookings Papers on Economic Activity*, no. 1. Washington, D.C.: Brookings Institute, 1984.

Lawrence, Robert Z., "Is Trade Deindustrializing America? A Medium Term Perspective," *Brookings Papers on Economic Activity*, no. 1. Washington, D.C.: Brookings Institute, 1983.

Leiss, William, "Industry, Technology and the Political Agenda in Canada: The Case of Government Support for R&D," *Science and Public Policy* Vol. 15, no. 1, 1988, pp 57-65.

Mansfield, Edwin, "Technological Change and the International Diffusion of Technology: A Survey.," in *Technological Change in Canadian Industry*, Volume 3 of the research studies prepared for the Royal Commission on the Economic Union and Development Prospects for Canada. Toronto: University of Toronto Press, 1985.

McFetridge, Donald G., *Government Support of Scientific Research and Development: An Economic Analysis*. Toronto: University of Toronto Press,

1977.

McFetridge, Donald G. and Jacek P. Warda, *Canadian R&D Incentives: Their Adequacy and Impact.* Toronto: Canadian Tax Foundation, 1983.

Milne, William J., "Industrial Policy in Canada: A Survey.," in F. Gerard Adams and Lawrence R. Klein, eds., *Industrial Policies for Growth and Competitiveness.* Lexington, Mass.: D.C. Heath, 1983.

Nelson, R. R., "Government Support and Technological Progress: Lessons from History," *Journal of Policy Analysis and Management,* no. 2, 1983.

Norris, Keith and John Vaizey, *The Economics of Research and Technology.* London: Allen and Unwin, 1973.

Organization for Economic Cooperation and Development, *Policies for Stimulation of Industrial Innovation: Analytical Report.* Paris: OECD, 1978.

————, *Objectifes et instruments des politiques industrielles: une etude comparative.* Paris: OECD, 1975.

Piekarz, R., "R&D and Productivity Growth: Policy Studies and Issues," *American Economic Review* Vol. 73, 1983.

Reich, Robert, "Making Industrial Policy," *Foreign Affairs,* 1982, pp 852-82.

Science Council of Canada, *Canadian Industrial Development: Some Policy Directions.* Ottawa: Supply and Services, 1984.

————, *Forging the Links: A Technology Policy for Canada.* Ottawa: Supply and Services Canada, 1979.

Tarasofsky, A., *The Subsidization of Innovation Projects by the Government of Canada.* Ottawa: Supply and Services Canada, 1984.

Thurow, Lester C., *Generating Inequality: Mechanism of Distribution in the U.S. Economy.* New York: Basic Books, 1975.

————, *The Zero-Sum Society.* New York: Basic Books, 1980.

Trebilcock, Michael J., *The Political Economy of Economic Adjustment: The Case of Declining Sectors,* Vol. 8 of the research studies prepared for the Royal Commission on the Economic Union and Development Prospects for Canada. Toronto: University of Toronto Press, 1986.

Treiman, Donald J., *Occupational Prestige in Comparative Perspective.* New York: Academic Press, 1977.

Chapter Seven
Socio-Spatial Dimensions of Innovation

Abonyi, A. and M. Atkinson, "Technological Innovation and Industrial Policy: Canada in an International Context," in M. Atkinson and M. Chandler, eds., *The Politics of Canadian Public Policy.* Toronto: University of Toronto Press, 1983, pp 93-126.

Barnes, T. and R. Hayter, *Restructuring in a Resource Economy: A British Columbia Case Study,* Paper presented at the North American meetings of the Regional Science Association, Toronto, Ontario, 1988.

Bradbury, J., "The Impact of Industrial Cycles in the Mining Sector: The Case of the Quebec-Labrador Region in Canada," *International Journal of Urban and Regional Research* Vol. 8, 1984, pp 311-331.

————, "International Movements and Crises in Resource Oriented Companies: The Case of Inco in the Nickel Sector," *Economic Geography* Vol. 61, 1985, pp 129-143.

————, "Strategies in Local Communities to Cope with Industrial Restructuring," in B. Van der Knapp and G.J.R. Linge, eds., *Social and Economic Change in Industrial Societies in the 1980s*. London: Croom Helm, (forthcoming).

Britton, J.N.H., "Research and Development in the Canadian Economy: Sectoral, Ownership, Locational, and Policy Issues," in R. Oakey and A. Thwaites, eds., *The Regional Economic Impact of Technological Change*. London: Frances Pinter, 1985, pp 67-114.

————, "Innovation Policies for Small Firms," *Regional Studies* Vol. 22, (forthcoming).

Britton, J.N.H. and M.S. Gertler, "Locational Perspectives on Policies for Innovation," in J. Dermer, ed., *Competitiveness Through Technology: What Business Needs from Government*. Toronto: Lexington Books, 1986, pp 159-175.

Britton, J.N.H. and J. Gilmour, *The Weakest Link: A Technological Perspective on Canadian Industrial Underdevelopment*, Background Study no. 43. Ottawa: Science Council of Canada, 1978.

Coffey, W.J. and M. Polese, "Local Development: Conceptual Bases and Policy Implications," *Regional Studies* Vol. 19, 1985, pp 85-93.

Dobilas, G., *Technology and Simultaneous Financial Markets: The Crash of October 1987*, Discussion paper prepared for the Department of Geography, London School of Economics, 1988.

Economic Council of Canada, *Making Technology Work: Innovation and Jobs in Canada*. Ottawa: Supply and Services Canada, 1987.

Gertler, M.S., "Industrialism, Deindustrialism, and Regional Development in Central Canada," *Canadian Journal of Regional Science* Vol. 8, 1985, pp 353-375.

————, "Economic and Political Determinants of Regional Investment and Technical Change in Canada," *Papers of the Regional Science Association* Vol. 62, 1987, pp 27-43.

————, "The Limits to Flexibility: Comments on the Post-Fordist Vision of Production and its Geography," *Transactions of the Institute of British Geographers*, M.S. Vol. 13, 1988, pp. 419-432.

————, "Some Problems of Time in Economic Geography," *Environment and Planning* Vol. 20, 1988, pp 151-164.

Hepworth, M.E., "The Geography of Technical Change in the Information Economy," *Regional Studies* Vol. 20, 1986, pp 407-424.

Holmes, J., "Industrial Reorganization, Capital Restructuring and Locational Change: An Analysis of the Canadian Automobile Industry in the 1960s," *Economic Geography* Vol. 59, pp 251-271.

————, "The Organization and Locational Structure of Production Subcontracting," in A.J. Scott and M. Storper, eds., *Production, Work, Territory*. London: Allen and Unwin, 1986, pp 80-106.

―――, "Technical Change and the Restructuring of the North American Automobile Industry," in K. Chapman and G. Humphrys, ed., *Technical Change and Industrial Policy*. Oxford: Basil Blackwell, 1987, pp 119-156.

―――, *Buyer-Supplier Relationships in the Automobile Industry: Towards a Post-Fordist Model*, Paper presented at the annual meeting of the Association of American Geographers, Phoenix, Arizona, 1988.

Lesser, B. and P. Hall, *Telecommunications Services and Regional Development: The Case of Atlantic Canada*. Halifax: Institute for Research on Public Policy, 1987.

Mackenzie, S., "Neglected Spaces in Peripheral Places: Homeworkers and the Creation of a New Economic Centre," *Cahiers de Geographie du Quebec* Vol. 31, 1988, pp 247-260.

MacPherson, A., "Industrial Innovation in the Small Business Sector: Empirical Evidence from Metropolitan Toronto," *Environment and Planning* Vol. 20, pp 953-971.

Miller, R. and M. Cote, "Growing the Next Silicon Valley," *Harvard Business Review* Vol. 63, 1985, pp 114-123.

Norcliffe, G.B., M. Goldrick, and L. Muszynski, "Cyclical Factors, Technological Change, Capital Mobility and De-industrialization in Metropolitan Toronto," *Urban Geography* Vol. 7, 1986, pp 413-436.

Rose, D., P. Villeneuve, and F. Colgan, "Women Workers and the Inner City: Some Implications of Labour Force Restructuring in Montreal, 1971 to 1981," in C. Andrew and B. Moore Milroy, eds., *Life Spaces: Gender, Household, Employment*. Vancouver: UBC Press forthcoming.

Chapter Eight

Standards

Adam, H. D., "Canada's National Standards System Current Concept," Standards Engineering Society, *Proceedings of Annual Meeting*, 1976.

Anderson, Tom, "International Standardization in Banking," *Canadian Banker*, August 1983, p. 30.

Besen, Stanley M. and Garth Saloner, *Compatibility Standards and the Market for Telecommunications Service*, Working Papers in Economics E-87-15, The Hoover Institution, Stanford University, March 1987.

Bochman, Gregor V., "Standards Issues in Data Communications," *Telecommunications Policy* Vol. 1, no. 5, December 1977, pp 381-388.

Bodson, Dennis, "The Federal Telecommunication Standards Programme," *IEEE Communications Magazine* Vol. 23, no. 1, January 1985, pp 56-62.

Boire, P. C., "Canadian Metric Conversion in the Eighties," Standards Engineering Society, *Proceedings* "of Annual Meeting," 1980.

Boire, P. C., "Metric Conversion in Canada," Standards Engineering Society, *Proceedings of Annual Meeting*, 1974.

Burtz, L. and E. Hummel, "Standard Setting in International Telecommunications," *Telecommunications Policy* Vol. 8, no. 1, March 1984, pp 3-6.

Canadian Standards Association, *Proceedings of the Third Conference for Consumer Representatives*. Rexdale: Canadian Standards Association, 1986.

Castrilli, J. F. and C. Clifford Lax, "Environmental Regulation-Making in Canada: Towards a More Open Process," in J. Swaigen (ed.), *Environmental Rights in Canada*. Toronto: Butterworths, 1981, pp 334-405.

Cerni, Dorothy M., *Standards in Process: Foundations and Profiles of ISDN and OSI Studies*, NTIA Report no. 87-170. Washington, D.C.: Department of Commerce, December 1984.

————, "The United States Organization for the CCITT," *IEEE Communications Magazine* Vol. 23, no. 1, January 1985, pp 38-42.

Cerni, Dorothy M. and E. M. Gray, *International Telecommunications Standards: Issues and Implications For the '80's*, NTIA Special Publication no. 83-15. Washington, D.C.: Department of Commerce, May 1983.

Chilton, David, "OSI Celebrates Quiet 10th Birthday," *Computing Canada* March 17, 1988, p. 37.

Cohen, E. J. and W. B. Wilkens, "The IEEE Role in Telecommunications Standards," *IEEE Communications Magazine* Vol. 23, no. 1, January 1985, pp 31-33.

Crane, Rhonda J., *The Politics of International Standards: France and the Color TV War*. Norwood: Ablex Publishing Corporation, 1979.

————, "Communication Standards and the Politics of Protectionism: The Case of Colour Television Systems," *Telecommunications Policy* December 1978, pp 267-281.

Department of Communications, *Communications in the Twenty-First Century*. Ottawa: Supply and Services Canada, 1987, pp 49, 53, 83.

Farrell, Joseph and Garth Saloner, "Standardization, Compatibility, and Innovation," *Rand Journal of Economics* Vol. 16, no. 1, Spring 1985, pp 70-83.

Fowler, Alvin G., "Lack of Standards Amounts to a Tower of Babel," *Canadian Datasystems* Vol. 15, no. 1, January 1983, pp 137-38.

Gould, Richard G., "Transmission Standards for Direct Broadcast Satellites: The System of the United States Satellite Broadcasting Company," *IEEE Communications Magazine* Vol. 22, no. 3, March 1984, pp 26-34.

Gouldson, Tim, "Standards Approval Made Easier: Group Provides One-stop Shop for Product Certification," *Computing Canada*, January 21, 1988.

Haighton, Robin, "MAP guiding efforts of GM Corp," *Computing Canada* March 17, 1988, pp 34-36.

Harrop, Michael, "Government Pledge to OSI Will Have Significant Impact," *Computing Canada* April 28, 1988.

Harter, Philip J., *Regulatory Use of Standards: The Implications for Standards Writers*. Washington, D.C.: Office of Standards Information, National Bureau of Standards, November 1979.

Hemenway, David, *Standards System in Canada, the UK, West Germany, and Denmark: An Overview*. Washington, D.C.: National Engineering Laboratory, National Bureau of Standards, April 1979.

————, *Industrywide Voluntary Product Standards*. Cambridge, Mass.: Ballinger Publishing Company, 1975.

Herr, Thomas J. and Thomas J. Plevyak, "ISDN: The Opportunity Begins," *IEEE Communications Magazine* Vol. 24, no. 11, November 1986, pp 6-10.

Hoppitt, Cliff, "ISDN Evolution: From Copper to Fiber in Easy Stages," *IEEE Communications Magazine* Vol. 24, no. 11, November 1986, pp 17-22.

Hughson, John, "Standards—Past, Present, Future," *Canada Commerce* October, 1984, pp 22-23.

Hummel, Eckart, "The CCITT," *IEEE Communications Magazine* Vol. 23, no. 1, January 1985, pp 8-11.

Hutchison, Margaret, "Understand the System and Make it Work for You: Standards Writing in Canada," *Canadian Plastics* October 1983, pp 31-34.

"Is MAP Succeeding or Stumbling?," *Computing Canada* March 17, 1988, pp 34-35.

Kindleberger, Charles P., "Standards as Public, Collective and Private Goods," *Kyklos* Vol. 36, no. 3, 1983, pp 377-396.

Kirby, Richard C., "International Standards in Radio Communication," *IEEE Communications Magazine* Vol. 23, no. 1, January 1985, pp 12-17.

Lanthier, Gregg, "EDI Moves into the Mainstream," *Computing Canada* March 17, 1988, pp 40-42.

Lecraw, Donald J., "Some Economic Effects of Standards," *Applied Economics* Vol. 16, 1984, pp 507-522.

———, *Voluntary Standards as a Regulatory Device.* Ottawa: Economic Council of Canada, July 1981.

Legget, Robert F., *Standards in Canada.* Ottawa: Information Canada, 1970.

Liebovitch, Evan, "Standards Remain a Thorny Issue," *Computing Canada* April 28, 1988, pp 28-37.

Lifchus, Ian M., "Standards Committee T1—Telecommunications," *IEEE Communications Magazine* Vol. 23, no. 1, January 1985, pp 34-37.

Lohse, Edward, "The Role of the ISO in Telecommunications and Information Systems Standardization," *IEEE Communications Magazine* Vol. 23, no. 1, January 1985, pp 18-24.

Marshall, Sandra and Cameron MacDonald, *Bibliography of Standards and Standardization* n.p., March 1987.

Middleton, R. W., "The GATT Standards Code," *Journal of World Trade Law* Vol. 14, no. 3, May/June 1980, pp 201-219.

Mollenauer, James F., "Standards for Metropolitan Area Networks," *IEEE Communications Magazine* Vol. 26, no. 4, April 1988, pp 15-19.

Mosco, Vincent and Mary Louise McAllister, *Canada and the International Telecommunication Union: A Preliminary Investigation,* Ottawa: Department of Communications, March, 1986.

Mueller, Milton, "Technical Standards: The Market and Radio Frequency Allocation," *Telecommunications Policy* Vol. 12, no. 1, March 1988, pp 42-56.

"NLC a Pioneer in OSI Activity," *Computing Canada* April 14, 1988, p. 44-45.

Nslund, Ruben. "Setting Technical Standards for Improved Communication Flows." *Telecommunications Policy* Vol. 9, no. 4, December 1985, pp 273-275.

Neu, Terry, "A Threat to the United Unix Front," *Computing Canada* April 28, 1988, p. 37.

"Not All Users Ready for MAP, Survey Finds," *Computing Canada* March 17, 1988, pp 34, 36.

Nusbaumer, Jacques, "The GATT Standards Code in Operation," *Journal of World Trade Law* Vol. 18, no. 6, Nov./Dec. 1984, pp 542-552.

OECD, *The Information Economy: Policies and International Consensus. Theme III: Improving International Rules of the Game*, High Level Meeting of the Committee for Information, Computer and Communications Policy. Paris: OECD, November 2, 1987, pp 11-12.

Olley, Robert E., "Consumers and Standards," *International Consumer* 1979.

———, *The Role of the Canadian Standards Association in the Development of Telecommunications Standards in Canada*, Canadian Business Telecommunications Alliance, Annual Conference, Edmonton, Alberta, Sept. 11, 1985.

Panko, Raymond R., "Standards for Electronic Message Systems," *Telecommunications Policy* Vol. 5, no. 3, September 1981, pp 181-197.

Peiser, H. Steffen and John A. Birch., "Standardization in Support of Development," *Proceedings* of a Seminar, October 1977. Washington, D.C.: U.S. Department of Commerce, National Bureau of Standards, May 1978.

Lapp Philip A., *A Study of the Implementation of DOC's Role in Information Technology Standardization*, Ottawa: Philip A. Lapp Ltd., December 1983.

———, *A Study of the Role of the Department of Communications in Telecommunications Standardization*, Ottawa: Philip A. Lapp Ltd., June 1982.

Reddy, Mohan N., "Voluntary Product Standards: Linking Technical Criteria to Marketing Decisions," *IEEE Transactions on Engineering Management* Vol. 34, no. 4, Nov. 1987, pp 236-243.

———, *The Role of Voluntary Product Standards in Industrial Markets*, Ph.D. diss., Case Western Reserve University, 1985.

Salter, Liora, *Mandated Science: Science and Scientists in the Making of Standards*. Dordrecht: Kluwer Academic Publishers, 1988.

Selvaggi, Philip S., "The Development of Communications Standards in the DoD: A Detailed Overview of Procedures in the Military Standards-Making Process," *IEEE Communications Magazine* Vol. 23, no. 1, January 1985, pp 43-55.

Sherr, Sava I., *Communications Standards and the IEC*, Vol. 23, no. 1, January 1985, pp 25-27.

Sirbu, Marvin A. and L. E. Zwimpfer, "Standard Setting for Computer Communication: the Case of X.25," *IEEE Communications Magazine* Vol. 23, no. 3, March 1985, pp 35-45.

Standards Council of Canada. *The National Standards System of Canada: The Second Five Years 1976/1980*, Ottawa: Standards Council of Canada, October 1976.

"Standards Unfold as They Should," *Computing Canada* March 17, 1988, p. 10.

Standing Committee on Communications and Culture, *A Broadcasting Policy for Canada*. Ottawa: Supply and Services Canada, June 1988, pp 210-215.

Symposium on Methods for Determining Geometric Road Design Standards, *Road Research: Goemetric Road Design Standards*, Paris: OECD, 1977.

Tang, W. Victor, "ISDN &208; New Vistas in Information Processing," *IEEE Communications Magazine* Vol. 24, no. 11, November 1986, pp 11-16.

Tilson, Michael, "The Importance of a Non-Proprietary Standard: Unix Release 4 Must be Made Widely Available, Says Developer," *Computing Canada* April 28, 1988, p. 38.

Toth, R. B. ed., *Standards Activities of Organizations in the US*. Washington, D.C.: National Bureau of Standards, 1984.

Toutan, Michel, "CEPT Recommendations," *IEEE Communications Magazine* Vol. 23, no. 1, January 1985, pp 28-30.

Veall, Michael, R., "On Product Standardization as Competition Policy," *Canadian Journal of Economics* Vol. XVIII, no. 2, May 1985, pp 416-425.

Verman, Lal C., *Standardization: A New Discipline*, Hamden: Archon Books, 1973.

Chapter Nine

Technology Assessment

Alecxe, Kenneth, and Graham F. Parsons, eds., *New Technology in the Prairies*. Regina: Canadian Plains Research Centre, University of Regina, 1986.

Armstrong, Joe E. and Willis W. Harman, *Strategies for Conducting Technology Assessments*. Stanford: Stanford University Press, 1977.

Barrett, F. Derm, "Technology: the Permanent Wave," *Business Quarterly* Vol. 50, Spring 1985, pp 43-52.

Beaulards, Gordon E. and Peter N. Duinker, *An Ecological Framework for Environmental Impact Assessment in Canada*. Halifax: Institute for Resource and Environmental Studies, Dalhousie University, 1983.

Berger, Thomas, *Northern Routes, Northern Homeland. The Report of the Mackenzie Valley Pipeline Inquiry*. Toronto: James Lorimer & Co., 1977.

Bischof, J., *Anik-B Delivery Project. A 12 month Performance Assessment*. Ottawa: Department of Communications, Communication Research Centre, December 1981.

Bogumil, R.J., "Technology and Politics," *IEEE Technology and Society Magazine* Vol. 1, no. 2 June 1982 pp 2, 27-28.

Booth, Peter J., *The Market for Videotex, Teletex and Related Services*, Vancouver: Wescom Communication Consultants, November 1985.

Boothroyd, Peter and William Rees, *Impact Assessment from Pseudo-Science to Planning Process: An Educational Response*, Planning Paper no. 3. Vancouver: University of British Columbia, 1984.

Botting, Dwight, Dennis Gerrard, and Ken Osborne, eds., *The Technology Connection. The Impact of Technology in Canada*. Vancouver: CommCept Publishing Co. Ltd., 1980.

Brannigan, Augustine; and Sheldon Goldenberg, eds., *Social Responses to Technological Change*. Norwood, Conn.: Greenwood Press, 1985.

Caissy, Gail, "Developing Curriculum for the Information Age: How Must Education Change To Meet Future Needs," *Education Canada* Vol. 26, no. 2, 1986 pp 21-25.

Cameron, C.A., Information Technologies of Social Change: An Introduction to the Social Impacts Subcommittee of the Canadian Videotex Consultative Committee. Fredricton: University of New Brunswick, April 1982.

Campbell, Robert Malcolm, "Technology, Democracy, and the Politics of Economic Regeneration," Journal of Canadian Studies Vol. 20, no. 4, 1985-86, pp 158-172.

Canadian Environmental Assessment Research Council, Philosophy and Themes for Research, Hull: CEARC, 1986.

———, Social Impact Assessment: A Research Prospectus, Hull, CEARC, 1985.

Carpenter, Stanley R., Technology Assessment and Appropriate Technology. Ottawa: Supply and Services Canada, 1980.

Clarke, Thomas E. and Jean Reavley, Educating Technological Innovators and Technical Entrepreneurs at Canadian Universities. Ottawa: Science Council of Canada, May 1987.

Coates, Vary T., "Technology Assessment: Some Aspects Related toInformation Technology," in Norbert Szyperski, et al., eds., Assessing the Impacts of Information Technology. Braunschweig: F. Vieweg, 1983.

Coates, Vary T. and Thecla Fabiau, "Technology Assessment in Europe and Japan," Technology Forecasting and Social Change Vol. 22, nos. 3 &4, 1982.

Collingridge, David, The Social Control of Technology. London: Frances Pinter Ltd., 1980.

Cordell, Arthur J., The Uneasy Eighties: The Transition to an Information Society. Ottawa: Science Council of Canada, 1985.

Cornford, Alan B., "Integrating Planning and Project Assessment With Environmental and Social Management," Proceedings of the International Workshop on Impact Assessment for International Development. Barbados: 1987, pp 379-396.

Day, J.C., "Regulating Coal Development: The British Columbia Experience," Proceedings of the International Workshop on Impact Assessment for International Development. Barbados: 1987, pp 694-714.

Demirdache, A.R., " Technology Assessment—The Process. A Canadian Perspective" Proceedings of the Conference on the Human Context for Science and Technology. Ottawa: Supply and Services Canada, 1980, pp 189-207.

Department of Communications, Telidon Reports. Ottawa: Department of Communications, various years.

———, Proposals For Mobile Satellite Service. Ottawa: Department of Communications, 1984.

———, Direct to Home Satellite Broadcasting for Canada. Ottawa: Department of Communications, June 1983a.

———, Telidon-Trials and Services. Ottawa: Department of Communications, 1983b.

Dickson, D., "Europeans Embrace Technology Assessment," Science Vol. 231, February 1986, pp 541-542.

Einseidel, Edna, "Media Agendas and the New Technologies: Nurturing the Information Gap," Science and Public Policy Vol. 11, no. 6, December 1984 pp 378-380.

Einsiedel, Edna and Sandra Green, "VCR's in Canada: Usage Patterns and Policy Implications," *Canadian Journal of Communication* Vol. 13, no. 1, 1988, pp 27-37.

Evans, Allan S. and Riley Moynes, *People, Technology and Change.* Toronto: McGraw-Hill Ryerson, 1980.

Federal Environmental Assessment Review Office, *Environmental Assessment in Canada: 1985 Summary of Current Practices.* Ottawa: Supply and Services Canada, 1986.

Fried, J., "Intergenerational Distribution of the Gains from Technical Change and from International Trade," *Canadian Journal Of Economics* Vol. 13, no. 1, February 1980, pp 65-81.

Gardiuer, W. Lambert, "Family and Technology in the Home," *Canadian Home Economics* Vol. 36, no. 3, 1986.

Gibbons, John H. and Holly L. Gwin, "Technology and Governance," *Technology and Society* Vol. 7, 1985, pp 333-352.

Godfrey, D. and D. Parkhill, eds., *Gutenberg Two: The New Electronics of Social Change.* Toronto: Press Porsepic, 1980.

Hetman, Francois, " From Technology Assessment to an Integrated Perspective on Technology," in Margalam Srinivasan, ed., *Technology Assessment and Development.* New York: Praeger, 1982, pp 36-54.

Hills, Philip, "Human Communication in an Age of Electronic Revolution," *Science and Public Policy* Vol. 11, no. 6, December 1984, pp 335-337.

Hoos, Ida R., "Societal Aspects of Technology Assessment," *Technological Forecasting and Social Change.* Vol. 13, 1979, pp 191-202.

Hoffmaster, Barry, "Socio-Medical Ethics in Canada" in *The Human Context for Science and Technology.* Ottawa:Social Sciences and Humanities Research Council of Canada, 1980, pp 351-386.

Ide, T.R., Eric Manning and Alphonse Quimet, *The Computerized Society. Implications for Canada.* Toronto: Canada Studies Foundation, 1980.

Johnson, Patrick G., "Review of Selected Technology Assessment Studies of Information Technologies in the United States of America," in Norbert Szyperski et al., eds., *Assessing the Impacts of Information Technology.* Braunschweig: F. Vieweg, 1983.

Johnston, Ron and Philip Gummet, eds., *Directing Technology.* New York: St. Martin's Press, 1979.

Kroker, Arthur and Marie Louise Kroker, "Mediascape," *Canadian Journal of Political and Social Theory* Vol. 10, nos. 1 & 2, 1986, pp 60-65.

Kurchak, Marie, *Telidon The Information Providers.* Ottawa: Department of Communications, 1981.

Lang, R. and A. Armour, *The Assessment and Review of Social Impacts.* Ottawa: Federal Environmental Assessment and Review Office, 1981.

Leiss, William, *Colloquium Overview: Movements in Environmental Awareness,* Mimeo. Burnaby, B.C.: Department of Communication, Simon Fraser University, undated.

Lesser, Barry and Pamela Hall, *Telecommunications Series and Regional Development: The Case of Atlantic Canada.* Halifax: Institute for Research on

Public Policy, 1987.

Levy, Edwin, *Justice and Technology*, unpublished paper, Vancouver, Department of Philosophy, University of British Columbia, 1985.

Lorimer, Rowland, "Implications of the New Technologies of Information," *Technology Studies* Vol. 16, no. 3, April 1985, pp 106-210.

Maclaren, Virginia and Joseph B. Whitney, eds., *New Directions in Environmental Impact Assessment in Canada.* Toronto: Methuen, 1985.

Mann, J. Fraser, *Computer Technology and the Law in Canada.* Toronto: Carswell, 1987.

Mazur, Allan, *The Dynamics of Technical Controversy.* Washington, D.C.: Communications Press Inc., 1981.

McCallum, John S., "Canada and Technological Change," *Business Quarterly* Vol. 50, Spring 1985, pp 18-20.

McNulty, Jean, "The Political Economy of Canadian Satellite Broadcasting," *Canadian Journal Of Communication* Vol. 13, no. 2, Spring 1988, pp 1-15.

McPhail, T.L. and B.M. McPhail, eds., *Telecom 2000: Canada's Communication Future.* Calgary: University of Calgary Press, 1985.

McQueen, J.R., "Appeal to the High Priests of Technology," *Optimum* Vol. 15, no. 1 1984, pp 68-80.

Megaw, W.J., " Prospects For Man," *Science Technology, and Economy.* Toronto: York University, 1984.

Meisel, John. "'Newspeak' and the Information Society," *Archivaria* Vol. 19, Ottawa, Winter 1984-85, pp 173-184.

Melody, William H., *Development of the Communication and Information Industries: Impact on Social Structures,* Symposium on the Cultural, Social and Economic Impact of Communication Technology, 1983.

Melody, William H. and Dallas Smythe, *Factors Affecting the Canadian and U.S. Spectrum Management Process: A Preliminary Evaluation,* Ottawa: Department of Communications, March 1985.

Ministry of Transportation and Communication (Ontario), "Mobile Satellite Service in Canada," *Ontario Comment,* Ministry of Transportation and Communication, January 7, 1985.

Moriarity, Andrew, "Biotechnology: A Development Plan for Canada," *Canadian Research* Vol. 14. no. 3, May 1981, pp 20-23.

Mosco, Vincent, "Book Review of Telecom 2000: Canada's Communication Future," *Canadian Journal Of Communication* Vol. 12, no. 2, 1986, pp 71-77.

O'Brien, David M. and Donald Marchand, eds., *Politics of Technology Assessment: Institutions, Processes, and Policy Disputes.* New York: Lexington Books, 1982.

O'Neill, John, "Biotechnology. Empire, Communications and Bio-Power," *Canadian Journal of Political and Social Theory* Vol. 10, Nos.1-2, 1986, pp 66-78.

Organization for Economic Co-operation and Development, *Social Assessment of Technology.* Paris: OECD, 1978.

————, *Assessing the Impacts of Technology on Society.* Paris: OECD, 1983.

Olsen, John Lawrence, *Strategies for Alternative Technology Assessment in the Information Society,* Master's thesis, Vancouver, Simon Fraser University,

1983.

Overduin, Henry, "Book Review of The High Cost of High Tech, The Dark Side of the Chip," *Canadian Journal of Communication* Vol. 12, no. 2, Winter 1986, pp 79-82.

Pergler, P., *The Automated Citizen: Social and Political Impact of Interactive Broadcasting.* Montreal: The Institute for Research on Public Policy, 1980

Peterson, E.V., *Cumulative Effects Assessment in Canada: An Agenda for Action and Research,* Ottawa: CEARC, 1987.

Peterson, Lorne, "Social Dangers in the Information Revolution," *In Search* Winter 1980.

Porter, Alan L. and Frederick A. Rossini, "Technology Assessment/Environmental Impact Assessment: Toward Integrated Impact Assessment," *IEEE Transactions on Systems, Man and Cybernetics,* August 1980, pp 417-424.

Priscoli, Jerry Delli and Peter Homenuck, "Consulting the Publics," in Reg Lang, ed.,"" *Integrated Approaches to Resource Planning and Management.* Calgary: University of Calgary Press, 1986.

Rees, William E., *Reflections on the Environmental Impact and Assessment Process,* discussion paper. Ottawa: Canadian Arctic Resources Committee, 1979.

————, "Environmental Assessment and the Planning Process in Canada" in S.D.Clark, *Environmental Assessment in Australia and Canada.* Vancouver: WestWater Research Center, University of British Columbia, 1981.

————, *Comment on Demirdache and Carpenter,* Proceedings of the Conference on the Human Context for Science and Technology. Ottawa: Supply and Services Canada, 1980, pp 204-208.

Robinson, Peter, "Social Implications of the Information Revolution," *Canadian Datasystems* Vol. 11, no. 11, 1979, pp 53-55.

Rosenberg, D.M., "Recent Trends in Environmental Impact Assessment," *Canadian Journal of Fisheries and Aquatic Sciences* Vol. 38, no. 5, 1981, pp 59-62.

Rosenberg, Richard S, *Computers and the Information Society.* New York and Toronto: Wiley, 1986.

Rossini, Frederick A., *An Overview of Forecasting Methodologies,* Technology and Science Policy Program, Georgia Institute of Technology, no date.

Roy, David J. and Maurice A.M. de Wachter, *The Life Technologies and Public Policy.* Montreal: Institute for Research on Public Policy, 1986.

Royal Society of Canada, *Hermes. The Communications and Technology Satellite,* Ottawa, Royal Society of Canada, 1977.

Sadler, Barry, ed., *Environmental Protection and Resource Development: Convergence for Today.* Calgary: University of Alberta Press, 1985.

————, "The Regulation of the Red Deer River: Conflict and Choice," in Derek Sewell and Mary Barker, eds., *Water Problems and Policies.* Victoria, B.C.: University of Victoria, Department of Geography, 1980.

————, "Impact Assessment in Transition," in R. Lang, *Integrated Approaches to Resource Planning and Management.* Calgary: University of Calgary Press, 1986.

Serafini, Shirley and Michel Andrieu, *The Information Revolution and its*

Implications for Canada. Ottawa: Supply and Services Canada, 1981.

Sheridan, William, "Feedback for Safety," *Policy Options*, Vol.7, 1986, pp 45.

Shirley, Steve, "Social Consequences of the Electronic Revolution," *Science and Public Policy* Vol.11, no.6, 1984, pp 350-351.

Slotin, Lewis A., *Biotechnology in Canada*, Ottawa: Minstry of State for Science and Technology, 1980.

Soete, Luc, "Science, Technology and Long Term Structural Change," in W.J. Megaw, ed., *Prospects for Man*. Toronto: York University, 1984, pp 119-157.

Solntseff, N., "Personal Computers: An Assessment," Canadian Information Processing Society, *Proceedings* of Session 80, 1980.

Swan, Neil, "Technology and Timing Standards" in W.J. Megaw, ed., *Prospects for Man*. Toronto: York University, 1984, pp 59-75.

Telesat, *Study of the Use of Anik-C for Direct-to-Home and Community Television Distribution Services*, Ottawa: Supply and Services Canada, 1981.

Tester, Frank, *Social Impact Assessment: Coping with the Context of our Times*, Ottawa: Human Context for Science and Technology, Social Sciences and Humanities Research Council of Canada, 1980, pp 249-271.

Thompson G.B., "Technology and the Information Society," *In Search* Vol. 7, Spring 1980, pp 26-31.

Vanier Institute of the Family, *A Family Perspective on Microcomputer Communications*, Ottawa: Vanier Institute, April 1982.

Von Buchstab, Victor, "Microelectronics Research: Canadians Aim for a Foothold in this Super-Industry," *Canadian Research* Vol. 15, no. 1, 1982, pp 25-34.

Weinstein, Betty, *The Impact of Microelectronics on Society and Education* Annual Conference of the National Council of the Canadian Federation of University Women, University of Waterloo, 1981.

Chapter Ten

Risk

Journals:
Risk Abstracts
Risk Analysis
Science, Technology and Human Values, (especially the Special Issues Vol. 11, no. 3/4, 1987).
Science Vol. 236, no. 17, 1987.

Books and Articles:

Burton, I. and R. McCollough,, eds., *Living with Risk*. Toronto: University of Toronto, Institute for Environmental Studies, 1982.

Douglas, M., *Risk Acceptability According to the Social Sciences*. New York: Russell Sage Foundation, 1985.

Douglas, M. and A. Wildavsky, *Risk and Culture*. Berkeley: University of California Press, 1982.

Fischhoff, B., Christopher Hope and Stephen R. Watson, "Defining Risk,"

Policy Sciences Vol. 17, 1984, pp 123-139.

Gratt, Lawrence, *The Definition of Risk and Associated Terminology for Risk Analysis,* Society for Risk Analysis, Committee on Definitions, 1986.

Jasanoff, S., *Risk Management and Political Culture.* New York: Russell Sage Foundation, 1986.

Kaplan, S. and Garrick, B.J., "On the Quantitative Definition of Risk," *Risk Analysis* Vol. 1, 1981, pp 11-28.

Krewski, D. and P. Birkwood, "Risk Assessment and Risk Management," *Risk Abstracts* Vol. 4, 1987, pp 53-61.

Kunreuther, H., ed., *Risk: A Seminar Series.* Laxenberg, Austria: International Institute for Applied Systems Analysis, 1982.

MacCrimmon, K. and D. Wehrung, *Taking Risks: The Management of Uncertainty.* New York: The Free Press, 1986.

Mazur, A., *The Dynamics of Technical Controversy.* Washington, D.C.: Communication Press, 1981.

Nelkin, D., ed., *The Language of Risk.* Beverly Hills CA: Sage, 1985.

Rogers, J. and D. Bates, eds., *Risk: A Symposium on the Assessment and Perception of Risk to Human Health.* Ottawa: Royal Society of Canada, 1983.

Rowe, W.D., *An Anatomy of Risk.* New York: Wiley, 1977.

Salter, Liora, *Mandated Science: Science and Scientists in the Making of Standards.* Dordrecht: Kluwer, 1988.

Sprent, Peter, *Taking Risks.* London: Penguin, 1988.

Risk Assessment

Covello, V. and M. Merkhofer, eds., *Risk Assessment and Risk Assessment Methods. The State-of-the-Art,* National Science Foundation, Washington, D.C., 1984.

Environmental Health Directorate, Health Protection Branch, Health and Welfare Canada, *Risk Assessment/Risk Management: A Handbook For Use Within The Bureau Of Chemical Hazards,* Ottawa, 1988.

Great Britain, Royal Society, "Risk Assessment: A Study Group Report," *Proceedings of the Royal Society of London* Vol. 376, London, 1983.

McColl, R.S., ed., *Environmental Health Risks: Assessment and Management.* Institute for Risk Research, University of Waterloo Press, 1986.

National Research Council (U.S.), Committee on the Institutional Means for Assessment of Risks to Public Health, *Risk Assessment in the Federal Government: Managing the Process.* Washington, D.C.: National Academy Press, 1983.

Office of Science and Technology Policy (U.S.), "Chemical Carcinogens: A Review of the Science and its Related Principles," *Federal Register* Vol. 50, 1985, pp 10372ff.

Paustenbach, D. J., ed., *Environmental Risk Assessment: A Textbook of Case Studies.* New York: Wiley, 1987.

Schraeder-Frechette, K.S., *Risk Analysis and Scientific Method.* Boston: Reidel, 1985.

Task Force on Health Risk Assessment (U.S.), *Determining Risks To Health.*

Dover, Mass.: Auburn House Publishing, 1986.

Risk Communication

Special Issues of Journals and Edited Collections:
"Communicating Risk: The Media and the Public." Special Issue, *Journal of Communication* Vol. 37, no. 3, Summer 1987.
Covello, V.T., David B. McCallum and Maria T. Pavlova, eds., *Effective Risk Communication.* New York: Plenum, 1989.
Davies, J. C., Fredrick W. Allen and Vincent T. Covello, eds., *Risk Communication.* Washington, D.C.: The Conservation Foundation, 1987.
Leiss, W., ed., *Problems and Prospects in Risk Communication* Waterloo, Ont.: Institute for Risk Research, University of Waterloo Press, 1989.

Articles and Books:

Baram, Michael, "Chemical Industry Accidents, Liability, and Community Right to Know." *American Journal of Public Health* Vol. 76, no. 5, 1986, pp 568-572.
———, "Risk Communication and the Law for Chronic Health and Environmental Hazards," *The Environmental Professional* Vol. 8, 1986, pp 165-178.
Covello, V., Paul Slovic and Detlof von Winterfeldt, "Risk Communication: A Review of the Literature," *Risk Abstracts* Vol. 3, 1986, pp 171-182.
Edwards, Ward and Detlof von Winterfeldt, "Public Values in Risk Debates," *Risk Analysis* Vol. 7, 1987, pp 141-158.
Ibrekk, H. and M. Granger Morgan, "Graphical Communication of Uncertain Quantities to Nontechnical People," *Risk Analysis* Vol. 7, 1987, pp 219-259.
Kasperson, Roger, "Six Propositions on Public Participation and their Relevance for Risk Communication," *Risk Analysis* Vol. 6, 1986, pp 275-281.
Keeney, Ralph and Detlof von Winterfeldt "Improving Risk Communication," *Risk Analysis* Vol. 6, 1986, pp 417-424.
Krimsky, S. and A. Plough, *Environmental Hazards: Communicating Risks as a Social Process.* Dover, Mass.: Auburn House, 1988.
Mazur, Allan, "The Journalists and Technology: Reporting About Love Canal and Three-Mile Island," *Minerva* Vol. 22, 1984, pp 45-66.
O'Hare, Michael, "Improving the Use of Information in Environmental Decision Making," *Environmental Impact Assessment Review* Vol. 1, 1980, pp 229-250.
Sandman, P., *Explaining Environmental Risk.* Washington, D.C.: U.S. Environmental Protection Agency, Office of Toxic Substances, 1986.
Sharlin, Harold, "EDB: A Case Study in Communicating Risk," *Risk Analysis* Vol. 6, 1986, pp 61-68.
Slovic, Paul, "Informing and Educating the Public About Risk," *Risk Analysis* Vol. 6, 1986, pp 403-415.
U.S., National Research Council, Committee on Risk Perception and Communication, *Improving Risk Communication.* Washington, D.C.: National Academy Press, 1989.

Risk Management

Brickman, R., Thomas Ilgen and Sheila Jasanoff, *Controlling Chemicals: The Politics of Regulation in Europe and the United States*. Ithaca, New York: Cornell University Press, 1986.

Covello, V., "Decision Analysis and Risk Management Decision-Making: Issues and Methods," *Risk Analysis* Vol. 7, 1987, pp 131-139.

Covello, V. and J. Mumpower, "Risk Analysis and Risk Management: An Historical Perspective," *Risk Analysis* Vol. 5, 1985, pp 103-120.

Covello, V., Joshua Menkes and J. Mumpower, eds., *Risk Evaluation and Management*. New York: Plenum Press, 1986.

————, *Uncertainty in Risk Assessment, Risk Management and Decision Making*. New York: Plenum Press, 1986.

Crouch, E.A.C. and R. Wilson, *Risk Benefit Analysis*. Cambridge, Mass.: Ballinger, 1982.

Environmental Protection Agency (U.S.), *Risk Assessment and Risk Management: Framework for Decision Making*. Washington, D.C.: Environmental Protection Agency, Washington D.C., 1984.

Fiksel, Joseph, "Toward a De Minimis Policy in Risk Regulation," *Risk Analysis* Vol. 5, 1985, pp 257-269.

Fowle, C. D., A.P. Grima and R.E. Munn, eds., *Information Needs for Risk Management*. Toronto: University of Toronto Institute for Environmental Studies, 1988.

Interdepartmental Working Group on Risk-Benefit Analysis, *Risk-Benefit Analysis in the Management of Toxic Chemicals*, Ottawa: Agriculture Canada, 1984.

Lave, L.B., ed., *Enhancing Risk Management*. New York: Plenum Press, 1987.

Leiss, William, *The Risk Management Process*, Working Paper, Ottawa: Agriculture Canada, 1985.

Mazur, A., "Bias in Risk Benefit Analysis," *Technology in Society* Vol. 7, 1985, pp 25-30.

Mumpower, Jeryl, "An Analysis of the De Minimis Strategy for Risk Management," *Risk Analysis* Vol. 6, 1986, pp] 437-446.

National Research Council, Associate Committee on Scientific Criteria for Environmental Quality, *Strengths and Limitations of Benefit-Cost Analyses Applied to the Assessment of Industrial Organic Chemicals Including Pesticides*, (Monographs I-VI). Ottawa: 1985.

Nicholson, W., ed., *Management of Assessed Risk for Carcinogens*. New York: New York Academy of Sciences, 1981.

Otway, M. and H. Peltu, eds., *Regulating Industrial Risks*. London: Butterworths, 1985.

Stanbury, W. T. and I. Vertinsky, *Guide to the Application of Cost-Benefit Analysis to Regulation*. Ottawa: Office of Privatization and Regulatory Affairs, 1988.

Starr, C., "Risk Management, Assessment and Acceptability," *Risk Analysis* Vol. 5, 1985, pp 97-102.

Versteeg, H., *The Conflict between Law and Science*, Unpublished ms., Ottawa, 1988.

Victor, P., "Techniques for Assessment and Analysis in the Management of Toxic Chemicals," *Proceedings of the National Workshop on Risk- Benefit Analysis*. Ottawa: Agriculture Canada, 1985.

Risk Perception

Covello, V., "The Perception of Technological Risks: A Literature Review," *Technological Forecasting and Social Change* Vol. 23, 1983, pp 285-297.

Covello, V., W.G. Framm, J. Rodricks and R. Tardiff, eds., *The Analysis of Actual Versus Perceived Risks*. New York: Plenum Press, 1983.

Fischoff, Baruch, "Managing Risk Perceptions," *Issues in Science and Technology* Vol. 2, 1985, pp 83-96.

Fischhoff, B., Sarah Lichtenstein and Paul Slovic, "Lay Foibles and Expert Fables in Judgements about Risk," *The American Statistician* Vol. 36, 1982, pp 240-255.

———, *Acceptable Risk*. New York: Cambridge University Press, 1981.

Fischhoff, Baruch and D. MacGregor, "Judged Lethality: How Much People Seem to Know Depends on How They're Asked," *Risk Analysis* Vol. 3, 1983, pp 229-235.

Horisberger, B. and R. Dinkel, eds., *The Perception and Management of Drug Safety Risks*. New York: Springer-Verlag, 1989.

Johnson, B. and V. Covello, eds., *Social and Cultural Construction of Risk*. Boston: Reidel, 1987.

Kahneman, D. and A. Tversky, eds., *Judgement under Uncertainty*. New York: Cambridge University Press, 1982.

Kasperson, R., Halina Brown, Jacques Emel, Robert Goble, Jeanne Kasperson and Samuel Patrick, "The Social Amplification of Risk," *Risk Analysis* Vol. 8, 1988, pp 177-187.

Krewski, D., E. Somers, and P.L. Birkwood, "Risk Perception in a Decision-making Context," *Environmental Carcinogenesis Reviews* C5 1987, pp 175-209.

Lindell, Michael K., and Timothy C. Earle, "How Close is Close Enough: Public Perceptions of the Risks of Industrial Facilities," *Risk Analysis* Vol. 3, 1983, pp 245-253.

MacGregor, Don and Paul Slovic, "Perceived Acceptability of Risk Analysis as a Decision-making Approach," *Risk Analysis* Vol. 6, 1985, pp 245-256.

Rapoport, Anatol, "Subjective Aspects of Risk," *Risk Abstracts* Vol. 3, 1986, pp 1-10.

Vertinsky, I. and D. Wehrung, "Risk Perception and Drug Safety Evaluation," Working Paper, Ottawa: Health Protection Branch, Health and Welfare Canada, 1989.